DATE DUE

CRISIS IN THE ISRAELI KIBBUTZ

CRISIS IN THE ISRAELI KIBBUTZ

Meeting the Challenge of Changing Times

ର

Edited by

Uriel Leviatan, Hugh Oliver,
and Jack Quarter

PRAEGER

Westport, Connecticut
London

Library of Congress Cataloging-in-Publication Data

Crisis in the Israeli kibbutz : meeting the challenge of changing
   times / edited by Uriel Leviatan, Hugh Oliver, and Jack Quarter.
      p.   cm.
   Includes bibliographical references and index.
   ISBN 0-275-95838-8 (alk. paper)
    1. Kibbutzim. I. Leviatan, Uri. II. Oliver, Hugh, 1929–
III. Quarter, Jack.
   HX742.2.A3C75   1998
   307.77′6′095694—dc21   97–26902

British Library Cataloguing in Publication Data is available.

Library of Congress Catalog Card Number: 97–26902
ISBN: 0-275-95838-8

First published in 1998

Praeger Publishers, 88 Post Road West, Westport, CT 06881
An imprint of Greenwood Publishing Group, Inc.

Printed in the United States of America

The paper used in this book complies with the
Permanent Paper Standard issued by the National
Information Standards Organization (Z39.48–1984).

10 9 8 7 6 5 4 3 2 1

Contents

Introduction: The Kibbutz in Crisis   vii
   Uriel Leviatan, Jack Quarter, and Hugh Oliver

1   Kibbutz Demography   1
   Stanley Maron

2   Winds of Change   13
   Shlomo Getz

3   Work in the Kibbutz   27
   Menachem Rosner

4   Organization in Kibbutz Industry   41
   Michal Palgi

5   The Changing Identity of Kibbutz Education   57
   Yechezkel Dar

6   Attitudes of Parents toward Their Own Role and That of the
   Caregiver in Two Sleeping Arrangements for Kibbutz
   Children   73
   Ronit Plotnik

7   Second and Third Generations in Kibbutzim—Is the
   Survival of the Kibbutz Society Threatened?   81
   Uriel Leviatan

8   The Governmental System of the Kibbutz   97
   Avraham Pavin

9   Women in the Changing Kibbutz   111
   Gila Adar

10 Individual Needs and Public Distribution in the Kibbutz   119
    Yaakov Gluck

11 Aging—The Kibbutz Experience   131
    Uriel Leviatan

12 Inter-Kibbutz Organizations and Cooperatives   147
    Daniel Rosolio

13 Summary and Conclusions   159
    Uriel Leviatan, Jack Quarter, and Hugh Oliver

References   165

Index   179

About the Contributors   185

Introduction: The Kibbutz in Crisis

Uriel Leviatan, Jack Quarter, and Hugh Oliver

The Israeli kibbutz is experiencing major changes. Crises that erupted ten years ago because of economic problems have led to major social and ideological changes. Basic kibbutz principles and values have been questioned. The underlying debate is about what values should govern kibbutz functioning: Collective and altruistic values are clashing with individual and egocentric values in determining policies and directions for the future of the kibbutz society.

One result of the changes is the irrelevance of much research about the kibbutz. The analyses written prior to the current crises need updating. This volume explores the changes under way.

KIBBUTZIM UNTIL THE RECENT PAST

Until very recently, an outsider visiting a kibbutz would have seen a tightly knit communal society of about 150–200 families living alongside each other and sharing a common ideology, mutual responsibility for each other, social activities, and their means of livelihood. Although kibbutzim are a type of commune, they have always differed from other communes in their adoption of modern values, such as pursuing scientific knowledge for application to social and economic activities, keeping up-to-date with modern technologies, being open to innovation, and (within the boundaries of a modest life) not opposing improvements in the standard of living. Even though they were few in number and located primarily in the countryside, kibbutz members did not attempt to withdraw from the surrounding society but purposely involved themselves in it as an expression of their mission to both influence and serve society. Rather than staying secluded from the rest of society as most communes do, kibbutzim have been open to visitors, the media, cultural inflows, and outsiders.

Although the kibbutz population was always small (only about 3 percent of
Israel's population), kibbutzim have achieved a prominence both in terms of the
country's social life and its economy. For many years kibbutz society has served as
a symbol of success in many domains. For example:

1. In politics, a disproportionate number of the country's leaders, including
   prime ministers, have had roots in the kibbutz movement.

2. Comparative research conducted from the late 1960s through the 1980s
   showed that kibbutz economic performance surpassed that of others both
   in farming and in industry (Barkai, 1977; Rabin, 1991; Melman, 1971;
   Don, 1988; Peleg, 1980; Leviatan, 1975b). At present, the kibbutzim are
   responsible for about 35 percent of Israel's agriculture sales, about 6
   percent of industrial production, and about 10 percent of Israeli exports.
   Moreover, kibbutzim have provided a good standard of living for their
   members.

3. During the years 1970–1985 (see Maron's chapter in this volume), the
   membership of kibbutzim increased by about 2.5 percent each year, which
   illustrates their attractiveness to their own youth and to youth from the
   outside. (About half of the new members came from outside the kibbutz.)
   This rate of growth, surpassing the growth of the Jewish population in
   Israel, was by itself a major accomplishment, as decline is the rule in
   modern rural communities both in Israel and abroad.

4. Kibbutzim introduced innovative educational, organizational, and social
   arrangements such as sleeping houses for children and communal education (see Dar's and Plotnik's chapters), care for the elderly (Leviatan's
   chapter), and organizational solutions to potentially alienating jobs and
   to the ill effects of hierarchy (Palgi's and Rosner's chapters; Leviatan and
   Rosner, 1980). In addition, the kibbutz movement was a prime contributor to the creation of a secular Jewish culture in Israel.

5. These and other innovative attempts at solving problems faced by other
   parts of industrial society have generated considerable interest in this
   society, including that from academic researchers. To date, there are close
   to six thousands research publications about the kibbutz—half in lan-
   guages other than Hebrew.

6. The Israeli public has always had a positive attitude toward kibbutz society,
   even when the general political mood turned away from the Labor ideology (which the kibbutzim spearheaded) after the political upheaval in
   Israel in 1977. Opinion surveys during the years 1977–1985 (Leviatan,
   1981) showed that about 60 percent of the public had positive feelings for
   the kibbutzim and only 6–8 percent expressed negative feeling. In addition, about two-thirds held the opinion that kibbutz life was viable and in
   many ways superior (including education). About half of the respondents
   even supported the view that kibbutzim should have an influence on
   Israeli politics disproportionately greater than their size.

7. Finally, the very survival of the kibbutz movement for almost a full century (the first kibbutz was established in 1910) is indicative of its success. There are few examples of nonsecluded, communal societies that have survived for so long.

CONDITIONS FOR PAST SUCCESSES

The success experienced by kibbutzim over such a wide range of domains resulted from abiding by three important principles: holding on to their defining values while constantly (and innovatively) adapting their concrete expression to changing circumstances; maintaining a dynamic balance between the values of collectivism and the values of individualism and seeking congruency among the principles of conduct exercised in the different life domains

Constant Values and Their Dynamic Expression

Although the kibbutz movement has undergone many changes, until recently the values guiding development have remained constant. This point is extremely important because over the years there has been a tendency among outside observers of kibbutz life to view the kibbutz in static terms—as a constant (e.g., Darin-Drabkin, 1962; Leon, 1969; Blasi, 1978). It is not the kibbutz that has remained constant, but its values.

The constancy of values was upheld over the first eight decades of kibbutz existence, but their translation into practical arrangements of kibbutz life changed from one period to another. Changes included the work domain (kinds of jobs, level of technology, size of work group, organizational structure, etc.), expressions of community governance (institutions and bodies of governance, topics discussed, dynamics of decision making, etc.), and consumption (what was consumed, methods of distribution of goods and services, level of consumption, etc.). Change was also introduced in other domains, such as education, family, culture, and leisure. However, a deeper look into the differences in practical arrangements over time would show that they were mostly on the surface. In effect, the differences have, until recently, been expressions of the same governing values of kibbutz life: solidarity among members, collectivity in pursuit of goals, democracy in governing the life of the community, the goal of maximum self-development for every member, the mission of service to the larger society, and an equality among members in rights and obligations which takes into account the uniqueness of each person's needs and abilities.

This dialectic of dynamically adapted social arrangements and constant values was key to kibbutz success.

Balanced Collectivism and Individualism

The changes introduced over the years in kibbutz life resulted not only from external pressures, but also from the reaction of the kibbutz to the constant and contrasting pulls of two of the major forces that empowered kibbutz life: collectivity for the sake of community and individuality for the sake of self-fulfillment. Although the tendency is to view the kibbutz in simplistic terms as an expression of communal and utopian ideals, kibbutzim are complex societies that, from their inception, were based on a synthesis of differing and seemingly conflictual values. On the one hand, kibbutzim were founded upon values of collectivism. For example, the means of production were owned by the community, the children had a common educational experience that included living in their own houses, and members ate their meals in a common dining hall. On the other hand, individual expression was also evident in many of the practices. For example, decisions were taken in meetings following extensive discussions by members; the goods and services of the community were allocated according to the needs of members; the educational system (which was influenced by John Dewey and the progressive tradition) emphasized art, music, and various forms of individual expression; and work assignments usually involved attempts to accommodate individual preferences (when this could not be done, arrangements would be negotiated whereby members would do work that interested them for part of the week and work that the kibbutz required for the other part).

In the pioneer period, during which the kibbutzim were defensive settlements attempting to establish a basic level of agriculture both to support their members and, subsequently, to support a Jewish homeland in Palestine, individualism was viewed as a luxury, and the good of the community was the predominant value for making decisions. If, for example, someone wanted to go on to higher education, he or she would have to leave the kibbutz. With time, changes occurred in the life of the kibbutz that led to greater individualism, but the individualism operated within communal arrangements. In effect, the introduction of greater opportunities for individuals was viewed as a way of strengthening the communal structures and the collective values upon which they were based. Yet even though, out of necessity, collectivism was accentuated in the pioneer years, individualism was not ignored. And when it became practical to incorporate individualism into kibbutz life, it took a central role alongside collectivism—leading to a balance between them. The policy was to take both into account in decisions about practical life arrangements. Moreover, this balance between collectivism and individualism was a major component of the strength of the kibbutz in attracting members, in maintaining their commitment, and in eliciting the highest levels of motivation and identification.

Congruency among Domains

During the transformations that they experienced in their first eighty years, the kibbutzim understood what theoreticians (e.g., Katz and Kahn, 1978) have only recently come to identify as an important condition for successful functioning of social organizations: the congruence among their subparts in principles of conduct. Social systems whose parts function in a framework of incongruent principles are likely to experience inside tensions, strife, and wasted energy. And, what is particularly important in the kibbutz case, the smaller the social system, the more danger-ous for it are the outcomes of incongruence.

In the past, kibbutzim avoided this danger of incongruity. They constructed all their subsystems (domains) along commensurate principles of conduct with, of course, appropriate adaptation to fit the features of specific domains. For example, work units in farming, services, and education were all structured along principles similar to those of committees in the public domain: Those in charge were "coor-dinators" rather than "managers"; the units had planned rotation in leadership and administrative positions, and they exercised direct democracy through general assemblies and through decentralization into committees; informal interactions were the rule; and even the social structure of the school community operated as a mini-kibbutz. Likewise, when industry was introduced, it was forced to adopt a management structure that complied with kibbutz principles.

THE TURBULENT LATE 1960s AND EARLY 1970s

During the turbulent period of the late 1960s and early 1970s, five major changes occurred concurrently in the kibbutz external and internal environments and tested the three guiding principles that had influenced kibbutz life for so long.

1. Kibbutzim went through an industrial revolution, turning within a few years from economies based solely on farming to mixed economies in which industry contributed about half of their net income (see Palgi's chapter).

2. A revolution occurred in higher education. Within a few years, education that had formerly been restricted was offered to each member. To illus-trate: in 1964 there were only one hundred kibbutz members studying in academic settings; this number grew to four hundred in 1968 and to seventeen hundred in 1972, while membership grew at that time at a rate of only 2 percent per year (Leviatan and Orchan, 1982).

3. The first large age cohorts reached retirement age, thus forcing kibbutzim to deal with the needs of members from young to old (see Leviatan's chapter on aging).

4. For the first time, the kibbutzim experienced the intake of many new members without a background in kibbutz ideology—because of the marriage of kibbutz-born members to outsiders (both from Israel and from abroad). This change introduced the potential for the community to become less homogeneous in its basic values.

5. For the first time, large numbers of kibbutz-born members decided to leave the kibbutz (see Leviatan's chapter on second and third generations; Rosner, Ben-David, et al., 1990).

These major changes in the external and internal environments could have had serious consequences for the kibbutzim. Some of these changes encouraged greater individualism (such as the diversification of knowledge and careers and the increased heterogeneity of members) and so altered the balance between collectivism and individualism. The industrial revolution threatened kibbutz principles of managerial conduct and therefore the important condition of congruence among domains. But in general the kibbutz movement reacted by viewing the transformations to its environments not as threats (which would have led, perhaps, to stonewalling their introduction as long as possible), but as opportunities to exercise its goals, principles, and values on a higher level. We use the industrial revolution in the kibbutzim to illustrate this point.

The introduction of industry at first threatened the kibbutz values of equality and direct democracy in organization and management. Industrial managers demanded hierarchical authority, similar to that of their colleagues outside the kibbutz (which, had their demands been accepted, meant the surrender of the power rendered to institutions of direct democracy such as the workers' assembly and workers' committees). They also insisted on doing away with managerial rotation and argued for viewing the profit-making potential of the industrial branch as the sole goal to be pursued and for ignoring other goals such as offering appropriate jobs according to members' training, capabilities, and needs. In addition, the introduction of industry created much greater professional heterogeneity among members (due to its more diverse occupations), thereby threatening the social fabric of the kibbutz community, which was based on commonality of interests and knowledge concerning the public domain. Industrialization also led to demands to let go of the restrictions on the employment of hired workers. Although major debates ensued, these potential threats were treated as opportunities for strengthening both collectivism and individualism, while preserving the same balance between them and restating kibbutz values and principles in innovative ways that harmonize with the new conditions posed by industry.

Eventually, in the mid 1970s, the debate about changes from basic kibbutz values was decided in favor of keeping to the principles of kibbutz management and of shaping industrial management along the lines of other work branches and community bodies. However, those kibbutz principles were now adapted to the features of industry and were detailed and articulated in formal resolutions (see Leviatan and Rosner, 1980: "Resolutions"). Programs were developed in the kibbutz management training center. Capital-intensive and knowledge-intensive technologies were sought as the preferred ones for kibbutz industry (in contrast to the first industries which were labor intensive with low levels of needed knowledge). This direction was adopted so that industry could offer appropriate jobs to the large waves of graduates from the institutions of higher studies and so that the need for hired labor could be averted. It proved singularly successful, both economically and socially. Findings showed that kibbutz industry far surpassed comparable industry outside. Other findings showed that the stronger the adherence of a kibbutz industry to kibbutz principles of management, the more successful it was (Barkai, 1977; Leviatan and Rosner, 1980).

PRELUDE TO THE CHANGES OF THE MID-1980s

The successes described in the previous section (starting at the beginning of the 1970s) were also the beginning of a new era of handling both the delicate balance between individualism and collectivism, and the relationship between values and social arrangements. These successes depended to a great extent on the ideological commitment of members, the beliefs they shared about kibbutz values, and their willingness to conserve those values. But the success in absorbing the major transformations of those years apparently reduced ideological commitment and commitment to the importance of promoting it among members and youth in schools (see Dar's chapter). It was believed by many that ideological commitment developed by itself among members simply because they lived on a kibbutz. This did not happen; ideology is not an infectious phenomenon that one gets by sheer exposure to it. Thus, when the number of new members without an ideological background became sizable, and the leadership of the individual kibbutzim and of the federations no longer regarded overt emphasis on ideology as an important focus of its functioning (as it was in earlier years), the seeds were planted for a very different reaction to the next period (mid-1980's) of major transformations. These are analyzed in the present volume, but first, we tell the story of what ignited the crisis.

THE ECONOMIC CRISIS AND ITS ECONOMIC EFFECTS

The next important transformation in the kibbutz environment came about in the mid-1980s. It is what kibbutz lingo refers to as "the crisis." The year 1985 signifies the onset of that crisis, which started for economic reasons and later became both social and ideological. To understand the onset, we need to provide a brief outline of the Israeli economy at that time.

At the beginning of the 1980s, the Israeli economy was gripped with a hyperinflation that reached an annual rate in mid-1985 of 400 percent. Not only was such inflation directly devastating for the economy and society, but it also had an indirect effect on business; it precluded any rational bookkeeping and many businesses lost track of their financial status.

To combat inflation, the government came up with a plan in June 1985 that was supported by both labor and industry. The basic ingredients of the plan were as follows: freezing both wages and the exchange rate for foreign currency and keeping the interest rate at a very high level. To illustrate: the real interest rate was 85 percent for the first six months after initiation of the economic plan, but came down to 25 percent the following year and to about 16 percent the year after. At that time, four of the five large Israeli banks were essentially nationalized because they had been baled out of bankruptcy by the government in 1983.

Inflation was checked by the plan (declining to 25 percent within the first few months), but the economic price for society, particularly for producers, was horrendous. The high interest rates drove many businesses to bankruptcy—for instance, out of the one hundred largest companies in Israel in 1988 (as registered by

Dun and Bradstreet of Israel), about a sixth either declared bankruptcy or were on the brink of doing so. Hardest hit were manufacturers, who depended upon credit both for their investments and for their working capital.

As a result, businesses laid off workers and unemployment grew at an alarming rate. No workers were added to Israeli industry between 1985 and 1989, although the civilian labor force grew by 157,000. Unemployment grew by almost 33 percent from 6.7 percent to 8.9 percent (and an addition of about 45 percent to the unemployment ranks) during the years 1985–1989. Many manufacturing businesses became importers of their previous products. By doing so, they did not need as much capital (avoiding interest charges that go with it); they also did not need as many workers (avoiding the salaries and interest charges that accompany a work force). The business cycle was much shorter and therefore in need of less operating capital, and businesses could depend upon the credit of their overseas suppliers for their operating capital (with a much lower interest rate). By using this strategy, Israel was in effect reducing the unemployment of other countries at the expense of Israeli workers. The net result was economic stagnation and a much reduced market for whoever still remained as a producer of goods or services.

EFFECTS OF THE ECONOMIC PLAN ON KIBBUTZIM

Kibbutzim as business enterprises have a constant need for economic growth to create additional jobs for the new members. In addition, unlike any other business enterprise, kibbutzim are both employers of their members and the community responsible for their members' occupation. Thus, laying off members from work is not a viable solution because the unemployment of many members could destroy the community. And this is so even without taking into account the detrimental morale problems.

As a result, even with the new economic situation in Israel, kibbutzim have had to continue borrowing money in order to create jobs for the new members and to preserve the old jobs. In the mid-1980s, kibbutzim were at the historical peak of their growth rates—about 2.5 percent per year (as illustrated in Maron's chapter), which meant the addition of about fifteen hundred young members every year to the work force. Indeed, during the years 1985–1989, the kibbutz industrial work force grew by twenty-seven hundred workers, compared to no growth in the whole of Israel (one should remember that the kibbutz population was less than 3 percent of the Israeli population).

The freezing of the exchange rate also had a detrimental effect on kibbutz economy, which was export oriented both in its industry (providing 10 percent of Israel's industrial exports) and in most of its farm products. In addition, governmental policies of liberalizing markets to do away with central planning and subsidies for farming produce further harmed kibbutz economies, which still depended heavily on farming.

Finally, most kibbutzim have been dependent financially on loans from financial institutions (government or banks), as their enterprises were established without any capital of their own. To sustain the growth of the kibbutz population, it was necessary to continue borrowing heavily from financial institutions; but because of the superb economic performance of the kibbutzim over the years and the mutual-guarantee arrangement among all kibbutzim vis-à-vis their creditors, the banks were never reluctant to loan money. Unfortunately, these same arrangements made kibbutzim perhaps overly eager to borrow.

This combination of worsening outside conditions (hyperinflation, high interest rates, slow economic growth, worsening commerce ratio for producers between input and output, and deteriorating exports) and worsening inside conditions (the need for new jobs and expanded production together with too easy access to credit) led to an economic crisis in the kibbutz movement. Within a few years, the kibbutzim developed a high level of debt, and their economic performance deteriorated. In 1988 the kibbutzim of the two major federations (TAKAM and the Kibbutz Artzi) owed their creditors about $4.4 billion (U.S.), whereas their income was only about $3.1 billion (U.S.)—a ratio of close to 1.4:1. Six years earlier, the total debt of the same kibbutzim was $1.4 billion (U.S.) against $2.7 billion of income—a ratio of about 0.5:1. In other words, the debt more than tripled during a period when there was only a small increase in income.

The creditors (the banks and the government) accepted some responsibility for the excessive interest rates. They also understood that if the kibbutzim were to go bankrupt, they might well go down with them (the kibbutzim were among their largest debtors). Thus, they accepted responsibility for about a third of the debt. However, independent economists who analyzed the debt felt this figure was understated by half. Intensive negotiations started among the three parties involved in the debt: the government, the banks, and the kibbutzim. Although the first agreement between creditors and the kibbutzim was signed in 1989, and a consequent agreement was signed in 1996, no debt was officially erased until the end of 1996 (and, even then, for only a very few kibbutzim).

This financial crisis had a devastating impact upon the kibbutzim and their members. In 1988 (it took two or three years for the banks to understand the real gravity of the situation), lines of credit were closed and many kibbutzim experienced a sharp decline in their standard of living. They also lacked investment capital to modernize their technology. But these outcomes were less serious than the devastating blow to morale and self-confidence. The outside media, and even some kibbutz leaders, blamed the principles and the values that guided the kibbutz economy and not government policies. (The analyses that pointed the blame at the excessive interest rates were published later, but by then very few people paid attention to those analyses.)

The mood among many members was to view themselves as incompetent and their way of life as inefficient. Many kibbutzim looked externally for solutions, accepting as fact that the kibbutz system was inferior. And thus kibbutzim were flooded by consultants—most of them outsiders, but also some insiders who had lost their faith in the kibbutz system. Most of the consultants did not appreciate the collective values of the kibbutz and offered solutions to the economic problems that would structure kibbutz business in ways similar to any other business. These solutions emphasized individualistic values while weakening collectivist values.

(Several chapters in this volume, those by Getz, Rosner, Palgi, Pavin and Gluck, analyze the impact of these suggestions upon the kibbutz.) Thus, kibbutzim began to discuss ideas such as creating boards of directors in industry, lifting restrictions on the employment of hired workers, doing away with managerial rotation, linking contribution and remuneration, abandoning direct democracy in the control of kibbutz businesses, and removing restrictions against members working outside the kibbutz.

INTRODUCTION TO THE CHAPTERS

The economic benefits of the consultants' recommendations for the kibbutz businesses have yet to be proven. Meanwhile, changes in managing economic organizations spilled over into other domains of kibbutz life. In the kibbutz, the generic name for all these suggestions is "changes." Thus, this volume deals with the major changes that are now being introduced in kibbutzim and how they differ from past practice.

The chapters describe the changes that are being considered and implemented by kibbutzim. Each chapter focuses on a particular aspect of kibbutz life. The changes described should allow the testing of the thesis proposed earlier: that successful survival of kibbutzim depends on a balance between the contrasting values of collectivism and individualism, on adherence to the basic principles that define kibbutz distinctiveness, and on the congruency of social arrangements among the various domains within the kibbutz. In the concluding chapter, we evaluate this thesis by analyzing the outcomes of the changes described in the various chapters.

Because different aspects of life on the kibbutz interact with each other, some of the chapters inevitably cover similar material. However, such material is always presented from the particular perspective of the author.

Stanley Maron's chapter, "Kibbutz Demography," provides a demographic update from the most recent trends available. This paper represents a handy source of information for anyone interested in a statistical snapshot of the modern kibbutz.

Shlomo Getz's chapter, "Winds of Change," provides a comprehensive overview of the changes that have occurred in the kibbutzim during the years 1989–1996. Getz argues that these changes represent the decommunalization of the kibbutz.

"Work in the Kibbutz" by Menachem Rosner, looks at the impact of the changing kibbutz values on the work arrangements. Rosner argues that the kibbutzim are adopting a hybrid model—a combination of conventional practices (a market and hierarchical approach) and of traditional kibbutz practices (a communal and cooperative approach). He questions whether such a hybrid arrangement can endure.

Michal Palgi's chapter, "Organization in Kibbutz Industry," traces the growth of kibbutz industries and discusses dilemmas related to their development, including their impact upon other domains of kibbutz life. Palgi discusses whether (as a result of industrial pressures) the deterioration of direct democracy in the kibbutz is inevitable.

"The Changing Identity of Kibbutz Education" by Yechezkel Dar, provides an overview of the changes that are occurring in kibbutz education. Dar argues that these changes are eroding the communal structures of the kibbutz.

Ronit Plotnik's "Attitudes of Parents toward Their Own Role and That of the Caregiver in Two Sleeping Arrangements for Kibbutz Children" compares how parental attitudes have been affected by having children sleep in their parents' houses as opposed to the *bet yeladim* ("children-house") that was more traditional. Plotnik's research highlights some of the adjustments that parents are experiencing.

From the founding of the first kibbutz in 1910, there has been an evolution from a single-generation society to a society with at least three and, in some instances, four generations. The chapter by Uriel Leviatan, "Second and Third Generations in Kibbutzim—Is the Survival of the Kibbutz Society Threatened?," analyzes the sources of commitment to kibbutz life of the subsequent generations. Leviatan takes a hard look at the rising numbers of kibbutz-born leaving the kibbutz and examines various explanations of this phenomenon.

Avraham Pavin's chapter, "The Governmental System of the Kibbutz," describes the historical development of governing institutions in kibbutzim up to the present time and the changes that have taken place recently. He analyzes the effects upon kibbutz functioning of the introduction of several innovative institutions and of the disappearance of others.

The failure of the kibbutzim to achieve gender equality is a sour point in their history. Gila Adar's chapter, "Women in the Changing Kibbutz," describes the past and discusses the potential outcomes of the changes in kibbutzim upon this matter. The chapter weighs the further dangers to gender equality that may come with the changes against the opportunities the changes may offer. It suggests the importance of intentional structural changes for achieving gender equality.

Yaakov Gluck's chapter, "Individual Needs and Public Distribution in the Kibbutz," surveys the development of methods of distribution since the establishment of the first kibbutzim and the ideological arguments that were at their base. Special attention is given to the new approaches and how they might affect the future of the kibbutzim.

The members of all societies grow old, but kibbutz members are exceptional. "Aging—The Kibbutz Experience," by Uriel Leviatan, describes the aging process as it is experienced by the kibbutz population and how societal arrangements contribute to longevity. He also looks at the relevance of the data for other societies.

Daniel Rosolio's chapter, "Inter-Kibbutz Organizations and Cooperatives," presents an overview of organizations that the kibbutz movement has developed to deal with the movement's activities (nationwide and regional). He discusses the impact upon these organizations of the changes in the kibbutzim and points to a trend of decentralization (into regional organization) and from solidarity among kibbutzim based on common ideology to partnerships based on local interests.

1
Kibbutz Demography

Stanley Maron

At the end of 1995, there were in Israel 269 kibbutzim. They had a total population of 124,600 and together formed the largest communitarian movement in the world. Although kibbutzim are spread throughout the state, most are located in the remoter parts of Galilee or in the Jordan and Jezreel valleys to the north or in the Negev to the south (see Table 1.1).

Kibbutzim began primarily as agricultural settlements. Though they form fewer than 3 percent of Israel's total population, they still represent a quarter of the rural population. (Israel's population, both Jewish and Arab, is overwhelmingly urban, with more than half concentrated in just a dozen cities in the center of the country.) In recent years, however, accelerated urbanization has brought expanding towns up to, and even around, formerly remote kibbutzim. By the mid-1990s, more than a quarter of kibbutzim were already near or within urban areas. Undoubtedly, this process of urbanization will have an important influence on the future of the kibbutz. Meanwhile, kibbutzim remain an important part of rural Israel.

The kibbutz population is divided into four movements (see Table 1.2). The largest is the United Kibbutz Movement, usually known by its Hebrew acronym, TAKAM; it comprises about 60 percent of the kibbutz population and 167 kibbutzim. The second largest is the Kibbutz Artzi movement of Hashomer Hatzair, about just over 32 percent of the kibbutz population and 84 kibbutzim. The third largest is Kibbutz Dati or the nationalist religious kibbutz movement, with more than 6 percent of the kibbutz population and 17 kibbutzim. The remaining 2 kibbutzim belong to an ultraorthodox movement representing more than 1 percent of the kibbutz population. In the 1970s, in order to draw closer to the kibbutz model, six collective moshavim joined TAKAM as an associated group. As in kibbutzim, economic operations in collective moshavim belong to all the members, but consumption is private in separate households. When discussing total kibbutz population, the data in this chapter refer to kibbutzim only but include those collective moshavim when using TAKAM data.

Table 1.1
Geographical Dstribution of Israel's Rural Population, 1995

Area	Kibbutz Settlements	Other Rural Settlements	Kibbutz Population	Other Rural Population
Galilee	56	104	26,700	50,000
Jordan Valley	21	32	10,000	15,500
Jezreel Valley	48	61	26,400	38,900
Golan Heights	10	22	2,400	9,200
Central Israel	51	208	27,900	113,000
Judean Hills	8	55	3,600	21,200
Negev	66	137	25,500	88,500
West Bank and Gaza	9	120	2,000	48,300
Total	269	739	124,500	384,600

Source: Central Bureau of Statistics, Government of Israel.

Table 1.2
Kibbutz Population by Federation, 1995

Movements	Number of Kibbutzim	Population	Percentage
TAKAM	167	74,100	59.9
Kibbutz Artzi	84	39,200	31.7
Kibbutz Dati	17	8,100	6.5
Poeley Agudat Israel	2	2,400	1.9
Total	269	123,800	100.0
TAKAM-Moshavim	6	2,100	

Source: Central Bureau of Statistics, Government of Israel.

Kibbutzim range in size from small communes with a few dozen members up to large communities with populations of more than a thousand. As can be seen in Table 1.3, almost 80 percent of the total kibbutz population is concentrated in kibbutzim that have at least four hundred men, women, and children.

Most kibbutzim were formed by young people, and therefore it is not surprising that the kibbutz population has been consistently younger than the surrounding Jewish population—and remains so in the 1990s. However, the aging process has now brought the kibbutz population to the full span of years, with quite a few members aged sixty-five and over. In addition, many kibbutzim invite parents of

Table 1.3
All Kibbutzim by Population Size, 1993

Population	Number of Kibbutzim	Percentage	Total Population	Percentage
1,000 or more	9	3.3	10,920	8.7
900–999	5	1.9	4,691	3.7
800–899	5	1.9	4,242	3.4
700–799	19	7.0	14,325	11.3
600–699	33	12.2	21,111	16.7
500–599	41	15.2	22,857	18.1
400–499	44	16.3	20,014	15.9
300–399	46	17.0	16,145	12.8
200–299	31	11.5	8,040	6.4
100–199	22	8.1	3,238	2.6
0–99	15	5.6	480	0.4
Total	270	100.0	126,063	100.0

Source: Central Bureau of Statistics, Government of Israel.

members to live there during their final years, close to their children and grandchildren. Together, that makes for a significant number of aged comparable in proportion to the surrounding Jewish population, as can be seen in Table 1.4. Although the kibbutz population grew by 38 percent between 1972 and 1995, there have been no unusual structural changes apart from results of the aging process. In 1972, 77 percent of the population was forty-four years of age or younger and in 1995, a generation later, 72 percent.

TRANSFORMATION FROM A COMMUNE TO A KIBBUTZ

The earliest kibbutzim, formed from 1910 onward, were really communes and were part of a relatively widespread trend which saw many communes established in Palestine during the first quarter of the twentieth century. Owing to economic difficulties and to a high degree of mobility of the members, all the urban communes formed at that time dissolved, while the agricultural communes eventually became kibbutzim scattered throughout the remoter parts of Israel.

Communes are formed by mobile individuals who come together for shared living. Members are unified by bonds of ideology, friendship, and mutual feelings, and the social fabric is dependent upon individual decisions to remain together. But that is a weak basis for shared living, as the experience of thousands of

Table 1.4
Changes in Age Structure 1972–1995 (Percentages)

| Years of Age | Kibbutz Population | | | Jewish Population |
	1972	1983	1995	1995
0–14	28.7	31.3	26.3	27.2
15–24	23.9	17.6	19.9	16.9
25–34	15.7	16.7	14.3	13.6
35–44	9.1	12.2	11.7	13.7
45–54	8.4	6.9	10.9	10.1
55–64	10.0	6.2	6.2	7.5
65–74	3.1	6.7	5.1	6.6
75+	1.1	2.4	5.5	4.4
Total (percent)	100.0	100.0	100.0	100.0
Total (#)	89,700	115,500	124,000	4,495,100
Median Age:				
Kibbutz	23.9	25.7	27.3	
Jewish	25.3	27.6	29.2	

Source: Central Bureau of Statistics, Government of Israel.

contemporary communes in many parts of the world has demonstrated. Communes become more enduring communities after the formation of a core of families that have a clear group interest in stability and permanency. At that stage, matters concerning the care of children—particularly their education, health, and housing—become more important than private views and feelings. Mobile individuals are pushed to the periphery and become a minority. In the process, the original group of individuals is transformed into an organic social body that then reproduces itself and thereby ensures its continued existence.

By way of illustration, a report published in 1922 showed the extent to which mobility of individuals plagued the early kibbutzim. In the year of the report, Degania was twelve years old and had thirty-three members, but only six of them had been in the founding group. Other kibbutzim that were eight years old or less had even worse records. Mahanaim had thirty-three members, of whom only four had been in the founding group; Kfar Giladi had thirty-six members, of whom only four had been in the founding group; Ayelet Hashahar had thirty-three members, of whom only seven had been in the founding group; and Kiryat Anavim had forty-two adults, of whom only five had been in the founding group. Other reports from the same and later periods confirm that a high degree of mobility plagued the kibbutzim during their early stage of formation.

A study of the demographic data for twelve of the oldest kibbutzim shows that their formative period was in the late 1920s. The data indicate a strong connection between continuity and familial bonds. In 1922, those twelve kibbutzim had a total population of 855. Men outnumbered women two to one, and 80 percent of the men were single. There were only ninety-eight children. By 1930, the population in those kibbutzim had almost doubled, singles were in the minority, and the extent of family growth is demonstrated by the increase in number of children from 98 to 472.

GROWTH OF KIBBUTZ POPULATION

There are two sources of population growth—natural reproduction and migration. Only a combination of the two can give an accurate account of real growth. During the initial period of consolidation (usually the first decade), there is a good deal of movement into and out of the kibbutz. At that stage, a favorable balance of migration is essential for growth. Once a strong familial core is formed, however, continued growth comes primarily from natural reproduction, and often the balance of migration is negative.

Comprehensive data for births and deaths, as well as for those entering and leaving kibbutzim, are not available for any extended period. However, the data that are available indicate that, in the long run, more growth comes from within the kibbutz (natural reproduction) than from outside (migration). That trend has accelerated in most kibbutzim as they reach their third generation. Data for TAKAM (seen in Table 1.5) show that the source of net growth between 1986 and 1994 has been from those born and/or raised in a kibbutz.

Table 1.5
Changes in Adult Population of TAKAM by Source, 1986–1994 (Percentages)

Source	Composition of Population		Change for Each Group
	1986	*1994*	*1986–1994*
Kibbutz sons and daughters	29.4	43.5	+54.4
Trainees	6.5	5.3	–15.9
Absorbees from Israel	28.4	22.2	–18.1
Absorbees from abroad	8.3	8.2	+3.2
Youth movements from Israel	13.7	10.8	–17.3
Youth movements from abroad	13.8	10.0	–24.2
Total	100.0	100.0	+4.4

The adult population includes members and candidates aged eighteen and over.

Source: Department of Information, TAKAM.

Table 1.5 lists kibbutz sons and daughters, those born in a kibbutz to members or those who came to a kibbutz in childhood together with their parents. Trainees are various categories of youths who came to a kibbutz without their parents to study and work. Absorbees from Israel or from abroad are people who joined a kibbutz as individuals (rather than as part of a group). The remaining two categories refer to graduates of youth movements, who tend to join a kibbutz in groups.

As natural reproduction, or growth from within, becomes the major source of population increase, the proportion of kibbutz sons and daughters in the adult population (members and candidates) increases until they become a majority. In the more veteran kibbutzim, those born and/or raised in a kibbutz now form more than half of the adult population. In the year 1994, 43.5 percent of all members and candidates in TAKAM were from the second, third and even fourth generations. The next largest group comprised families and individuals who had joined on their own initiative or through marriage (30.4 percent). Those who had come directly from youth movements in Israel or abroad formed a third group (20.8 percent). The remaining 5.3 percent were made up mainly of youths who had come to the kibbutz for their education and had stayed on. In the older kibbutzim, those born and raised in the kibbutz form a clear majority and, together with their parents and marriage partners, represent the large familial core of the kibbutz.

FORMATION OF FAMILIES

Formation of a familial community has been the characteristic trait of kibbutzim. That process has seen family units expand over three or four generations, all living together in a shared household. The kibbutz, functioning as a communal household, provides protection for the family and makes for greater stability within the family. Divorce rates in the kibbutz population have been consistently low. In the early 1990s, the rates averaged 3.0 per 1,000 men and women aged fifteen and over as against 4.0 in the surrounding Jewish population.   '

The establishment of kibbutzim as familial communities did not come easily. Founding members of early kibbutzim were usually in their late teens or early twenties and imbued with revolutionary ideas about building an ideal community. Almost all agreed that the nuclear family would be an impediment to achieving that goal, and they determined to replace it by group arrangements that would provide more opportunities for women; reduce the tendency of parents to regard their children as their "private property"; and, by restraining egotism and encouraging widespread sharing, promote a more moral life.

As it turned out, nature proved stronger than ideology. Couples paired off and had children. The principle of shared consumption shaped the formation of a communal household within which nuclear families soon expanded into larger familial units embracing several generations—also groups, but not in the sense anticipated by the founding members. From that point of view, evolution of the kibbutz has been characterized until very recently by transition from a society of mobile individuals to a stable familial community. In most kibbutzim, a majority of the children grow up alongside their grandparents and are in daily contact with the whole cycle of life, from infancy to old age. For them, the kibbutz is a natural habitat, and yet the influence of the surrounding market society cannot be denied.

Members of the second generation began to come of age in significantly large numbers from the end of the 1950s, and they proved to be predominantly family-oriented. Data available for fifty-eight kibbutzim show that in 1957 only 9.3 percent of their members came from the second generation. During the following five years, the number more than doubled (from 1,003 to 2,181) and by 1967 had risen to 3,654 , or 29 percent of total membership. There were similar developments in the rest of the kibbutz population. While the new members from within the kibbutz did not contribute directly to increasing population numbers, they brought about a radical change in the character of the kibbutz: They married early and had more children than their parents.

NATURAL REPRODUCTION

During the 1960s and early 1970s, early marriage led to a rapid increase in population. In 1960, the marriage rate in kibbutzim was 11.7 as against 7.7 in the surrounding Jewish population. Between 1963 and 1971, the crude birth rate (number of births per 1,000 persons in the average permanent population) rose from 20.9 to 29.8, and the annual number of births from 1,667 to 2,549. The general fertility rate (number of births per 1,000 women aged fifteen to forty-nine) grew from 101.6 to 109.3, and total fertility (estimated average number of children per woman) from 2.7 to 3.3. Those rates of growth exceeded comparable rates in the surrounding Jewish population.

During those years, there was rapid industrialization in kibbutzim, and the standard of living rose appreciably. Meanwhile, members of the second generation proved devoted parents, and child raising became a central part of their way of life. A start was made in changing sleeping arrangements for the children from collective dormitories in separate children-houses (a hallmark of the early kibbutz educational system) to their parents' apartment, which soon became the focal point of social life. At the same time, apartments were enlarged, and provisions were made for more private consumption.

Such changes improved the kibbutz image as a favorable environment for family life and seem to have been a major influence in bringing about a sharp increase in the number of people joining kibbutzim from outside, particularly urban Israeli families. Between 1971 and 1986, the kibbutz population grew by 47 percent from 86,300 to 126,700; the growth in the children's population led the way due both to absorption of young families with their children and to the overall increase of the fertile population. There was, however, a falling off in the crude birth rate, although, at first, this was obscured by overall growth.

A serious financial crisis that erupted in 1985 changed some demographic trends. The most immediate and clear consequences were a sharp drop in the absorption of new members from outside and an increase in the number of people leaving their kibbutz. The migration from the kibbutzim brought into clear focus the declining birth rate of the core population. Between 1985 and 1993, the crude birth rate dropped from 24.0 to 15.2, and the general fertility rate from 97.0 to 59.7. There was a parallel drop in births in the surrounding Jewish population, showing that the causes were deeper than the specific conditions within kibbutzim. Adult population in kibbutzim remained at approximately the same level, while the children's population declined because of fewer births.

Many observers jumped to the conclusion that there was a direct connection between the economic problems of the time and the fall in births. A detailed examination of the data proved that theory only partially correct. In effect, the crude birth rate had fallen between 1971 and 1985 from 29.8 to 24.0, while the number of births had risen from 2,549 to 2,975. That situation changed when the crude birth rate continued to fall and reached 15.2 in 1993, while the number of births fell to 1,938.

Members of the third generation, mostly grandchildren of veteran members, began to make a massive appearance in the adult population during the late 1980s. Their behavior has been characterized by deferment of marriage and, consequently, a reduction in the number of children. The result has been a major shift in the composition of the familial core (see Table 1.6). In 1972, 22.3 percent of the men and 50.8 percent of the women aged twenty to twenty-four were married; in 1995, the figures for TAKAM show only 1 percent for men and 4 percent for women. Such a shift implies a radical change in life-style and reflects a much deeper involvement in the youth culture of the surrounding market society.

A direct consequence of deferred marriage is that mothers tend to be older at the time of giving birth—as has been happening at an accelerating pace in the kibbutz population since the 1970s (see Table 1.7). In 1972 almost 40 percent of all births were to mothers aged twenty-four or younger, while in 1992 the figure was

Table 1.6
Changes in the Percentage of Married Persons by Age Group

Age Group	Men		Women	
	1972^1	1995^2	1972^1	1995^2
20–24	22.3	1.0	50.8	4.0
25–29	71.2	19.6	83.1	40.3
30–34	89.1	69.9	89.6	85.0
35–39	92.6	86.2	91.5	89.7
40–44	92.4	90.0	92.8	88.3
45–49	91.5	91.3	91.2	86.2

1 All of the kibbutz population.
2 TAKAM members and candidates only.

Source: Central Bureau of Statistics, Government of Israel; and Department of Information, TAKAM.

Table 1.7
Age of Mother at Time of Birth (Percentages)

Age Group	1972	1985	1992
15–19	3.3	0.5	0.8
20–24	36.3	13.5	9.5
25–29	36.4	37.0	30.9
30–34	14.7	30.7	36.2
35–39	8.0	16.4	18.5
40+	1.3	1.9	4.1
Total	100.0	100.0	100.0

Source: Central Bureau of Statistics, Government of Israel.

just over 9 percent. At the same time, in 1972 24 percent of the births were to mothers aged thirty and older while in 1992 the figure was 57 percent. The demographic changes parallel trends in the advanced market societies of North America, Europe, and Japan. As women delay motherhood, the age gap between children and parents widens, with psychological consequences that have yet to be fully understood.

EDUCATIONAL LEVELS

The kibbutz educational system enjoys a large measure of autonomy. Almost all kibbutz children are educated in kibbutz schools staffed by teachers trained in one of the two educational colleges run by the kibbutz movement. Education was for many years dominated by a policy emphasizing equality. In recent years, more attention has been paid to encouraging individual development and excellence. Even in the pre-state period, kibbutzim required of their children twelve years of schooling, with the goal of bringing all of the children to the same level. Adult education was widely encouraged for all age groups. The ideal was an erudite laborer.

As can be seen in Table 1.8, most TAKAM members who have higher education have studied in disciplines connected with work in the kibbutz context. For the men, the major disciplines of study have been engineering and economics; for the women, the major disciplines of study have been education and medicine (mainly nursing, social work and alternative medicine). The data in Table 1.8 are doubtless representative of the entire kibbutz population.

EMPLOYMENT STRUCTURE

Productive labor is a central part of kibbutz ideology. In 1994, two-thirds of the men and more than a quarter of the women worked in agriculture or industry (see

Table 1.8
Higher Education among Members of TAKAM Aged Twenty and Over by Field of
Study, 1995

	20–29	30–39	40–49	50–59	60+	Total
Men						
Engineering	197	681	704	336	148	2,066
Economics	106	266	382	255	170	1,179
Education	21	76	142	97	129	465
Medicine	28	50	56	26	21	181
Social Sciences	77	153	248	206	170	854
Natural Sciences	64	183	290	154	105	796
Other	262	386	381	260	229	1,522
Total	755	1,795	2,203	1,334	972	7,063
Women						
Engineering	115	141	101	30	11	398
Economics	87	149	149	84	47	516
Education	260	731	1,143	595	440	3,169
Medicine	141	343	450	199	138	1,271
Social Sciences	170	195	255	137	133	890
Natural Sciences	71	114	113	39	19	356
Other	418	431	547	303	187	1,886
Total	1,262	2,104	2,758	1,387	975	8,486

Source: Department of Information, TAKAM.

Table 1.9). In recent years, the fastest-growing part of the kibbutz economy has been tourism and accompanying services. For the most part, men are concentrated in the productive and commercial branches, while almost half of the women are employed in services, especially education (in the broad sense, care of children as well as teaching).

The structure of employment by branches gives only one side of the picture. Division by occupation gives another side (see Table 1.10). Academization of teaching and nursing has led to an increase in academics, particularly women. Growth of the kibbutz economy, especially industry, has led to a 50 percent increase in managerial, clerical, and marketing personnel. The number of kibbutz members specializing in agriculture has been dropping steadily.

Table 1.9
Changes in Employment by Economic Branch (Percentages)

	Men		Women	
	1972	*1994*	*1972*	*1994*
Agriculture and fishing	46.7	36.6	9.4	11.8
Industry and quarrying	21.3	32.1	20.0	17.3
Tourism, commerce, and finance	5.6	9.3	15.7	14.8
Transportation and storage	4.1	2.7	3.8	7.8
Public and community services	7.7	7.7	22.3	26.1
Personal and other services	9.1	9.5	26.4	22.1
Other	5.5	2.1	2.4	0.1
Total (percent)	100.0	100.0	100.0	100.0
Total (#)	27,845	37,700	27,010	39,800

Source: Central Bureau of Statistics, Government of Israel.

Table 1.10
Changes in Employment by Occupation (Percentages)

	1972	1994
Academic and scientific	2.8	4.9
Liberal professions and technical	13.5	14.3
Administration and management	1.7	3.9
Clerical	9.5	13.6
Sales and marketing	1.3	4.2
Services	22.4	21.8
Agriculture	23.5	15.8
Skilled workers	18.5	15.6
Unskilled and other workers	2.4	5.9
Unknown	4.4	—
Total (percent)	100.0	100.0
Total (#)	54,855	77,700

Source: Central Bureau of Statistics, Government of Israel.

TOWARD THE FUTURE

Deferred marriage and fewer children represent trends characteristic of market societies, but they run counter to the formation of large familial communities. Should the present trend continue, it would bring about a change in the internal structure of the kibbutz and raise serious questions about the future of the kibbutz movement. Rapid urbanization is another process that threatens the future of the kibbutz. Much will depend on the ability of kibbutz members to adapt to change without forgoing basic principles of communal life.

2
Winds of Change

Shlomo Getz

KIBBUTZ AND CHANGES

Concern with change is not a new phenomenon in the kibbutz. Throughout its existence, the kibbutz movement has been engaged in controversies about changes in its way of life and to its institutional structure. Yet change was never considered as a comprehensive concept but was limited to a specific area. Since the mid-1980s, however, following a severe economic and social crisis, the scope and intensity of change proposed and accepted have been exceptional. Topel (1995), for instance, collected information about 118 different changes proposed in thirty-four kibbutzim in 1992–1993.

The need for change is seen by kibbutz members as evolving from the ever widening gap between reality and the existing organizational structure and system of values of the kibbutz. The new reality stems from two different causes: causes outside the kibbutz to which the kibbutz must adapt and internal causes related to the changing needs of kibbutz members. In kibbutz discourse, change may be expressed in such terms as "adaptation to the surroundings" (reflecting, on the one hand, the impact of external causes) or "personal responsibility of the members" (reflecting, on the other hand, the impact of internal causes).

Although the need for constant change in kibbutzim has always been accepted among the kibbutz population, the present differs from the past in that the focus is on the meaning of change for the kibbutz way of life—whether change represents change *within* the system or change *of* the system.

Several writers (e.g., Pavin, 1995; Rosolio, 1995; Ravid, 1994) discuss whether the change the kibbutz has undergone in recent years is a technical normative adjustment to the demands of a changing reality or a major change of the kibbutz value system. They believe it to be the latter. Rosner and Getz (1994) explain the change as the transition from a society run by principles of cooperation to the

introduction of market and hierarchy mechanisms in the internal kibbutz structure—which, they conclude, may lead to the loss of identity of the kibbutz as a
commune.

This chapter examines the main changes in the kibbutz since the crisis of the
mid-1980s. I start by describing the extent of the changes and the response of
kibbutz members in several areas of kibbutz life: consumption, work, organizational structure and democracy, allocation of rewards, and integration with the
surrounding environment. I then discuss the meaning of the changes for the
kibbutz way of life.

What I have to say is based on information about changes collected from all the
kibbutzim in Israel. Each year since 1990, a questionnaire has been sent to the
general secretary of each kibbutz asking about the implementation of a series of
changes. Information about thirty-five changes was collected in 1990 and about
fifty in 1996. Over the years, some of the changes were omitted because they had
been fully implemented; meanwhile new changes had been introduced. Most of
these changes are documented in Table 2.1. Data about kibbutz members' attitude
toward changes are based on surveys conducted yearly (since 1989) by Palgi and
Sharir (1995) from a sample of about one thousand members from all the secular
kibbutz communities.

THE PROCESS OF PRIVATIZATION

A prominent subject of kibbutz discourse is the concept of privatization. There
are members who view it as the major change which the kibbutz is undergoing; and
indeed, out of all of today's widespread changes, privatization is the most prominent
in the daily life of the kibbutz member. The changes in other areas—as in kibbutz
democracy and in the organizational structure of the economy in general and the
work branches in particular—are less felt (although their influence may be greater).
The overwhelming nature of privatization is so strong that even changes which are
not necessarily an expression of privatization are still considered by many members
to be a part of the privatization process. In the minds of many, privatization has
become synonymous with change itself.

As a theoretical concept, privatization was first introduced at the start of the
1980s—in Britain, during the tenure of Margaret Thatcher as prime minister, and
in the United States, during the presidency of Ronald Reagan. It signifies the sale of
public enterprises and services to private ownership (in effect, inversion of the
concept of nationalization). In the language of the kibbutz, the concept carries a
slightly different meaning—that is, the transfer of consumer budgets from kibbutz
control to personal control by the member. While kibbutz control meant that
kibbutz governing institutions could decide about priorities in spending the consumer budget, privatization of a domain meant the distribution of the public
budget to individual members in equal shares and the introduction of user fees.
Privatization in the kibbutz encompasses two areas: consumption and services; and
labor.

Table 2.1
Diffusion of Changes among Kibbutzim, 1990–1996

	Cumulative Percent Adopting by Year						
	1996	1995	1994	1993	1992	1991	1990
Consumption							
Comprehensive private consumption budget	76	71	61	66	66	59	54
Charging members for electricity	68	67	69	60	57	44	26
Pay for recreation activity from personal budget	40	32	34	28	33	25	25
Charging members for meals in dining hall	38	25	16	7	6	NA	3
Pay for higher education from personal budget	10	7	7	4	3	3	1
Work							
Encouraging external labor	67	68	72	67	77	69	65
Members' responsibility to choose job	57	50	46	41	40	27	19
Organizational Structure and Democracy							
Board of directors in factories	66	64	63	52	51	37	23
Secret ballot instead of vote in assembly	50	46	43	41	33	20	7
Economic branches as profit centers	42	32	34	29	39	26	18
Partnership with private investors	30	26	28	21	21	22	12
Abolishing obligatory rotation of managers	30	25	19	14	16	7	8
Co-ownership with other kibbutzim	29	24	23	25	27	28	30
Creation of a representative council	29	32	31	23	24	19	8
Separating the economy from the community	28	22	18	13	16	7	6
Replacing committees by officeholders	24	26	19	14	17	11	7
Calculating shadow wages	21	13	10	8	10	6	7
Formation of internal control committee	19	14	13	10	11	7	5
Board of directors in agriculture	26	26	24	17	15	12	9
Allocation of Rewards							
Extra pay for additional hours worked	15	11	5	3	3	3	2
Extra pay for officeholders in difficult jobs	6	3	3	1	2	2	2
Connection between work and budget	16	11	11	7	5	NA	NA
Integration							
Employing hired laborers instead of members	55	54	55	47	46	29	20
Children-houses for outside children	89	83	84	74	72	67	55
Selling services	63	69	64	60	57	57	48

NA = not asked.

PRIVATIZATION OF CONSUMPTION SERVICES

Kibbutz consumption has gone through various incarnations since the early days of kibbutz life. During the 1970s and the early 1980s, a more or less stable method became well established. Much of the consumption and services was communally given to members, and the members were allowed free access to them (for example, food, laundry, basic health services, and so on.) In addition, each member was allotted a small personal budget, which was distributed in an egalitarian way. Various budgets were placed at the disposal of committees, which allocated them to members according to personal need (starting from an additional budget for clothing up to the acquisition of higher education or housing). While this method served well the kibbutz dictum "to each according to his or her needs," it also, according to some members, led to many distortions—because it rendered the members dependent upon the committees.

In time, as the kibbutz became multigenerational and heterogeneous, members' needs became more and more diversified, reflecting, at least in part, the rest of Israeli society, which was becoming a society of consumers. In this situation, the members found it more and more difficult to supply their unique, nonbasic needs from the budget placed at their disposal. At the same time, kibbutz institutions found it difficult to distribute the budgets according to principles that were accepted and agreed upon by all sections of the population. Dissatisfaction grew when the economic situation in the kibbutzim took a turn for the worse and the total sum of budgets to be distributed declined. The idea of privatization arrived on the scene to solve these problems.

The basic assumption of privatization is that the transfer of budgets to the members' control enhances economic consumer-efficiency and enlarges the individual's room to maneuver according to his or her preferences. In addition, the individual's dependence upon the kibbutz committees decreases. The result is the member's greater satisfaction as a consumer. However, in addition to considerations of efficiency, arguments of principle have also been heard in kibbutz discourse. It has been said that the purpose of privatization is "to transfer responsibility" to the member's shoulders, to allow the member more autonomy. The argument is that the kibbutz way of life, in which all the needs of the member are supplied to him or her by the system, leads to degeneration and lack of initiative, whereas the individual should act according to his or her considerations and be responsible for his or her actions.

Public budgets targeted for privatization lay in two domains:

1. Services that the kibbutz supplied "as required" (such as meals in the dining hall and the consumption of electrical energy)
2. Budgets that were at the disposal of committees and were handed out according to clear criteria (such as a supplement for cigarettes) or in response to personal requests

Table 2.2 exemplifies the trend of privatizing these public budgets.

Table 2.2
Privatization in Consumption—Percentage of Kibbutzim Implementing

	1990 N = 135	1992 N = 191	1994 N = 204	1996 N = 221
Comprehensive private consumption budget (that includes up to 60–70% of all consumption budget)	54	66	61	73
User fee for electricity	26	57	69	70
Charging user fee for meals in the dining hall	3	6	16	37
Pay for recreation activity from personal budget	25	33	34	40
Pay for higher education from personal budget	1	3	7	10

The privatization of budgets is taking place in almost all the kibbutzim, and the method is similar in most. The sum that the kibbutz has allocated for a specific purpose is divided among all the members, either in equal shares or according to agreed-upon criteria (such as the size of the family). The heading of "comprehensive budget" includes various budgets which previously had been given to members as a distribution free of charge ("according to need"), but which they must now pay for—for example, such items as the daily newspaper, travel on public transportation, postal charges, personal hygiene products, and various basic necessities such as vegetables, eggs, and milk products. Each kibbutz decides what to list in the comprehensive budget and transfers to individual control the sum of money that is required for acquiring them. Even expensive items have been privatized—for example, payment for electrical consumption and trips overseas (generally arranged according to a queue of members).

The payment for meals in the dining hall was controversial for a long time. In public opinion surveys of the kibbutz movement (Palgi and Sharir, 1995), less than a quarter of those interviewed in 1989 supported such payments, but the rate of support has steadily grown from year to year, and in 1995, it reached as high as 55 percent. At first, few kibbutzim put into effect payment for meals; but starting in 1994, there was a significant increase, and by 1996, such payment was the rule in almost 40 percent of the kibbutzim.

This issue of the kibbutz dining hall has other aspects. The dining hall has never been just a restaurant but has served as a central daily meeting place for all the members of the kibbutz and as a forum for public affairs—the work schedule, the kibbutz general assembly, and various meetings. Nowadays, the dining hall is closed during the evening hours in one-third of the kibbutzim and also during breakfast in a smaller number. The dining hall, which used to be one of the more outstanding symbols of the kibbutz, is now becoming a restaurant that is open only for the noontime meal.

Permission to purchase a private automobile (not heard of a few years ago) also belongs to the area of consumption—but not precisely to the area of privatization. In the sense of transfer of budgets from communal to personal control, the purchase of a private car represents a situation in which the kibbutz does not intervene in the standard of living of the individual. In the past, the individual's standard of living was determined by the kibbutz—not only through the personal budget but also through reservations about what was permitted and what was forbidden within the limits of the budget. Items that were relatively expensive were generally supplied by the kibbutz, each kibbutz determining the rules whereby the item was supplied.

From the point of view of initial acquisition, and even more from the standpoint of ongoing expenses, the automobile is unique. It is an item whose cost exceeds the collective cost of all the other items that the kibbutz has been accustomed to supply to its members or enabled them to acquire from their personal budget. The continuing economic crisis has cast further doubt on the possibility that the kibbutz would find in the near future communal arrangements to place a personal car at the disposal of every family. The granting of permission to acquire a vehicle and to use it legitimizes, therefore, the private purchase of any item in which the member is interested. This proposal has been accepted in 40 percent of the kibbutzim. Yet it seems that in many kibbutzim, this was not a planned move but rather a lack of ability to implement decisions.

As mentioned, researchers of kibbutz life are divided in their opinions about the significance of the changes in consumption patterns—whether they signify change *within* or *of* the system. In a comparative study of the changes in consumer attitudes between the years 1978 and 1987 (Rosner, Gluck, and Goldenberg, 1991), it was found that no change had taken place in the value-oriented approaches of the subjects, despite the privatization of budgets that had already begun in many kibbutzim. Yet the granting of money instead of providing a service or satisfying a necessity is liable to lead to a situation in which the kibbutz no longer regards itself as responsible for fulfilling certain needs.

In all the budgets that have been privatized, it is accepted that once a specific need has been supplied by the transfer of a budget to the control of a member, the kibbutz should not be responsible for the supply of that need. Since the allocation is egalitarian, the transition is from the principle of "to each according to his or her needs" to an equality-based distribution in all those areas of consumption that have been privatized, and this represents a change in values. It is not a question of technical arrangements only, but rather of arrangements based upon new values aimed at the abolition of communal consumption. The transition to the granting of money signifies the introduction of market mechanisms into the kibbutz (Rosner and Getz, 1996).

The more intense the privatization of budgets becomes, the more the member pays for necessities and services. This could result in a situation in which all the services and necessities are privatized and the member receives a budget which is, in effect, a salary. The kibbutz then becomes a seller of services instead of a provider of services, and the considerations for activating the service or for the member's acquisition of it become the business of the marketplace—that is, economic profitability.

Transition to the granting of a budget instead of providing a service will likely lead members to consume certain services outside the kibbutz—ultimately to the point where there will no longer be any need for their existence within the kibbutz. For example, this might mean the termination of the kibbutz general store in which everything is bought with money—because the members prefer to buy at the shopping center of the nearby town where the selection is larger and there is sometimes no difference in price. Another example is personal services, such as barber shops and cosmetic treatments, where the selection is greater outside the kibbutz. Furthermore, for reasons of economic efficiency, it might be preferable to transfer certain services to a regional framework (as happens, in effect, in education).

Another possible result of the privatization process could be the reduction of services that the kibbutz provides to its members. But this has not happened. A recent survey in 180 kibbutzim of some forty types of services that exist in the kibbutz shows that instead of canceling services, the kibbutzim have chosen to open them up to customers outside the kibbutz. Examples of such services are children-houses, cosmetics, laundry services, recreational parks, and even nursing homes for the aged. This phenomenon may be temporary. Meanwhile, it answers several needs: Kibbutz members continue to receive services within the kibbutz (which they prefer because of the high degree of accessibility and because of the quality of the service), and the continuation of services ensures employment for the members who provide them.

PRIVATIZATION IN THE AREA OF WORK

Work per se is not generally conceived of as a part of the process of privatization. However, the principles that have guided the transition to the privatization of consumption are also evident in the area of work.

Two changes of principle have emerged in the concept of work in the kibbutz. First, there has been a transfer of the responsibility for work onto the member, following an approach similar to the one that has guided the privatization in the area of consumption—that is, treating the member as an autonomous adult who should support himself. In order to implement this principle, the kibbutz set up a new administrative body—"human resources"—one of whose functions is to assist the members in planning their professional futures.

Second, there has been a change in the concept of work from a value in its own right to work for livelihood as a value: The emphasis is on *livelihood*—that is, on the economic value of work. This change is linked to another change: the decline in ideological importance of the kibbutz productive units. One of the goals of the kibbutz at its inception was to maintain a self-sustaining economy. The allocation of members to workplaces was based more on the requirements of the work branches than on the needs of the members—and without economic efficiency of the work as the prime motive. This is exemplified by a well-known cartoon of kibbutz life. Says the work coordinator to a recent graduate of accounting: "OK, so you've just finished a course in accounting! Now go to work in the cow barn."

Nowadays, the goal is not to maintain a self-sustaining economy but to plan for the economic success of the kibbutz. Sometimes this may require members to work outside the kibbutz, even at the price of bringing in hired workers or cutting back a branch of work to the point of liquidation.

In current kibbutz discourse, one hears more and more the demand that the member should be responsible for his livelihood. To achieve true freedom, it is necessary to remove certain restrictions, such as those on work outside the kibbutz. The possibility of members working outside the kibbutz is also associated with increasing the sources of income for the kibbutz. And indeed many kibbutzim have officially decided to approve work outside on the condition that it generate income above a certain minimum level; others do not even make that condition at all.

Work outside the kibbutz has magnified another phenomenon: the increase in the number of hired workers in the kibbutz. The increase has occurred in most kibbutzim, partly because of an increase in production and partly because of the option of the member has to choose his or her place of work. In 1996, the idea of "personal responsibility for livelihood" was accepted in 57 percent of the kibbutzim (as opposed to 19 percent in 1990), and in 1996 the substitution of hired workers for members was accepted by 55 percent of the kibbutzim (as opposed to 20 percent in 1990).

In the background exist new concepts of business-oriented management in the kibbutz. Against this background, the change in approach has led to a situation in which the individual member has to cope with the external labor market (if he or she chooses to work outside the kibbutz) or even the one within the kibbutz—competing with potential hired workers from the outside. The conventional system of allocating work has given way to an approach that stresses counseling and guidance rather than allocation according to the needs of the work branches (44 percent of kibbutzim in 1996). In practice, even here market considerations are active—in particular, the labor market. The kibbutz member has to compete for his place of work. "Factory managers who would desire to maximize the profits of their enterprise would be faced with the dilemma whether to employ a member as against someone from the outside; their duty and privilege is to select the more efficient." This was written in 1992 in the weekly *Kibbutz* by Professor Kroll, a teacher of business administration and a kibbutz member.

The labor market within the kibbutz is merely symbolic (Rosner and Getz, 1996). It lacks the use of money as a driving mechanism, making it difficult to function as a market. The outcome is twofold:

1. Many kibbutzim which have decided on personal responsibility for livelihood do not know how to implement this idea under the existing conditions.
2. Pressure is created to introduce differential payments for work in order for a labor market to function.

ORGANIZATIONAL STRUCTURE AND DEMOCRACY

The normative kibbutz was characterized by a comprehensive organizational structure in which hierarchical levels were few and direct democracy prevailed. To prevent the creation of distinct status and accumulation of power and influence, a rotation system was introduced in all economic and public positions (Tannenbaum et al., 1974; Leviatan, 1978). The self-labor principle was strengthened by the reluctance to employ outside workers.

The economic crisis brought changes to the managerial approach and to its language. The new discourse began introducing such terms as "business managing" rather than "kibbutz management." It was suggested that the "firm" (a new term introduced instead of "productive branches") be separated from the "community" and that overall management of the economic activities should be attuned to the needs of the market, while the egalitarian and democratic principles should be implemented only in the communal sphere. This separation, it is supposed by supporters, will contribute to the economic efficiency of the kibbutz.

The main proposals are to have a board of directors in kibbutz industry; to change the kibbutz economic units into autonomous "profit centers"; and to calculate (but not pay to the members) differential "shadow wages" based on labor costs outside the kibbutz and thereby arrive at a more realistic and correct calculation of the economic cost of the business. Employment of hired laborers and rotation of managers should be based solely on economic considerations and should no longer be used as a tool to maintain the social structure of the egalitarian society. The business approach should also allow the participation of outside investors in kibbutz enterprises.

The most profound changes stemming from these suggestions have been the increase in employment of hired laborers and the establishment of boards of directors in factories and (occasionally) in agriculture (see Table 2.3). Profit centers exist in about 40 percent of the kibbutzim, often without the separation of the economy from the community, which can be problematic in a community accustomed to being comprehensive. To illustrate this problem, I found in a survey conducted in 1995 that a third of the kibbutzim separating the economy from the community failed to calculate differential shadow wages for members' work. Some of them did not have profit centers; others had changed the status of economic units into profit centers but allowed those centers only restricted autonomy.

Centralizing decision making was also suggested in the overall governing system of the kibbutz, leading to the creation of representative councils (usually of twenty to thirty members) which took over most of the functions of the general assembly. The diffusion of this change was rapid at the beginning of the 1990s, but then it stopped; some kibbutzim even abolished the council after a short trial.

Another suggestion was to establish a controlling committee for restricting the powers of managers and committees. Although considered a democratic device, such a committee implied loss of confidence in the executive body. However, despite the fact that spontaneous, face-to-face social relations in the kibbutz are tending to become impersonal and formal, and despite proposals to do away with principles

Table 2.3
Changes in Organizational Structure and Democracy—Percentage of Kibbutzim
Implementing

	1990 N = 135	1992 N = 191	1994 N = 204	1996 N = 221
Organizational Structure				
Separating the business from the community	6	16	18	27
Economic branches as profit centers	18	39	34	42
Employing hired laborers	20	46	55	72
Board of directors in factories	23	51	63	67
Abolishing obligatory rotation of managers	8	16	19	31
General Decision Making				
Formation of internal control committee	5	11	13	18
Secret ballot instead of vote in assembly	7	33	43	50
Creation of representative council	8	24	31	29

of direct democracy (that govern kibbutz functioning by law), this type of committee has not been implemented in most kibbutzim.

Still another popular new direction is voting in a secret ballot, which has been
implemented by half of the kibbutzim in 1996 and which thereby broadens direct
democracy, since it is unnecessary to participate in the assembly for voting. But the
possibility of reaching agreement after the exchange of ideas is lacking. The cost is
less communication, less possibility of reaching consensus, and less solidarity
among members. Although a voluminous body of research and theory argues that
democratic organizations become increasingly less democratic with the passage of
time (e.g., Michels and the "iron law of oligarchy"), it seems that with the kibbutz,
this process has not occurred. Contrary to the hypothesis, the older and bigger
kibbutzim have rejected more than the other kibbutzim the suggestion to reduce
direct democracy (Russell, Getz, and Rosner, 1996). Furthermore, the last public
opinion survey (Palgi and Sharir, 1995) shows that kibbutz members prefer direct
democracy: In 1995, only 44 percent supported the representative council, while 78
percent supported the secret ballot.

ALLOCATION OF REWARDS

The kibbutz is unique in the way it allocates rewards to members. Changes have
been proposed since the end of the 1980s, and if adopted, such proposals could
threaten the kibbutz identity. The first wave assumed that whereas "ordinary" work
should not be rewarded, additional work should be differentially paid. This inno-

vation was implemented in only a few kibbutzim. A few years later, a relationship between the number of work days and the personal budget was proposed in some kibbutzim, dealing with an issue of widespread concern—the "free riders." The proposal, which was to "penalize" those that worked less than the annual working days required, was rejected in most kibbutzim. Even kibbutzim which overcame the ideological barrier and implemented this change found that almost all members worked the required number of days.

These early proposals generated only a quantitative connection between work and payment—as opposed to qualitative, which is based on skill or managerial responsibility. As the market mechanism penetrated into the kibbutz culture, other proposals came into the open, in particular, differential payment for work based on qualitative measurement—namely, regular salary. More than thirty kibbutzim are discussing that possibility, but so far only very few (three or four) are implementing it. Another proposal introduces a modified version of a regular salary: The personal budget of the member should include a differential component according to his or her calculated potential salary (in the outside labor market). This component would represent 3 percent to 25 percent of the total budget (different proportions in different kibbutzim), while most of the budget would be distributed equally to all members, taking into consideration the size of the family. As shown in Table 2.4, such changes have been implemented in only a few kibbutzim.

The public opinion polls of Palgi and Sharir (1995) show an increasing readiness to accept differential rewards. In 1990, 43 percent of the members approved extra pay for additional hours worked; in 1995, the figure was 54 percent. Almost 60 percent in 1995 were agreeable to relating the personal budget to the number of working days. The proportion of members supporting differential wages according to individual income grew from 30 percent in 1993 (when the question was asked for the first time) to 43 percent in 1995. The question about a differential component had yet to be asked, but in 1996, 20 percent of the kibbutzim were discussing it. Materially and differentially rewarding work in the kibbutz is often justified as a way to overcome a lack of motivation by the members and, with common assets, the absence of feelings of ownership.

Table 2.4
Changes in Allocation of Rewards—Percentage of Kibbutzim Implementing

	1990 N = 135	1992 N = 191	1994 N = 204	1996 N = 221
Paying for overtime	2	6	5	15
Correlation between work and budget	NA	5	11	14
Differential salary	NA	NA	NA	2
Budget with differential component	NA	NA	NA	4

NA = not asked.

INTEGRATION WITH THE SURROUNDING ENVIRONMENT

Most of the changes the kibbutz has undergone are designed to affect the internal social and work arrangements of kibbutz life, but some deal directly with the relation of the kibbutz to the surrounding environment. The general idea is expressed in kibbutz discourse as "openness to the environment." The expression of that openness is bidirectional: It allows members to work outside the kibbutz, while opening the kibbutz to hired laborers; it enables the kibbutz to sell its services outside; and it allows nonmembers to live as residents on the kibbutz. The extent of diffusion of some of these changes is shown in Table 2.5.

The results of such changes are far-reaching. In the population of the kibbutz, no longer do members necessarily predominate. During the day, the kibbutz courtyard is full of hired laborers, children from surrounding towns and villages pour in to be cared for in the kibbutz children-houses, and random visitors come to use kibbutz services such as shops and alternative medicine centers. At the same time, about 20 percent of the members work outside the kibbutz, and the forecast for future years is about a third (Palgi and Sharir, 1995).

The social impact of this situation is of great significance. For the member working outside, the kibbutz may become only a place of residence—with himself or herself as a commuter. And the solidarity among members, which was partially based on everyday meeting and working together, will necessarily be weakened.

In 1996, about half of the kibbutzim offered apartments for rent to outsiders. Some kibbutzim reported that the reason they were not renting apartments was simply that they didn't have any that were empty. More than half of kibbutz members support this activity (Palgi and Sharir, 1995). Obviously, renting apartments introduces residents to the kibbutz who are not members, and as this process continues, the social identity of the kibbutz will become ambiguous: Will the kibbutz social entity comprise all residents or only those who belong to the commune? This problematic situation may be exacerbated by the sale of houses to outside residents. Although only a few kibbutzim have so far sold houses to outsiders, 40 percent of kibbutz members are ready to accept permanent nonmem-

Table 2.5
Integration with the Environment—Percentage of Kibbutzim Implementing

	1990 N = 135	1992 N = 191	1994 N = 204	1996 N = 221
Encouraging work of members outside	65	77	72	72
Accepting children from outside into children-houses for a fee	55	72	84	90
Selling various services	48	57	64	63
Partnership with private investors	12	21	28	30
Partnership with other kibbutzim	30	27	23	28

ber residents in their community (Palgi and Sharir, 1995). These residents who owned their houses on kibbutz land would then become an integral part of the community, but would not share ownership of means of production and all other communal assets. However, they would no doubt participate in the municipal activities and could legally be elected to the formal institutions of the municipal authority. In those kibbutzim which accepted nonmember residents, the community would be split into a "regular" community and a commune. It is not clear how stable such a social arrangement would be.

CONCLUSION

The process of intensive change in the kibbutz still continues after a decade. Some of the changes can be defined as adaptation or modification, but the overall impact may change the whole system of kibbutz life. Sometimes a change implemented as a minor modification has led to an unanticipated major outcome. In this context, I have discussed some of the sources of pressure for changing the system of allocating rewards and the development of a community in which the kibbutz is only one fragment.

From the kibbutz members' point of view, there are some principles that govern the proposed and accepted changes. Among them are the responsibility of the individual member to control his or her life, including consumption and work; the rational economic behavior that focuses on earning money as a target instead of developing the kibbutz assets; and integration with the socioeconomic environment.

The new directions the kibbutz is taking are toward markets and hierarchy that replace cooperation and lead to decommunalization of the kibbutz. Decommunalization can take two major forms: disintegration and assimilation. The first happens when all members of the commune leave the community; neither commune nor community exists any longer. Assimilation means that the commune becomes something else. One possibility is to become a private, for-profit firm. The organization continues to exist, but members disperse. The concrete community does not exist anymore. Another possibility is that members of the commune do not disperse but create a new form of community.

When a process of decommunalization occurs and when the direction is toward assimilation (as in the kibbutz), the process can end with the creation of a community based on principles other than those of the commune. It does not necessarily follow that the end of the commune will be the end of the community. Kibbutz experience in the last decade shows that this phenomenon is possible.

We are experiencing the emergence of a new form of community—a community built on the remains of the communal principle without rejecting all communal traits. To understand the nature of the new type of community, we have to examine not only change but also stability—principles that have not changed. Communal ownership of the means of production is one of these unchanged principles. There has been no proposal to change communal ownership, and members of the kibbutzim are against such a change. If this principle persists, a new form of commune might arise.

3
Work in the Kibbutz

Menachem Rosner

Work organization in the kibbutz raises three questions inapplicable in other work organizations. First, the social organization of work in the kibbutz is based on satisfying the needs of the individual (such as health, family, and personal interests) irrespective of the amount or the quality of his or her work. Thus, the first question to be asked about the social organization of work in the kibbutz is, what motivates kibbutz members to exert themselves when the satisfaction of their needs is already guaranteed?

Second, since money is not used as a medium of exchange (there are no wages), manpower supply and demand cannot be reconciled through a market mechanism; and since membership in the kibbutz is free and voluntary, coercion cannot be exerted. Another question that therefore arises from the uniqueness of kibbutz organization is, What ensures congruity between the available work force and the manpower requirements of the kibbutz?

Third, the organization of work in the kibbutz is based on democratic procedures, with workers in a given branch having the authority to make decisions. They elect the branch coordinator for a limited term, and it is his or her job to see that the decisions made democratically in the branch are carried out. Furthermore, the democratic organization of work in the kibbutz is demonstrated in the limited authority invested in the branches: They are part of the general organizational system of the kibbutz, whose policies are determined by the general assembly (or general meeting, as it is called in some kibbutzim)—that is, by the members of the kibbutz as a whole. How is it possible to guarantee that decisions are based on professional know-how and on an understanding of the problems that must be dealt with when most of those participating in the decisionmaking lack the necessary knowledge and can devote only a small part of their time to studying the problems that must be solved? In summary, can a system based on a democratic decision-making process, with lengthy discussions and general meetings, address professional and economic issues in such a way as to guarantee the economic efficacy required of branches and enterprises that must compete in the marketplace?

These questions of motivation to work, of congruence between the changing needs of the kibbutz and the wishes of the members, and of the possible conflict between professional or managerial authority and the democratic process have grown more acute with the social and economic development of the kibbutz. These unique kibbutz principles of work were appropriate when the kibbutz was small and its members were all of the same age and shared the same ideals. Are they still applicable to a large, heterogeneous multigenerational kibbutz with many branches and with complex industrial enterprises?

In the large, complex kibbutzim of today, tensions and conflicts have emerged between egalitarian, democratic principles and the increasing need for economic efficacy. In addition to the far-reaching changes in the political, economic, and technological environment, these tensions and conflicts have created a constant need for adaptation of the work environment.

In this chapter, then, I analyze and discuss the changing answers given, in different periods, to the following three basic questions:

1. How can the kibbutz, without a market mechanism, reach congruency between the needs of the kibbutz economic and social system and members' aspirations and abilities?

2. How can the kibbutz ensure work motivation without monetary incentives?

3. How can the kibbutz overcome the discrepancies between democratic decisionmaking and economic efficiency?

CHANGES IN THE CONCEPT OF WORK

From the outset, the concept of work in the kibbutz was not a monolithic one. It drew on several (sometimes opposing) sources, and its formation, as well as its development, was influenced by economic, security, and political exigencies. At different times, different elements have been given priority. During the pioneering period, kibbutz members had to set aside their intellectual and artistic abilities and give clear priority to those abilities necessary for the establishment and survival of the kibbutz settlements. Members were required to perform a limited variety of tasks—in agriculture and construction, in safeguarding the security of the settlement, and in providing services for kibbutz members and children.

In the 1960s, impressive economic development took place. Changes in agriculture required a higher level of professional knowledge and expertise, and industrial enterprises were set up in many kibbutzim. As a result, signs of inequality among various jobs and positions began to appear in the production branches with respect both to the professional level required to perform a given task and to the managerial responsibility and authority attached to various positions. At the same time, thousands of young people born in the kibbutz began for the first time to join the work force in the kibbutz movement. These young people attached greater importance to possibilities for personal development, particularly to work that conformed to their professional aspirations and offered them satisfaction, and they began voicing a demand for higher education.

Results from a study conducted in 1969 (Rosner et al., 1990) show, however, that although there were changes in the ideological approach to the concept of work, differences between the generations were negligible. In both generations, there was, on the one hand, support for the conservative position that kibbutz members should continue to work in production jobs, while on the other hand, there was support for the innovative position to broaden opportunities for higher education and self-fulfillment. Broadening higher education for young people, however, did not fit well with the expansion of industry in which much of the work did not require such an education. There existed also an unwillingness both to allow academic professionals to work in their professions outside the kibbutz and to use hired labor from outside the kibbutz to perform simple, non professional tasks.

However, there was continuity between the two generations in the value they associated with work. Most men of both generations claimed that work was the most important aspect of their lives (while most women ranked it second in importance—after family). Nevertheless, older men and women gave higher marks to the importance of work than did younger people. The value-based concepts of work in the kibbutz emphasized the noninstrumental nature of work and saw working as an end in itself. Ronen (1978), for instance, compared members of eleven kibbutzim with urban industrial workers employed by these kibbutzim. He found that the kibbutz members placed significantly more importance on self-realization than on extrinsic and material rewards. It seems, however, that the severe economic crisis in the 1980s and the efforts to overcome it have weakened this value-based conception of work.

Efforts were made to diversify the occupational structure by expanding, as an additional source of income, the service sector. In most kibbutzim, the number of members working outside the kibbutz increased substantially—contrary to the traditional value-based approach that almost all kibbutz members should work within the kibbutz branches. The rationale for the change was both to develop additional sources of income and to provide opportunities for self-realization in work. Contrary to the kibbutz value of "self-labor" (Leviatan, 1980b), the number of hired workers has been steadily growing, most of them working in the production lines of kibbutz factories. The need to overcome the economic crisis, seen as a menace for the future of the kibbutz, has legitimated a more instrumental conception of work, stressing the economic outcomes and weakening the conception of work as a value in itself. At the same time, there is a growing legitimization for individual self-realization, which may eventually diminish the priority of the instrumental-economic considerations.

AN ALTERNATIVE TO THE LABOR MARKET

To ensure congruity between the demands for manpower of the kibbutz occupational system and the abilities and aspirations of members, alternative mechanisms to the labor market have been developed. In the beginning, the occupational system was formed according to ideological and economic considerations. Demographic considerations were introduced later—creating places of work that were suitable for older people and that provided a technological challenge for young people. At this stage, the reference was to the needs of entire age or other social groups, not to the desires of any particular individual. Similar developments in recent years have reflected both direct and indirect consideration of individual desires for the long term.

An example of direct consideration is the acceptance of a member's wish to work outside the kibbutz, even when the income from this work is less than the possible alternative income within the kibbutz. An example of indirect consideration is the establishment of a particular industrial enterprise, taking into account not only economic considerations but also the desires and preferences of the members who will work in it.

Naturally, the establishment of a particular industry will affect the kibbutz for years to come. Decisions of this type are usually made in the kibbutz general assembly, where not only collective considerations (such as the potential for profit of various types of enterprise) but also social considerations (such as regard for the wishes of the members) and ideological considerations (such as avoidance of hired labor) are presented. An additional factor is the voluntary nature of work organization in the kibbutz: If members do not want to work in the factory that is set up, there is no way to force them to do so.

Because there was a direct connection between the occupational needs of the community and the aspirations of individual members, this potential conflict between individual and community did not develop in the early stages of kibbutz life. Committed to pioneer values, kibbutz members wanted to work in agriculture, which was what the community needed.

Collective needs could also influence individual members indirectly. For example, socialization for occupational positions available within the kibbutz system was accomplished by having the youth integrated from childhood into the team of one of the branches; children thus identified with the needs of the branch and hence with the needs of the collective. Here, however, even the founders faced a dilemma: While they wished for their children to remain farmers and manual laborers, at the same time they hoped that their children would also be like most of themselves— well educated and often intellectually and artistically oriented. As a result, the wish to provide a broad education caused secondary schools in the kibbutz to be designed as academic rather than agricultural or technical schools. This character of kibbutz education was important in the nurturing of occupational ambitions that went beyond the employment system of the kibbutz.

More complex, however, than long-term coordination between individual and community is short-term coordination to deal with the immediate changing needs of the system. The problem faced here by the kibbutz is to get members to agree to perform various jobs which they are not always interested in performing, even for a limited time. The success of work institutions in filling these jobs stems from their ability to persuade potential workers of their importance. Such success usually depends not on formal authority but on persuasive skills and the readiness of members to comply. To assist in solving such short-term placement problems, the kibbutz has developed two additional mechanisms:

1. Arrangements for duty by rotation in which members work temporarily, and for a fixed period of time, in branches in which they are unwilling to work on a regular basis—usually in services such as the dining hall or as helpers in the children-houses.
2. Employment of hired workers in filling positions where there is a lack of qualified or willing manpower.

The alternative to the labor market offered by the kibbutz has, therefore, been based on two principles: building an employment system that takes into account members' aspirations and shaping members' aspirations during the various stages of education to suit the nature of the kibbutz occupational system and to socialize the young into the branches of the kibbutz.

CURRENT TRENDS

The flexibility of the occupational system is limited by economic, environmental, and even ideological factors, such as the priority given to productive occupations in agriculture and industry. The ability of the kibbutz to influence members' aspirations is also limited. Thus, in the short term, we find numerous cases of a shortage of specialists in sought-after professions and a surplus in others, as well as members performing jobs they would prefer to give up. These limitations were felt especially during and following the severe economic crisis at the end of the 1980s. There was a need to increase immediately the number of members working in income-creating jobs and to reduce the number of those working in internal services. In the short term, it was difficult to accomplish these shifts. At the same time, there was a growing demand by members to work in their acquired professions, even if these professions were not needed in the kibbutz. In response to these difficulties, attempts were made in some kibbutzim to develop a quasi-market system with three major components: free choice of workplace by members; personal responsibility to find a workplace; and autonomy of work units in deciding whom to employ and whom to dismiss.

All three components are clearly at odds with the traditional (kibbutz) approach, where the choice of workplaces resulted from an agreement between the work institutions and the members, taking into consideration both kibbutz needs and individual preferences. Now it is the individual who decides, but it is his or her responsibility to find a job—no longer that of a kibbutz institution to find one for him or her. Free choice also includes the right to work outside the kibbutz. But the kibbutz continues to be responsible for the satisfaction of members' material needs, and members continue to receive both the monetary budget and the services supplied by the kibbutz—a situation which carries the seeds of conflict.

As members search for a workplace inside or outside the kibbutz they become units in the labor market. The work units can dismiss members that are surplus or do not meet the job requirements. If a member is without a job and doesn't find one during a limited period, his or her monetary budget will be reduced for each day that he or she is not working.

I define this system as a quasi market, since it lacks the major mechanism regulating the job market—monetary wages that represent the price of labor as determined by supply and demand. The quasi market is therefore a hybrid mechanism, combining elements of two contrasting social and economic governance principles: market principles versus principles of cooperation. This hybridity and lack of congruence probably explain why only some parts—but not others—of the quasi market have been implemented in many kibbutzim. Note the following (as of 1995): 68 percent of kibbutzim decide to encourage work outside the kibbutz; in 54 percent of kibbutzim, hired workers are employed to replace members so that members can freely choose their work; in 50 percent of kibbutzim, members are responsible for finding for themselves an appropriate workplace; but in only 11 percent of the kibbutzim has a link between the number of workdays and the monetary budget been created, and in only 2 percent are differential wages paid.

It is already clear that some of the proposals that have been implemented in many kibbutzim have created problems. The number of hired workers is increasing. The salaries earned by members working outside the kibbutz are sometimes lower than the salaries paid to hired workers replacing them. The main positive outcome is that more kibbutz members can now realize their professional aspirations.

A basic issue still remains unsolved: how to increase the fit between the kibbutz occupational structure and members' abilities and aspirations. In many kibbutzim, a change toward a more diversified occupational structure and more knowledge-based occupations is necessary; and this is true also from an economic perspective because the dependency of a kibbutz on one, or even two, manufacturing plants employing large numbers of hired workers is risky. Although many kibbutzim recognize the present occupational structure as a necessity in a transition period, they are looking toward a more postindustrial occupational structure. Fortunately, the traditional kibbutz work organization based on teamwork and self-management is a suitable environment for high-tech work organizations, while knowledge-based occupations are a better fit with kibbutz members' aspirations for professional self actualization.

MOTIVATION

In the introduction, I asked what motivates kibbutz members to exert effort at work when there is no direct connection between this effort and their standard of living. Different answers have been given to this question at different stages of kibbutz development. During the pioneer period, the assumption prevailed that the sole motivation was commitment to kibbutz values and identification with the kibbutz community. The first sociological studies of kibbutz society (conducted in the 1950s) revealed the importance of yet another factor: the social cohesion of the work group (Etzioni, 1959). The cohesion of the work group was perceived as "a functional alternative" to a decrease in the identification of members with the larger and more heterogeneous kibbutz communities and to the related weakening of informal social control stemming from the opinion of the whole community. It was found that the more cohesive work groups were those that kibbutz public opinion was less able to control. The inference from these findings was that social cohesion in these work groups created the basis for informal social control and compensated for the lack of such control by the community.

During the 1970s and the 1980s, more studies were conducted on the topic of work motivation and work commitment of kibbutz members, as compared to the motivation and commitment of other populations (e.g., Rosner, 1971; Eden and Leviatan, 1974; Tannenbaum et al., 1974; Ronen, 1978; Leviatan, 1980a; Palgi, 1984; Shimoni et al., 1994). The results of these studies may be summarized as follows:

First, work motivation, work commitment, and identification with work goals of kibbutz members were found to be higher than those of workers from other populations both in Israel and abroad.

Second, the higher level of work motivation and work commitment did not have corresponding similarities in the variable of satisfaction with work. All comparisons with other populations of workers failed to show any advantage (or disadvantage) for kibbutz members.

Third, material rewards or incentives did not play any role in promoting members' motivation or commitments. (Incidentally, no personal material rewards were used in kibbutz work organizations.)

Fourth, it was the work motivation and the commitment of members that best explained the organizational success of kibbutz enterprises, while satisfaction with work had no relation to organizational effectiveness for the business enterprises.

Finally, research across the years found that different factors assumed priority in determining levels of work motivation or commitment: identification with kibbutz values and with the community—during the pioneering period; social cohesiveness of the work team—during the 1950s and the 1960s; and the content of the job and the opportunity it offered for self-realization and autonomy—during the 1970s and the 1980s.

These findings led to efforts to enrich the content of work in the kibbutz occupational system, particularly in industry. Kibbutz industry (as it evolved in the late 1960s) avoided the use of technologies (such as the assembly line) likely to cause severe alienation among workers. Efforts were made to generate team spirit at work, and self realization through autonomy and control opportunities for workers became criteria for choosing an industry and setting up the organizational structure. Comparing job opportunities, job satisfaction, and commitment (from data collected in studies of kibbutz industrial plants in 1969, 1983, and 1993), researchers found a significant improvement in all the measures (Shimoni et al., 1994).

But in spite of these improvements in industry, growing aspirations for self-realization at work were hard to satisfy because of the limitations of the occupational structure. The 1990s, as mentioned earlier, saw the introduction of two developments meant to overcome such limitations: bringing in hired workers to relieve kibbutz members of unwanted jobs (e.g., shift work or "alienating" jobs) and allowing a growing number of members to work outside the kibbutz occupational structure.

In addition, demands were made to introduce material incentives in the workplace. There were several arguments to justify these demands: The desire to compensate for the weakening of the traditional incentive of identification with values; a wish for additional personal income—especially since personal consumption budgets had been reduced following the economic crisis; and the belief that such incentives would attract appropriate candidates to fill those managerial positions which many members were reluctant to accept. At first, only two limited material rewards were suggested: payment for additional hours worked and payment for holding difficult jobs. Because they stand in strong contradiction to the kibbutz principle of dissociation between contribution and monetary rewards, these proposals raised strong ideological opposition. In 1995, the first proposal was implemented in 22 kibbutzim (11 percent) and the second in only five kibbutzim (3 percent). Two kibbutzim decided to introduce a more comprehensive and far-reaching change: differential wages to members based on the wage scale in the general labor market.

Although only a few kibbutzim have introduced monetary incentives, there is a general search for ways to increase work motivation. Paradoxically, while outside the kibbutz there is growing awareness of the importance of nonmonetary (psychological and social) incentives, in the kibbutz, as an outcome of the economic crisis, the efforts in this direction have been reduced. There has been less investment in improving work content and conditions, in creating cohesive work groups, and in worker participation in decision making.

THE MANAGEMENT STRUCTURE OF KIBBUTZ WORK ORGANIZATIONS

Kibbutz work units in agriculture and in the services were formerly small (mostly less than ten workers) with little internal differentiation. There was usually only one managerial role: the branch coordinator whose main functions were organizational (work organization and allocation, relations with kibbutz economic officeholders, and relations with other branches). Marketing of agricultural products was through nationwide cooperative organizations, without direct involvement of the branch coordinators.

Coordinators fulfilled their role in addition to their regular job in production or services. Branch members participated in decision making mainly through informal discussions, while formal meetings were institutionalized only in the larger branches. The branch coordinator was elected by the branch members, and rotation of this office occurred regularly (Leviatan, 1978, 1992).

With the growth and internal differentiation in some of the branches, the managerial role became more institutionalized and differentiated from other work roles. Studies revealed problems related to this differentiation. Yuchtman-Yaar (1983) studied poultry branches and found a much higher percentage of managers desiring to leave the branch (42 percent) than of regular workers (16 percent). His explanation of this finding was based on equity theory (e.g., Adams, 1965). The assumption was that the input of managers in the branch was greater than that of other workers, and the managers expected, therefore, adequate outcomes. Since these expectations were not realized, they wanted to quit. The author suggested that equity could be achieved by increasing the managers' socio-emotional satisfaction. He took for granted the need for equality between coordinator and workers in material rewards.

The trend toward differentiation of special managerial roles developed much faster in kibbutz factories. In the first stage of industrialization (in the 1940s and 1950s), labor-intensive factories with large numbers of hired workers were established in some kibbutzim. In these factories, a hierarchical work organization developed, quite different from that prevailing in other kibbutz work units.

The development of hierarchical and bureaucratic organizational patterns based on hired labor was perceived by a majority of kibbutz members and leaders as opposed to kibbutz values. Efforts were made to develop a different type of kibbutz factory—more capital intensive and with an organizational structure that conformed to kibbutz principles, although preserving some hierarchical features (Leviatan and Rosner, 1980).

Research into industrial hierarchy in the kibbutz focused on the connection of hierarchical features with other characteristics of the bureaucratic model and on the mechanisms for overcoming drawbacks: for example, rotation of officeholders, equality in distribution of rewards, and decision making in a democratic framework with maximum participation among members.

Two theoretical aspects that relate to this topic are (1) How universal is the hierarchical model, with its nonegalitarian distribution of authority? (2) What is the principal reason for the existence of the hierarchical structure in organizations? Is it to coordinate the holders of various positions in the organization? Or is it to supervise work performance?

The answer to these broad questions was sought through several international studies (Tannenbaum et al., 1974; Bartolke et al., 1985). The findings demonstrated that most kibbutz enterprises (not employing hired workers) maintained the special character of kibbutz managerial components alongside a hierarchical structure: Rotation in management positions functioned well, and those who held managerial positions were elected democratically, either by the workers in the factory or by the kibbutz assembly.

From an examination of fifty-four industrial enterprises in the Kibbutz Haartzi movement in 1976, it was found that the average term of office for a manager was three and a half years (Rosner and Palgi, 1980). A different study (Leviatan, 1976) examined the effect of rotation on the efficiency of production branches (both agricultural and industrial) in the kibbutz. It was found that the best economic results were achieved in industrial enterprises whose managers held office for three to four years—as compared to enterprises whose managers held office for a longer or shorter time. It was also found that when the manager was not replaced after the optimal time, the level of communication between manager and workers diminished. And the more workers who (as a result of rotation) had held management positions, the greater the levels of motivation and identification with the enterprise. The same study also examined the effects of rotation on people who completed a term in a management position and returned to a lower position in the hierarchy. In a comparison between former officeholders and workers who had not held such positions, it was found that for a period of several years after completing a term of office, former officeholders were more influential and more involved.

EQUALITY IN DISTRIBUTION OF REWARDS

According to the common bureaucratic model, holders of higher offices in a hierarchy enjoy not only greater authority and influence but also other rewards such as higher salary, social benefits, greater prestige, and more interesting work. Although in kibbutz enterprises there are no differences in material rewards (except for role-related facilities such as use of a motor vehicle or opportunities for overseas travel), studies found some inequality in nonmaterial rewards: Managers had more opportunities for self-realization in their work as well as the greater authority and influence that came with the job. The inequality was more evident in opportunities for using existing skills, and less evident in opportunities for developing skills. In other words, the opportunities for using organizational and intellectual skills were greater in management jobs, but rank-and-file workers also had the chance to learn new things and to develop themselves, either within the framework of their jobs or by attending training courses (Rosner, 1971).

In comparison with workers from other countries, kibbutz members were offered more possibilities to move up in the hierarchy, but they were less willing to perform management roles (Tannenbaum et al., 1974), because of fear of exposure to criticism and difficulties in dealing with problematic workers.

DECISION MAKING IN A DEMOCRATIC FRAMEWORK

The desire to maintain a direct participatory democracy in all areas of kibbutz life, together with the endeavor to distribute influence and authority among as many people as possible, would seem to clash sharply with the nonegalitarian distribution of authority in the hierarchical managerial structure. Nevertheless, in bureaucratic and industrial organizations outside the kibbutz, many attempts have also been made to integrate various forms of democracy into the hierarchical structure. There are two distinct approaches: the political and the motivational. The political approach is based primarily on participation by representatives of the workers or of the trade union in decision making. A clear example of this approach is the German system of co-determination. The motivational approach is based on direct participation by the workers, particularly in decisions related to their own work. This approach evolved from the human relations management method, which favors a participatory style of management, particularly by lower management, toward their subordinates. The goal is not to grant formal rights of participation, but rather to develop an informal system of communication between the manager and his or her subordinates. Accordingly, the manager should consult the workers on various questions but has the authority to choose whether to accept their opinions.

In an effort to achieve work democracy, kibbutz industry sought to combine the political and motivational approaches: Ideally, there should exist formal frameworks both of direct democracy (for instance, the general assembly of plant workers) and of indirect democracy (for instance, the elected management personnel and committee members). At the same time, the group coordinators (who in their roles correspond to foremen elsewhere) should allow their subordinates to participate informally in making decisions.

Some studies (Rosner, 1971; Rosner and Palgi, 1980; Palgi, 1984) have found differences between the outcomes of formal political participation in the framework of the workers assembly and those of informal motivational participation within the framework of the work group. It was found that, on the one hand, formal participation of the workers in the assembly of plant workers was related neither to their satisfaction nor to their identification with the objectives of the plant. It had a positive effect, however, in other areas such as information flow in the plant and workers' confidence in, and attitude toward, the management. Participation within the work groups, on the other hand, contributed to the increased satisfaction of workers and, to an even greater extent, to their identification with the enterprise. It would therefore appear that formal participation in the workers assembly primarily affects organizational and collective factors, whereas participation in work groups affects personal and motivational factors (Rosner, 1971).

Although, in kibbutz industry, a combination of formal and informal participation alongside a management hierarchy preserves the fundamental principles of kibbutz democracy, the authority of the workers assembly is limited compared to that of the kibbutz general assembly. Its limitations arise from the coexistence of hierarchy on the one hand and democracy in the plant on the other, a combination not existing in the kibbutz assembly. Members participating in the plant assembly find themselves in an ambiguous position: The assembly is the center of authority, and the management, elected by the assembly, must carry out its decisions; but in the daily work process, most of the participants are subordinate to the holders of managerial positions. There is liable to be a clash between the roles of equal participant and subordinate. In the kibbutz assembly there is no such structural division between superiors and subordinates; for although many kibbutz members hold positions of authority (as branch managers, committee members and chairpersons), members that are superiors in one area might be subordinates in other areas, and lines of authority are not clear (Rosner, 1983b).

Despite these limitations, the combination of hierarchy, rotation, relative equality in distribution of rewards, and democracy constitutes a unique management structure that has functioned efficiently and effectively for several decades (Barkai, 1977; Don, 1977). But following the economic crisis in the 1980s, deviations from the normative model occurred in many industrial plants (see Palgi's chapter).

RECENT DEVELOPMENTS

The deviation from the normative model of work organization leads in two directions: strengthening of hierarchical structures and the introduction of quasi-market mechanisms.

An important change in the hierarchical structure has been the introduction of boards of directors, replacing both the workers assembly in plants and the kibbutz general assembly as major decision-making bodies and reducing the role of the general assembly to that of a yearly shareholders meeting. Managers are professionals nominated from above—not officeholders elected from below for a limited term. The general trend is toward conformity with patterns prevailing in Israel outside the kibbutz.

The trend toward establishing a hierarchy is evident in the fact that in some kibbutzim, the payment by the plant to the kibbutz for the work of kibbutz members is based on the differential wages prevailing outside the kibbutz. At the same time, in almost all kibbutzim, there is no connection between a member's hierarchical position and his or her standard of living. This incongruity might explain why, among plant top managers, there is a stronger support than in the general public for the introduction of differential salaries.

The extent of these trends is not the same in all kibbutz plants. A recent study on boards of directors in kibbutz plants reveals major differences in the degree of involvement of the board in the internal management of the plant. In the more involved boards (less than a third), there are predictably more deviations from the normative kibbutz model of management.

While the weakening of the role of workers and kibbutz assemblies is common, there are also differences in managerial patterns and in the relationship between industrial enterprises and the kibbutz. The main reason for these differences is the percentage of hired workers. Similar to findings in previous studies, the management in plants with a higher percentage of hired workers is more like that outside the kibbutz. The employment of hired labor is also strongly correlated with the introduction of changes in other areas of kibbutz life.

Changes in the direct and participatory democratic system and trends toward hierarchy have also occurred outside the industrial plants. In some kibbutzim, boards of directors have been introduced in the agricultural sector, and in other kibbutzim in all the economic branches—including services. The branch manager's authority and responsibility are stressed, and decision making by the work group has become more limited.

In many kibbutzim a partial transfer of authority from the general assembly to other bodies has occurred. In some, the vote on decisions is no longer restricted to participants in the assembly; it is handled by a referendum open to all the members. In others, representative councils are elected, and a partial transition from direct to indirect democracy has occurred. Through the referendum mechanism, direct democracy continues, but members' participation in deliberations before the vote is restricted. In many kibbutzim, a smaller number of committees are now operating and those that exist are not as active, and the authority of central officeholders is thus enhanced through centralization.

The implementation in the past of the normative model had an important theoretical significance: It showed that organizations can combine a limited hierarchical distribution of authority, a participatory structure of decision making, and an egalitarian distribution of material rewards. It therefore offered a valuable contribution to the contemporary search for postbureaucratic and participatory patterns of management.

SUMMARY AND CONCLUSIONS

In this chapter, I have discussed three basic issues of kibbutz work organization together with the changes in values, norms and organizational patterns related to them. I have paid special attention to the following changes occurring in recent years.

First, I have discussed the fit between the demands for specific work roles and jobs by the kibbutz occupational structure and members' ability and aspirations. As an alternative to the market system, the kibbutz developed mechanisms for reciprocal adaptation between collective demands and individual abilities and preferences. The economic crisis and its aftermath aggravated difficulties in the functioning of these mechanisms. These difficulties related to growing differentiation and complexity and resulted in suggestions to introduce a quasi-market system, which would transfer responsibility for work choice and for income to the individual member, while avoiding the regulatory mechanism of differential wages determined by the market. Due to the inconsistent and hybrid character of these suggestions, only a few of them have been implemented.

Second, I have addressed the issue of motivation, arising from the kibbutz principle of dissociation between members' contribution and their material standard of living. As an alternative to the monetary incentives prevailing outside the kibbutz, different motivational factors were stressed during different periods. In the pioneer period, work was perceived as a value in itself, and motivation was based on ideological commitment. In later periods, social cohesion of the work group was perceived both as a motivating factor and as a basis for internal social control. Gradually the importance of intrinsic work motivation was recognized, and the content of work and opportunities for self realization were seen as central motivators. Following the economic crisis, arguments were presented that these non monetary motivators were insufficient and that they should be supplemented by limited monetary compensations for overtime, night shifts, and so on. Although few kibbutzim have implemented these suggestions, the demand for the introduction of differential wages has become part of the public discourse.

Third, I described the possible contradiction between the kibbutz egalitarian and democratic values and the functional requirements of efficient work organization and management. In the past, the prevailing assumption outside the kibbutz was that a hierarchical and bureaucratic structure was the most efficient response to the functional requirement of industrial management. Contrary to this assumption, findings in kibbutz industry showed that the plants which conformed more to the kibbutz normative model of participatory management were economically more efficient.

The normative organizational model of kibbutz industry was based on a limited hierarchical authority structure combined with equality in the standard of living, rotation in managerial roles, formal and informal participation in decision making, and integration in the overall democratic kibbutz system. In the past, significant differences in the implementation of this model were found between plants employing mainly kibbutz members and plants with many hired workers. The recent sharp increase in the percentage of hired labor in industrial plants is creating problems for the future implementation of the normative model. Meanwhile, there is no evidence of positive economic outcomes resulting from employment of hired labor or the introduction of more hierarchical patterns.

Industrial society presently questions the suitability of the bureaucratic model for new technologies, for a more educated work force, and for demands for more-flexible organizations. These changes outside the kibbutz, leading to models with some similarities to the normative kibbutz model, might also have an impact on the future kibbutz model—similar to the impact that external management patterns have had on current changes in the kibbutz.

Finally, I have discussed the shift from a value-based collectivistic concept of work toward a more instrumental and individualistic concept. In the future, contradictions could arise between individual aspirations toward self-realization and instrumental economic forces.

In the organization of work (as well as in other areas), the kibbutz is in a transition period. While there is a weakening of the kibbutz alternatives to monetary incentives, to the labor market system, and to bureaucratic management, there is also a strong reluctance to accept the "conventional" patterns—patterns that are also being questioned outside the kibbutz. The outcome is a search for pragmatic solutions that have mostly a hybrid character, combining components of opposite social and economic governance systems. These hybrid solutions are sometimes inconsistent, and in the long term, it will probably be necessary to make a choice between contradictory directions. This choice will be part of a more general effort to redefine the identity of the kibbutz.

$\sim$

For almost a century the kibbutz has illustrated the feasibility of alternative solutions to the basic problems of work organization. The kibbutz social experiment occurred under rare conditions of new land, homogeneous small communities, and a mostly agricultural economy. Nevertheless, it seems that the lessons of this experiment might also be relevant for the high-tech, postindustrial, complex societies and economies of the future.

4
Organization in Kibbutz Industry

Michal Palgi

In 1996, there were 377 kibbutz industrial plants, which were distributed among the following categories: wood, furniture, and food—52 plants; metal and textiles—105 plants; plastic and rubber, electrical supplies and electronics, optics, chemicals, and pharmaceuticals—150 plants; quarries and construction materials—21 plants; ornamental products—19 plants; paper and printing—18; and industrial services—12 plants (Association of Kibbutz Industry, 1996). In addition, kibbutzim own recreational and tourist facilities that have burgeoned in recent years. In 1996, sales of products of industrial plants amounted to 3,505 million dollars (US), their exports reached 1073 million dollars, and they employed twenty-six thousand people. Even though the kibbutz constitutes only about 2.8 percent of the Israeli population (but 6.9 percent of Israel industrial workers), kibbutz industries account for 5.9 percent of Israeli industrial sales and 8.2 percent of Israeli exports (excluding diamonds). Industry presently comprises about 70 percent of kibbutz economic production and employs a similar percentage of kibbutz members. (In some kibbutzim, industry generates close to 100 percent of the economic revenues.) In short, many kibbutzim are essentially industrial communities in rural areas. How did this come about in communities whose stereotypical image is that of idyllic farmers and farmland?

Kibbutz society was founded on the basis of cooperative, democratic, and egalitarian principles. These principles, as well as conditions in Palestine at the time of the kibbutz's foundation, determined to a great extent its way of life and its organizational structures. The economy at the beginning of the century was based primarily on agriculture, and only in the 1960s did the tempo of industrialization increase. This industrial growth produced many debates about the way in which industry should be organized in order to preserve kibbutz values and the kibbutz way of life. Ultimately, kibbutzim accepted a pattern of industrial organization very different from that existing in society at large—a unique organizational structure based on kibbutz values, social structure, and culture. I refer to this as the normative model of kibbutz industry. However, following the economic and social crises of the 1980s, profound changes occurred. The normative model and the changes that kibbutz industries are now experiencing provide the focus of this chapter, but first it is necessary to give a brief description of how industrialization has evolved.

IDEOLOGICAL PRINCIPLES IN THE FOUNDATION OF THE KIBBUTZ MOVEMENT

"The kibbutz system of life is a new model of social life. . . . this is a comprehensive system in which members live, raise children, work and create, grow old and pass away. In fact, the kibbutz is a microcosm of an entire society" (Golomb and Katz, 1971, 7). In the early days of the kibbutz, at the beginning of this century, its members regarded working the land as their central purpose. As kibbutz ideology developed, it drew on Zionist, socialist, and humanist values and integrated them to form a coherent ideology of its own. The stated goals of kibbutz founders were to cultivate the land from the wild, to build a Jewish national entity in Israel (Palestine at the time), and to create a just society. In *Kibbutz Regulations* (the kibbutz bylaws), the introductory chapter on foundations of the kibbutz states: "The kibbutz is a free association of people for purposes of settlement, absorption of new immigrants, maintaining a cooperative society based on community ownership of property, self-sufficiency in labor, equality and cooperation in all areas of production, consumption and education." Similarly: "The kibbutz considers itself an inseparable part of the Hebrew workers' movement in Israel, which aspires to establish the Jewish people concentrating in Israel as a working society built on foundations of social cooperation." Thus, the main objectives of kibbutz society embrace three categories:

1. Zionist objectives: settlement, conquering the wilderness, absorbing immigrants, and securing and safeguarding state borders by settling along them.

2. Creation and development of a working class: creating a cooperative society based on community ownership of property and forming an inseparable part of the Hebrew workers' movement in Israel. "The founders of the cooperative settlements felt called upon to create a healthy Hebrew society and to make up for the lack of a normal working class" (Talmon-Garber, 1972, 49).

3. Creation of a just society: self-sufficiency in labor, equality, and cooperation in all areas of production, consumption, and education. For "while they (the founders of the kibbutz movement) devoted themselves to creating a working class for the sake of their people, they were guided by their socialist views to reject in principle a working class dependent on providers of work. The solution to this contradiction was the creation of

a reformed society and an economic reality based on ownership by the workers and self-sufficiency in labor" (Talmon-Garber, 1972, 49).

Within this ideological framework, industrialization was introduced. Historically, kibbutz industry was already beginning its gradual growth around the time of World War II, when 13.7 percent of production workers in kibbutzim worked in industry. At that time, industrial plants developed primarily from workshops for repairing tractors and pipe systems—for which there was a need combined with a skilled work force in the kibbutz. However, it was not until the 1960s that a major rise in the rate of industrialization occurred: Of the 320 kibbutz industrial plants operating in 1981, only 34 percent were established before 1960 (Association of Kibbutz Industry, 1982).

In the 1960s, changes in economic and demographic conditions hampered agricultural development and provided the impetus for industrial growth. The main reasons for the impetus to industrialize were as follows:

1. The market was saturated with agricultural products.
2. There was a shortage of such resources as land and water to increase agricultural production, and the quota of production of various crops allocated to many kibbutzim was insufficient to support the members. Yet the kibbutz population kept growing at a rate of 2–3 percent per year.
3. Government policy supported industrialization, particularly in border settlements. Kibbutzim constituted a large proportion of border settlements, making them eligible for government benefits (long-term loans and grants) for the advancement of industrialization.
4. Older kibbutz members, unfit for physical work in agriculture, were seeking alternative places of work.
5. Kibbutz members with technological abilities (especially the young) were seeking work in which they could employ these abilities.

But the need for industrialization per se cannot ensure its successful implementation. Success in developing industry in the kibbutz came about from certain characteristics of kibbutz society and of its members.

Ideology and Cultural Perspective

The kibbutz movement has always emphasized a future orientation. It welcomes changes to its life-styles and occupational structure, but seeks to adapt these changes to its values. This ideological characteristic of kibbutz society has had far-reaching importance for the growth of industry, involving changes to the entire work system of the kibbutz (Rosner, 1971). An additional characteristic of kibbutz society is the ideological emphasis placed on productive work. Originally considered synonymous with work in agriculture, the concept of productive work was easily broadened to include work in industry (Rosner, 1971).

Structural Characteristics of Economic and Work Organization of the Kibbutzim

The economic structure of the kibbutz was based originally on small agricultural and service branches. In the busy seasons, there was movement of workers from branch to branch as dictated by need and the desire to distribute the work load more equally. Thus, members grew accustomed to changes in their place of work, and the introduction of industry into the kibbutz was seen as just another added branch. It should, though, be emphasized that change in place of work within the kibbutz was not accompanied by any change of social environment, social standing, standard of living, economic security, eligibility for public office, or cultural life.

The kibbutz economic mix of different branches (and involvement, therefore, in different markets) was also of help in the successful introduction of industry. Starting an industrial business involves large expenditures, and initially losses may well exceed profits. That the industrial branch was one of many enabled the kibbutz to invest in it and to cover the initial losses with profits from other economic units.

Rosner (1971) summarizes the above characteristics as follows: "There exists in the kibbutz, then, the main conditions for success in the test not only of industrialization but of modernization in general—mobility and availability of human resources. They enable workers to be directed to changing objectives, and the demand for changing the place of work is seen not as something to oppose but rather as part of the normal course of life."

Experience and Education of Individual Members

Kibbutz members have, on average, a high level of formal education. Most founders of kibbutzim came from cities (whether in Israel or abroad) in order to realize the Zionist ideal of changing the occupational structure of the Jewish people from a nation of merchants to one of farmers who worked the land. They received their secondary education, and often higher education, before their arrival. Their education was applied to agricultural development in the kibbutz, and it later contributed to their speedy adjustment to industry. People born and educated in the kibbutz also received advanced agricultural training at a high technological level, and their experience improved their ability to adapt to industrial technology and to its economic and financial demands. In addition, job mobility in kibbutzim created in members the flexibility and adaptability required for industrialization.

Thus, already at the onset of the industrialization process in kibbutzim, kibbutz industrial workers had a high level of formal education compared to nonkibbutz workers. Palgi (1984), in a study conducted in 1976, found that kibbutz industrial workers had, on average, 12.2 years of schooling while nonkibbutz Israeli industrial workers had only 8.6 years of schooling. Similar results were found by Tannenbaum et al. (1974), who, in 1969, compared kibbutz industrial workers with those from four countries (Italy, Yugoslavia, Austria, and the United States): The kibbutz workers had the highest level of formal education. Currently the average level of education for industrial workers on kibbutzim—aged forty five years or younger—is about 15 years of schooling.

Availability of Managerial Resources among Members

Democratic patterns of management in the kibbutz help to develop managerial skills. Many members are appointed to managerial positions at work and within the social domain of the community; and since these functionaries are replaced by new appointees every year or two and most get trained in managerial skills for their temporary office, the number of members who can, if needed, fulfill managerial positions is large. Indeed, about 50 percent of kibbutz members held some type of managerial position (Palgi and Sharir, 1995) during the years 1988–1995.

However, side by side with the supporting conditions for successful industrialization, other aspects of kibbutz society—ideological, structural, cultural, and personal—served to hamper the development of industry. As described in the next section, solutions to overcome these impediments had to be found before industry could take a leading role in the kibbutz economy.

PROBLEMS WITH INDUSTRIALIZATION AND SOLUTIONS FOR OVERCOMING THEM

The first problem of industrialization in a kibbutz relates to the size of the industrial plants. The small number of members in each kibbutz (from fifty to one thousand, but most commonly between three hundred and four hundred) has precluded the development of large industries, particularly in light of the socialist ideal of not employing paid workers from outside the kibbutz.

To overcome the difficulty of limited membership in individual kibbutzim and the ideological imperative of not employing outside paid labor, the type of industry tended to be based on plants requiring heavy capital investment and low manpower.

The second problem had to do with taking people off working the land, and even more important, the alienation and fragmentation associated with factory work, in contrast to the wholesome characteristics associated with farm work. The solution to this problem was to organize and manage industry within the kibbutz economy in a way similar to how farm branches were managed and operated. Thus, because managerial rotation and democratic conventions were the practice in agricultural branches, they should therefore be the practice in industry as well—with, of course, adaptations appropriate to the specific structure of the industry.

Another obstacle was that routine industrial jobs seemed inappropriate for most kibbutz members: Whereas most had received a broad general education, only a few had specific technological training. The possibility of creating jobs that failed to utilize the capacities of the workers was cited as a major problem with the continuation of industrialization. The solution here was to emphasize what was at the time (early 1970s) a high knowledge-intensive type of technology.

Thus, there was an awareness in the kibbutz movements that industries must be established that would answer the needs of kibbutz members and of the kibbutz social system. Large industries were unsuitable because they required a large work force; heavy industry requiring great physical strength on the part of the workers was also regarded as unsuitable (in consideration of the elderly and of women in the kibbutz); and simple tasks of the conveyor-belt variety aroused opposition. These limitations imposed difficulties on the penetration of industry into the kibbutz, and some industries that were set up later had to be liquidated or sold out.

FORMALIZATION OF THE INDUSTRIAL ORGANIZATION IN KIBBUTZIM—THE NORMATIVE MODEL

Following suggested solutions to problems of industrialization in kibbutzim, industries were sought that possessed certain characteristics: high in capital requirement; not employing outside hired labor; small in number of workers; managed on principles of democracy with full participation of workers in decision making; and offering enriching and self-actualizing jobs to the member-workers while, at the same time, being viable economically and answering to the other needs of the community. Not all kibbutzim adopted these recommendations, but many did, particularly during the most intensive time of industrialization, the 1970s; and the recommendations became benchmark criteria against which kibbutzim would weigh their success in accomplishing the goal of industrialization.

In the mid-1970s the combined criteria and objectives of industrialization were summarized by kibbutz official political bodies to form the components of the normative model of managing industry in a kibbutz community. The following section describes how the kibbutz movement formally defined objectives for the industrialization process and the preferred characteristics of industries that would make them congruent with basic kibbutz ideological premises and principles of organizational conduct—as formulated during the late 1970s by the industrial councils of the Kibbutz Artzi and by the United Kibbutz Movement (UKM). (Detailed analyses of these formulations appear in Leviatan and Rosner, 1980, and Palgi, 1984.)

The four main objectives of kibbutz industry, according to these formulations, are as follows (Palgi, 1984):

1. Welfare of the individual members. As noted above, a workplace in which people of various skills can work and realize their abilities is a goal of prime importance in kibbutz industry. In the resolutions of the industrial council of the Kibbutz Ha'Artzi, the opening statement reads: "The industrial plant is part of the kibbutz home in which the member is given a framework for the expression of his creative ability, satisfaction of his natural need for work and occupation, belonging to a team, satisfaction of his aspiration to achieve, etc."

2. Profitability. Kibbutz industry serves to consolidate the kibbutz economy. However, profit is not the sole objective. "The industrial plant is intended to contribute maximally, within the framework . . . of kibbutz principles,

to the profitability of the economy of the kibbutz. Maximal profit is not the sole objective of the plant, but one of several."

3. Safeguarding kibbutz principles. Several domains are considered: dealing with the hierarchical structure—managers and managed—in a democratic society; safeguarding the principle of decisionmaking through direct democracy; safeguarding the principle of interaction between plant and kibbutz and preventing the creation of autonomous foci of power in the plant; and safeguarding the principle of self-sufficiency in labor.

4. Achievement of national objectives. A number of national goals which the kibbutz movement has adopted can be advanced through industry. For example, kibbutz industry can contribute to the national economy by maximal exploitation of existing production potential, promotion of exports, creating alternatives to imports, and defense production. Industry can also allow for new settlements in arid areas unsuited to agriculture. If industrial settlements are established as a source of livelihood, the national goal of settling all sectors of the country can be realized, even in areas in which it is difficult to sustain agriculture.

The normative model articulated by formal resolutions saw the organizational structure and decision-making practices in the industrial plant as the principal means of realizing most objectives of kibbutz industry. The following quotation illustrates this well: "In keeping with the special conditions of the kibbutz, economic objectives can be achieved most efficiently by means of an organizational structure that will fulfill the expectations of those members who work in the plant and their aspirations for independence and enhancement of content in their work that will allow them to fully realize their abilities and skills" (Kibbutz Artzi, 1977, 9).

Organizational Structure of an Industrial Plant

The normative model allows for maximal individual freedom, together with work in cohesive teams in which good relations and communications are maintained. Consequently, decisions can be made and executed in an optimal way. Leadership is rotated among team members and involves coordination of activities within the team and between the team and other teams. The plant is managed by distributing authority among various managerial functionaries, with a flat hierarchical structure. Holders of managerial positions serve for three to five years, after which they are replaced.

Decision Making

The normative model requires decisions to be made at several levels: plantwide; at the level of work teams or divisions within the plant; at the level of management; and at the level of plant committees. The emphasis on participation of workers in decision making is aimed at kibbutz members only and does not include hired workers—stemming from the conviction that by not formalizing roles of hired

workers, kibbutzim would be discouraged from hiring them. The following decision-making system is that which was proposed.

Plantwide. At least once a month, all workers in the plant gather for a briefing
(in addition to written information posted on bulletin boards, etc.) for a presenta-
tion of recommendations from the management and committees and for a discussion of current problems. It is emphasized that the plant assembly is not merely a
platform for presenting information but a decision-making body. In matters pertaining to investments, production plans, and long-term courses of study for plant
workers, the plant assembly may make only recommendations to the kibbutz
general meeting, the body that determines such issues. The plant assembly also
discusses appeals concerning decisions made by other bodies in the plant (management, committees, etc.) that were not brought before it for discussion.

Work Teams or Divisions. Teams meet as the need arises, particularly to deal with
work schedules, working conditions, work plans, and so on. They can also make
recommendations to the plant management or plant committees on matters of
general concern such as investment plans, exports, and training programs.

Plant Management. Management of the plant comprises three categories: central
managerial personnel of the plant; central officeholders of the kibbutz (for example,
the economic coordinator and treasurer); and representatives of plant workers, one
of whom is the chairman of the workers assembly. Management meets once a week
to discuss and decide current management matters and to formulate proposals for
consideration by the plant's assembly and kibbutz institutions. The executive
management deals only with urgent technical matters.

Plant Committees. The role of these committees is to deal with special problems at
the plant, to formulate proposals, and to bring them before the relevant bodies for a
decision. The following committees are commonly established: a marketing committee; a work committee to deal with such matters as manpower planning, personnel
problems, and workers' training; a technical committee; and a safety committee. It is
recommended that as many workers as possible be integrated into the committees.

The normative model of kibbutz industry provides, then, for both direct participation (workers assembly and kibbutz assembly) and indirect participation
(representatives of the rank-and-file workers in the managerial bodies). Only a few
decisions are made without consulting other plant or kibbutz bodies. Because the
industrial plant is one of several branches in the kibbutz and all its expenditures
and income belong to the kibbutz, the kibbutz assembly determines the production
plan, the investment plan, and the plant training program after these matters have
been discussed within the plant and in the relevant kibbutz committees. Thus, if an
investment is planned in a certain branch or for the training program of a certain
worker, the decision must be based on considerations related to all the productive
branches in the kibbutz.

Managers

The manager of an industrial plant is elected by the whole community. Often
no one within the plant possesses the skills necessary for managing it, and therefore

an outsider must be sought from among all members. The plant manager, furthermore, needs to have certain social skills, and the kibbutz must be certain that the person who assumes the management of so central a workplace will both enjoy public support and safeguard the integration of the plant into the kibbutz. Holders of other managerial positions are chosen by the plant workers since, as a rule, these managerial duties are performed in addition to the managers' regular jobs as workers.

The essence of the normative model of operating kibbutz industrial plants is well illustrated by the perception and expectations regarding managerial roles. In the early years of kibbutz industry, the attitude toward managers was ambivalent. On the one hand, this office was recognized to be more important than other roles; on the other hand, there was the wish to preserve strict equality among all members. There were reservations about forming ruling and ruled classes and apprehensions that industrial imperatives would establish an organizational culture alien to the kibbutz spirit. Thus, there were expectations that the plant manager would act like a branch coordinator for whose role the appropriate balance lay between being "equal" and being "more." These expectations are evident in the behavioral norms that have been established, such as the inclusion of the plant manager in the duty roster for night shifts, in cleaning the factory and its washrooms, and in similar jobs. Furthermore, when managers make business trips abroad, they have first to receive the approval of the kibbutz assembly; they are replaced every five years (the term used to be three years); and they are not assigned a specific vehicle for work but have to file a daily request with the vehicle coordinator. As for outward symbols, they are not called managers, but coordinators—that is, they are expected to coordinate workers' activities rather than control them. To emphasize equality, many plant managers come to work in the same blue work clothes and boots worn by workers on the production line.

In summary, the principal characteristics of the normative organizational model are as follows:

- Replication of the management norms of the agricultural branch within the framework of the industrial plant
- Participation of all plant workers in the decision-making process
- Information flow and the avoidance, through managerial rotation, of concentration of power
- Maintenance of norms and mechanisms that create good labor relations, a comfortable atmosphere at work, and the involvement and satisfaction of the workers
- A decision-making process that embraces not only economic and organizational considerations, but also social considerations
- Definition of the plant as an integral part of the kibbutz community.

But how has the normative model fared and what is currently happening to it? These questions are dealt with in the next section.

DESPITE SUCCESS, A DEMAND FOR CHANGE

The normative model for establishing industry in the kibbutz was implemented by many kibbutzim. Industry in those kibbutzim concentrated on technologies and markets where the principles of the normative model could be applied, and for many years kibbutz industry, judged by any criterion, enjoyed success. Production and export per worker were above average compared to similar plants in Israel (see, for example, data of the Association of Kibbutz Industry, 1996; Barkai, 1977; Leviatan and Rosner, 1980). The economic effectiveness of kibbutz industries exceeded that of comparable industries in Israel (Melman, 1971). In terms of utilization of human resources (increased motivation and contribution), their internal functioning proved to be superior to that of industrial plants outside the kibbutz (Tannenbaum et al. 1974; Palgi, 1984; Bartolke et al. 1985). And the better performing plants were those which adhered more closely to the recommendations of the normative model (Leviatan, 1975b).

Kibbutz industrial plants still hold this exceptional economic position within Israeli industry, as demonstrated by Rabin (1991) in a comparison of about fifty kibbutz industries with a similar number of comparable (in size and branch of technology) Israeli industrial companies traded in the stock market. The kibbutz plants excelled on all measures of business effectiveness. Another example of the relative business success of kibbutz industrial plants is shown in the latest analysis of the performance of Israeli industrial plants by the Israeli branch of the appraisal firm of Dun and Bradstreet (Dun and Bradstreet, 1996). Fifteen of the top one hundred and fifty Israeli manufacturing companies are kibbutz plants and six others are kibbutz regional factories. Therefore, twenty one plants out of the 150 (about 14 percent) are industrial plants that are owned by kibbutzim, while the kibbutz population accounts for only about 2.8 percent of the total Israeli population. Interestingly, and of much relevance to the topic of this chapter, the top three of the fifteen kibbutz industrial plants belong to kibbutzim that strongly adhere to the normative kibbutz model of running industry.

Research found that kibbutz industrial plants allowed workers more participation than other Israeli plants (Palgi, 1984). Workers in kibbutz plants were better able to influence conditions in their place of work, including financial matters and the work schedule. Compared to workers in private or Histadrut (the association of Israeli workers)-run industry and to workers in other countries, kibbutz industrial workers had more opportunities for advancement, to do interesting work, to study, to use their skills and knowledge, and to decide how the work would be carried out (Palgi, 1984; Bartolke et al., 1985). Principles such as managerial rotation were adopted in a large number of kibbutz plants, with the expected social and productivity benefits (Leviatan, 1978).

And yet, following the economic crisis that surfaced during the mid-1980s, there was a crisis of confidence in the kibbutz mode of industrial management. Extensive criticism was leveled at the following: that frequent rotation led to a situation in which unqualified people were running the plants; that the decision-making process was slow and caused important decisions to be delayed; and that the decision-making process allowed considerations to be introduced that were unrelated to the plant—leading to decisions that were economically unsound. It was also maintained that because the industrial plant of today is too sophisticated for all the workers to participate actively in the workers assembly, the assembly should become a forum for conveying information and no longer a forum for discussion of problems. These criticisms against the components of the normative model have resulted in suggestions for alternative approaches.

CHANGE IN ORDER OF PRIORITY GIVEN TO DIFFERENT GOALS OF INDUSTRIALIZATION

The first focus for change has been to reorder priorities among objectives that an industrial plant in a kibbutz should strive to achieve. Top priority is given to economic viability. Profitability has become the overriding concern for industry, and in many kibbutzim, flexibility is now permitted with regard to other goals such as individual welfare and safeguarding kibbutz principles. Thus, unprofitable plants may be closed, even if they provide jobs for the elderly and disabled; and in the setting up of new plants, less consideration is given to the needs of the worker and more to future profitability. (In the past the opposite was true.)

Changes have also occurred in the application of kibbutz principles, principles which kibbutz industry was to safeguard. Today, many hold to the opinion that a hierarchical structure with a clear division of authority among the various levels is essential. The top managerial positions are still chosen democratically by decision of kibbutz members—but solely according to criteria of economic efficacy. Similarly, the principle of direct democracy has become more "flexible," so that the mechanism of representative democracy is legitimized in various areas of decision making. As a result, the workers assembly in many kibbutz plants now meets only once or twice a year instead of monthly. The decision-making powers have been given instead to different committees and various managerial bodies.

Finally, the economic dependence of the plant on the other productive branches or on community institutions in the kibbutz has sometimes rendered it impossible to adapt to new economic conditions. This has led to justification for an almost complete separation between economic (primarily industrial plants) and community affairs—in contrast to the original concept of safeguarding the integration of the different sectors. Thus, there are cases where the plant has money to invest in various welfare projects for its workers or may arrange for them to travel to exhibitions abroad, whereas, at the same time, the community is reducing members' budgets or putting a limitation on consumer spending, studies are being cut, vacation travel is canceled, and even budgets for higher education are curtailed.

CHANGES TO THE NORMATIVE ORGANIZATIONAL MODEL

The New Model: A Board of Directors

The second focus of change relates to the criticism that kibbutz management norms no longer seem to answer the needs of industry in all the kibbutzim. There are now two extreme, almost contradictory, models in kibbutz industry: the normative model (described earlier) that still operates in many industrial plants and a radically new model adopted by some other plants. Most of the kibbutz industrial plants are located somewhere in the middle. The new model introduces into the plant management a new body taken from business outside the kibbutz: a board of directors composed of both members of the kibbutz and outsiders nominated for their expertise in the business of the plant. By the end of 1994, boards of directors had been set up in approximately 60 percent of the large industrial plants in the kibbutz movement (see Getz's chapter). Most of these boards demand complete autonomy for the plants: autonomy in the choice of workers and nearly absolute autonomy in policies of investment, production, training, and so on. This demand negates equality of power among kibbutz members and the integration of the plant in the kibbutz. The manager of the plant is chosen by the board of directors and serves for a longer term than in the normative model. Rotation as a social and ideological norm is no more practiced; and, for the managerial position, nomination of candidates (who do not necessarily have to be kibbutz members) is made by a professional panel.

Thus, the decision-making process takes place almost entirely within the plant, not within the framework of the kibbutz. Most issues related to long-term policy are brought before the board of directors. The workers assembly has little authority and serves primarily as an opportunity for information dissemination and announcements. Contrary to the normative model, decisions about the employment of workers, including members, follow conventional business criteria, with almost no acknowledgment of social considerations.

It is interesting that support for the introduction of the board of directors comes from two contrasting points of view: The first wishes to conserve the control of the community over the plant management, while the second is focused upon protecting the plant from the kibbutz. The first group argues as follows. If the plant manager and management are autonomous in making decisions relating to the plant, they are liable to compromise the kibbutz financially—because most of the decision makers (rank-and-file kibbutz members) lack sufficient expertise to understand the proposed decisions or have enough confidence to intervene. The establishment of a board of directors consisting of knowledgeable experts in industrial matters can protect the kibbutz from arbitrary actions by the plant manager, introduce better auditing methods, create ongoing communication with the kibbutz, and safeguard kibbutz interests.

The arguments of the second group, which advocate protection of the plant from the kibbutz, run as follows. The board of directors has autonomy in making decisions related to investments and manpower. Thus, noneconomic considerations have no place in its deliberations, and the plant no longer requires approval by the kibbutz for each step it takes. The kibbutz cannot remove or put members to work in the factory without permission of the management. Employment policies are determined on an economic basis, allowing the plant to operate more efficiently. The manager is chosen in a professional manner, and if she or he fails, the board of directors can replace her or him without regard (unlike in the past) for social considerations.

Not much research is as yet available to support any of the contentions raised by these two opposing lines of argument. However, the introduction of a board of directors is shaping up as a mixed blessing. A recent study (Buchalted and Klipper, 1996) shows that from among three hundred and fifty kibbutz industrial plants, those that have boards of directors have higher levels of sales, yet these industrial plants operate at lower levels of profitability and they pay higher rates for labor than those that do not have boards of directors.

Other Changes

Changes in Ownership Structure. While in the past, ownership of the industrial plant was solely in the hands of its kibbutz, now there exist about a dozen kibbutz industrial plants which are public on the Israeli stock market where up to 50 percent of their stocks are traded. Other plants (several dozen) have created partnerships with outside capital under various legal definitions. These moves are encouraged by the kibbutz movements as a way to diversify financial risks of the kind that proved disastrous during the crisis of the 1980s.

The Office of Plant Manager. As already stated, the plant manager is no longer required to follow the norm of managerial rotation. Most kibbutz members (approximately 70 percent) now think that if the plant is successfully managed by a kibbutz member, he or she should be allowed to retain this position for many years (Palgi and Sharir, 1995). But an even more significant change is that the plant manager need not be a kibbutz member. If there is not a suitable manager in the kibbutz, it is thought preferable to hire a professional manager from outside rather than to have the plant run by a poor manager. (About 20 percent of top industrial managers were found in a recent unpublished study Rosner and his associates to be either members of other kibbutzim or professional managers from outside the kibbutz movement.) Yet the commitment of a plant manager who is not a kibbutz member to the norms of kibbutz life is obviously tenuous, and the methods of management tend to undergo change.

Workers in the Plant. Organizational culture—hitherto based on confidence in the workers, their identification with the plant, the existence of formal and informal communication channels, direct relations with the managers, and participation in unpleasant tasks—has undergone change in some plants. The senior managers, especially in those plants that have established boards of directors, are not part of the team of workers, and informal communication has been reduced. In addition, some managers refuse to employ kibbutz members who do not have the necessary skills.

One of the problems liable to arise in the near future is a lack of jobs for the physically handicapped, which until now had been guaranteed by kibbutz industrial plants. In the past, almost every worker was accepted as a natural outcome of the belief that the kibbutz has a duty to provide work for all its members, limitations or merits notwithstanding. But it also made economic common sense: Employment of a handicapped person who can contribute even a little is less costly to the kibbutz than having that person as a health or social liability. Now, management in some plants argue that from their (narrow) perspective of the plant's efficiency, it is not in their interest to employ members who are not in their prime. Indeed, some illustrative examples of this approach have already been recorded. For instance, in one plant the top manager demanded that older kibbutz workers should leave the plant as they were not as efficient as young hired laborers from outside. The angry reaction in the community was so intense that management backed off. In another plant the manager required that older people who worked in the plant would be only those of whom he approved and that they should work "voluntarily"—that is, the kibbutz would not get any transfer of money for their work.

Hired Workers. Until the mid-1980s, there was a downward trend in the percentage of hired workers employed in kibbutz industry—from about 60 percent in 1969 to about 20 percent in 1983. This downward trend stemmed from ideological considerations and from the problematic existence of two forms of discipline within the same organization: discipline arising from identification and internalization of values (that of kibbutz members) and discipline arising from necessity (that of hired workers). But since 1989, and resulting from the adoption of the new model, hired work is again on the rise. In 1990, 29.9 percent of kibbutz industrial workers were hired; in 1994, 50.9 percent and in 1996, 56.4 percent were hired. In plants with boards of directors, hired workers constitute the majority of production workers.

SIGNIFICANCE OF THE CHANGES FOR OTHER DOMAINS OF LIFE IN THE KIBBUTZ

During its years of existence the kibbutz has prided itself on the involvement and identification of its members with their workplace. Studies showed that the special qualities and qualifications of its members were among the strongest kibbutz economic advantages and that its main strength was apparent when it could recruit members at times of difficulty to make special efforts and to contribute to unforeseen work demands. The changes that many kibbutz industries have introduced, and which (according to present trends) many more might introduce, create a distance between members' personal lives and the welfare of the kibbutz and result in alienation from their work-place because they are no longer involved in decision making. This alienation is, of course, also true for the hired workers, but the latter are at least compensated by material benefits related to their efforts, while for kibbutz members who work in industry extra effort or special achievements are not compensated by material benefits.

True, in the past, kibbutz workers in industry also did not benefit personally from their work. But before the changes, they could at least feel that they had control over their work life and the future of their workplace through the democratic decision-making process that prevailed. This is no longer so in many plants.

Therefore, an increasing number of workers feel as if they are hired labor but without any of the benefits (salary and fringe benefits) of that position. This brings them to look first after their own personal interests and only later after the general good of the plant—as demonstrated by Leviatan (1995), who has shown that, for the first time, the motivation level of industrial workers is below that of farm workers. As a result, a new type of relationship is developing between managers and workers; a passage from a cooperative relationship and the pursuance of common goals to rivalry, contradictions, and conflicting goals.

Such adversarial relationships at the industrial workplace have a spillover effect on other domains of life on the kibbutz. Thus, the bureaucratic and the sometimes conflictual relations between workers and management are imitated by workers in other workplaces. It happens because the kibbutz is a closely knit community, and the industrial plants in most of them dominate in norm setting, since they represent the single largest workplace for members. The effect of the changed organizational culture can be felt even within the community's social domains. Domains such as education, health care, and mental health are also experiencing a transformation from an informal relationship based on trust into a stricter and much more formal relationship. For instance, members are limited in the hours and times they may approach officeholders for assistance or consultation; they may get help only after it is approved by a professional and not, as it used to be in the past, according to their request.

Members in central managerial positions enjoy in some kibbutzim (where the changes are significant) almost unlimited power in the community. In the few kibbutz communities (two at the moment) where differential remuneration has already been introduced, the high-ranking managers get the highest "salaries." The demand for the introduction of differential salaries in these kibbutzim came from their industrial managers, who argued that such an arrangement would better motivate their workers. There is no proof as yet that workers' motivation has been raised by the introduction of differential remuneration, but one outcome is clear: In one kibbutz that introduced differential monetary remuneration for members, holders of managerial positions receive three times as much as rank-and-file workers.

One attitudinal outcome that has resulted from the changes is that members who are high-income producers are highly esteemed while, in the past, this esteem was reserved for hard workers.

These changes are also having a profound impact on the kibbutz's organizational culture. While in the past, emphasis was placed on egalitarian work relations and the equal value of all types of work, today greater value is placed on personal achievement and organizational efficiency. It is fair to surmise that this process is transforming the organizational culture of kibbutz industries into that of traditional industrial plants elsewhere.

LEARNING FROM THE KIBBUTZ EXPERIENCE

The changes that kibbutz industries are presently experiencing relate to an ongoing argument in the literature that deals with the origins and causes of change: whether it is due to economic failure of the ongoing system (e.g., Williamson, 1975, 1991; Ouchi, 1980; Granovetter, 1985, 1991) or to ideological shifts (e.g., Meister, 1973).

The approach that emphasizes economic causes of change argues that when one organizational model fails economically, the organization switches to another model. For example, when a model based on hierarchy and power relations fails to be effective, the organization switches its principles of conduct to economic and market relations (as Williamson argues) or into some sort of "cooperative relations," to which different researchers give different names: clan (Ouchi, 1980); commune (Butler, 1983); or network (Powell, 1990). The common argument here is that the economic conditions of an organization trigger the change in principles of conduct.

By contrast, Meister (1973) studied what he called "the iron law of degeneration of direct democracies" and looked into the demise of cooperatives and voluntary associations in France and Italy. He argued that it is the ideology—values and attitudes held by members and leadership—which changes and which leads to changes in principles of organizational conduct. Ideology, according to Meister, is what leads to passage from a cooperative model into a hierarchical or market model—not failure in the economic conduct of the organization. That is, even economically successful cooperatives or other direct democracies may go through a process of decommunilization to become organizations that are hierarchically ruled or ruled by principles of the free economic market.

Meister pointed out the characteristics of such changes as he found them in dying cooperatives. These characteristics are very similar to what is currently observed in some kibbutzim: a change from members' intensive involvement in their organization to members' apathy for the organization; a change from direct democracy in the organization into indirect democracy; a change from cohesive social relations to conflicts between managers and workers; a change from ideological commitment to economic considerations as the only criteria to evaluate one's conduct; and a change from rewarding all organizational members equally to differentially rewarding them according to managerial position.

The changes occurring in kibbutzim are much in line with what Meister describes and are clearly in the direction of both hierarchy relations and economic or market relations. This, then, should allow us to test the contrasting hypotheses about the origins of change in organizations. Palgi (1994) offers a first test of the rival hypotheses in her study. Her findings are that in the kibbutz both ideological and economic conditions are responsible for changes from a cooperative model into a market or a hierarchical model, but the ideological have primacy over the economic conditions.

The conclusion from all this is ironic. A failure in functioning might bring about change in an organization. Paradoxically, however, the change is often to a model that has already been tried elsewhere but failed. Thus, kibbutz plants are trying the market and hierarchical models—stricter supervision over workers, representative democracy, material rewards, and so on. Meanwhile, plants in western industrialized societies are trying to introduce elements from the cooperative model—worker ownership, worker participation, autonomous groups, quality circles, group discussions, expression groups—because their market and hierarchical models have failed them.

5
The Changing Identity of Kibbutz Education

Yechezkel Dar

The ideal type of kibbutz education can be characterized by six structural traits: duality of communal educational institutions and family; centrality of the peer group in the socialization process; merging of the educational system and the community; a multifaceted, multifunctional school; autonomous but task-oriented adolescence; and a short passage from adolescence to adulthood. Although it may have taken a toll on individual autonomy, the "hidden curriculum" of this education has helped to inculcate a prosocial orientation, emotional moderation, and a strong sense of commitment to communal life and to the kibbutz as a place. All of these factors are important to the fulfillment of the role of kibbutz member. Now the rapid social change of the last decade is eroding this structure of kibbutz education and thus jeopardizing its capacity to socialize children into a communal life-style.

The uniqueness of the kibbutz phenomenon originated not only because of its communal design but also because it represented a model for a new and just Jewish society. Consequently, education was required both to sustain a particular social structure and to promote a willingness to deal with objectives within the wider society. Although the achievement of such aims accents intergenerational conformity and continuity, it precludes social isolation and leaves itself open to external messages calling for educational innovation and change. Moreover, since its inception, kibbutz education has functioned in a dual context of extreme collectivism coupled with individual autonomy. The potential conflicts and contradictions inherent in such a combination may partly explain the educational system's transient makeup.

This chapter examines the declining ability of kibbutz education to socialize young people for communal life. To begin with, I describe the normative structure—ideal-type in the Weberian sense—of kibbutz education which endured to the late 1960s and early 1970s.[1] This normative ideal of kibbutz education then serves as a frame of reference for discussing the changes that are currently occurring as a result of more general changes in kibbutz communities.

NORMATIVE MODEL OF KIBBUTZ EDUCATION

The model of kibbutz education was established in the 1930s and the 1940s and is based on two premises which the kibbutz shares with many other communal societies: that the commune is fully responsible for the education of its members' children, who are also perceived as the ensuing generation to be primed for the role of kibbutz member; and that education is a process shared between the family and communal educational agents. Educating the next generation enhances three objectives. The first objective is to embue children with a commitment to the values of egalitarianism and sharing; of a needs-based conception of justice (as opposed to allocation of benefits based on the contribution of each individual); of work (mainly manual) as an end in itself; of participatory, democratic decision making; of the advance of social justice extending beyond the borders of the kibbutz; and of national responsibility. This task involves fostering the ability to make moral judgments, to engage in the clarification of values, and to take stands on social and political issues. The second objective is to foster skills necessary for a communal life-style: playing down one's ego; investing in work and society without direct material reward; effectively operating within interpersonal relationships which are simultaneously task- and solidarity-oriented; and withstanding pressures which are engendered by reciprocal dependency and by overlapping social networks. The third objective is to promote emotional commitment to the community: to the shared enterprise, to one's fellow members of the kibbutz, and to the landscape of one's childhood. Six structural characteristics derive from these objectives.

STRUCTURAL CHARACTERISTICS OF THE NORMATIVE MODEL

Two Foci in the Child's Life

The educational institute (whose team bears most of the responsibility for the instrumental and ideological education of the child) and the family (which provides the supportive and expressive milieu for the child) are the two distinct but coordinated foci in the child's life. Though the two foci are complementary, the division of labor between educators and parents is not without tension. The child spends with the family only very few hours of leisure time a day. Thus the parents and the parents' apartment represent the domain of the "me" and "mine" for the child—what is private and individual—as opposed to the "we" and "ours" characterizing the group in the communal children-use (where the young child lives about twenty hours a day). The demarcation between these two domains allows the child to negotiate with adults, thus extending his or her liberty.

Centrality of the Age Group

A stable and continuous comprehensive age group supports the child as both progress through educational stages, switching age-graded homes and educators, yet staying together all the time.[2] The group constitutes a center in the child's life which competes with the family both as a locus and an influence. It is in this group that the child lives and sleeps, learns, participates in formal and informal activities, spends leisure time, and makes friends.

Such a functional totality enhances the group's power of control and reduces the private domain in the life-space of the individual child. Conflicts that inevitably arise in interpersonal relations are counterbalanced by positive sentiments that develop in a system of longitudinal and intense interaction, marked by close, semi-sibling relations (Faigin, 1958; Ross, et al., 1992) in which the individual child learns to cooperate in the attainment of common objectives and to consider others when striving for personal goals (Bar-Yosef, 1959).

Merging of Community and Education

Merging is reflected in the unity of educational agencies (Segal, 1955; Golan, 1961): the children-house, the peer group, the family, the school, and the community. All have to cooperate in both the formal and the informal educational systems. Because education is integrated into the community, role models and guidance are not confined to parents and professional educators. Every kibbutz member may serve as a model or a mentor. On the one hand, ideological indoctrination cannot stray too far from reality because children are able constantly to examine the significance of educational messages. On the other hand, socialization is strengthened whenever the educational messages are in step with social reality. Seeing parents and educators share beliefs and activities fortifies the children's sense that they are children not only of their parents but also of their kibbutz. The sentimental attitude of the kibbutz members towards their children serves to reinforce this feeling.

Education and community are integrated in yet one other way. Education, including school, is a prominent topic on the kibbutz agenda. Educational and community work assignments are interwoven, and a rotation of educational and noneducational work roles in members' jobs allows nonprofessionals to participate in educational activity (Ben-Peretz and Lavi, 1982). The kibbutz principles of organization—its economy, history and philosophy, as well as its close environment—are subjects of study in school. Children and adolescents participate significantly in the kibbutz work force. They also take part in most of the communal festivities. Their *rites des passages*—beginning and end of school years, bar-mitzvah, school graduation, and acceptance into the commune as members—are times of festivity for the entire community. The merging of education with the community is also fortified by the semiautonomy of kibbutz education from the state educational system.

A Multifaceted School

The kibbutz school is a nonselective, nontracked institution that combines academic, vocational, aesthetic, moral, social, and ideological education without giving primacy to the functional over the moral and expressive (Golan, 1961). Subjects of study are interdisciplinary: Each subject is framed as a "project" associated with topics pertaining to the child's immediate environment, as well as, at the more general level, to culture, society, and science (Alterman, 1973). This approach to education accords real-life questions priority over knowledge, and critical thought over mere information acquisition. The process of learning, which is based on experimentation and investigation, is just as important as the end product of learning—knowing. Effort, morally proper behavior, and contribution to society are valued as much as academic accomplishments (Lavi, 1973). In line with this approach, manual work is accorded important educational value and is integrated in the curriculum (Bar-Lev and Dror, 1995).

Group work and collective achievement are given priority over the personal. Although individual study is encouraged, cooperation is valued more than competition. A flexible method of evaluation replaces the standard grading system, and preparation of projects is preferred to exams. There is no selection whatsoever. Ability grouping, aimed more at aiding poor students than at advancing the academically gifted, is confined to a narrow area of the curriculum (mostly in studying English and math) and applied only in the upper grades. Completion of twelve years of study has been encouraged, even at a time (up to the 1960s) when this was a privilege among the general populace in Israel.

The weakening of instrumental emphases (as compared to moral and expressive) reduces the problem of control and helps to promote the personal authority of the educator and the student's intrinsic motivation. The teacher's responsibility extends beyond studies and the classroom to initiating a close personal relationship with his or her students. At variance with the teacher's traditional role of being restricted to authoritative transmission of knowledge, the kibbutz educator serves as an informal intermediary between the adult society and its culture and the particular needs and subculture of the students.

Task-Oriented Autonomy of Adolescence

Adolescent autonomy is exercised in a task-oriented context, albeit one that is steered by adult educators. It is sustained by the belief that adolescents need independence and behavioral leeway; that they are responsible enough to be entitled to personal freedom and group autonomy; and that this very autonomy may have a moral, socializing effect (Golan, 1961).

Autonomy is embodied in the Adolescent Society, a multi-age structure of several one-age educational groups, usually from ages twelve or thirteen to eighteen (seventh grade to end of high school). The Adolescent Society represents a miniature simulation of the organizational structure of the kibbutz and is characterized by an interplay of formal and informal activities, institutionalization and role playing, and independence coupled with adults' tacit guidance. The freedom given allows for experimentation with various social and public roles and for relatively unconstrained development of moral autonomy (Kohlberg, 1971).

However, the instrumental context, which permits access to such valuable social roles as acting as counselors to younger children and as officials in the system of self-government, minimizes marginality and social deviation of individual students and channels personal and group experimentation into paths that conform to the central social values (Zellermayer and Marcus, 1972). In addition, a workload of 80 to 90 days a year—the teenagers' contribution to the economy of the community as well as to the cost of their upkeep—aids in the framing of the student's life-space.

A significant aspect is the continuous presence of real-life issues of daily living, including clashes that need to be resolved between individual and group norms. Dealing with these kinds of moral problems entails framing them in moral terms: equality, fairness, rights, and responsibilities; encouraging an open and diverse expression of reasons why the group should decide one way or another; having nonauthoritarian educators who present points of view that challenge the prevailing view of the group; and resolving each problem through a binding group decision (Snarey, 1987).

Short Passage to Full Social Adulthood

This characteristic is promoted through early adoption of responsible roles in the workplace, in the family, and in the community. Transformation into full social adulthood immediately follows obligatory military service. The groundwork for this relatively smooth transition is laid during the task-oriented adolescence, especially through participation in the kibbutz work force during high school, which serves as a bridge between the adolescent and the adult role. This bridging is facilitated by the fact that the adoption of responsible work roles does not require any formal certification or prior formal training. Rapid transition into full adulthood is also facilitated by the prevailing concept of social mission, which curbs the moratorial tendency of young people from seeking individualistic self-actualization; the constant economic growth and organizational development of the kibbutz, which provides many new job openings for young members; and a strong orientation in young people to establish families of their own (Shepher, 1969).

It is the conjunction of these six structural characteristics that have provided the kibbutz educational model with exceptional socialization strength.

CONCEPTUAL FOUNDATIONS

This model of education came into being initially as a practical solution to the needs of an egalitarian and communal society—a society that sought to allow women significant equality in fulfilling its pioneering mission, by freeing most of them from house chores and child-rearing tasks (Ron-Polani, 1960). The articulation of an educational conception was only subsequently achieved (Dror, 1984).

Kibbutz education borrowed ideas from several sources. It is the special integration of these ideas, rather than their originality, that makes this education unique. One of several conceptual foundations for the kibbutz education model was drawn from the socialist-Zionist synthesis, which emphasized egalitarianism, productivity, and a pioneering elite. Adopted from socialist thought was the idea of a "new family," one based on emotional ties and reciprocation as opposed to the bourgeois family based on property ties and authority. The critical attitude toward the traditional family helped to legitimize the restricted role of the family in education. Also from this source was drawn the idea of fashioning a "new person": educated, liberated, creative, emotionally balanced, and sensitive to others, to social justice, and to the needs of the collective.

One may also detect in kibbutz education the influence of Marx's conception of noninstrumental education that produces a creative, many-sided child. The achievement of this aim requires the coalescence of intellectual and bodily activities and the blurring of disciplinary lines between the humanities, arts, sciences, and engineering—all this as a basis for making human work a creative activity (Zilbersheid, 1994). Such ideas may be seen in the multiplicity of educational aims, the interdisciplinary curriculum, and the importance of manual work in kibbutz education.

Furthermore, the pedagogic underpinning of kibbutz education drew from the autonomous youth culture of G. Wyneken (Wyneken, 1913; Yitzhaki, 1976) and S. Bernfeld (Bernfeld, 1921; Yitzhaki, 1977) and from the German youth movement Vandervogel (Becker, 1984). These emphasized the power of youth to change the world (an antithesis to the enervated society and decadent culture of the adult world) as well as the moral, prosocial educative characteristics of the community of peers. Whereas Wyneken regarded education as a leverage for cultural, apolitical change, Bernfeld associated the emancipation of the child with that of the working class and viewed the school community as a cell of the socialist youth movement. This view allowed Bernfeld to transfuse the concepts of youth culture and the educative group into the Zionist youth movements in Europe. Kibbutz education reflected these ideas in its appreciation of adolescent autonomy, of the idea of the teacher as educator and of the notion of children and adolescent societies as key educational structures.

Another (although indirect) influence was exerted by progressive education—a blend of educational currents that flourished at the beginning of this century with the aim of bringing education closer to the needs of both society and children—as highlighted by radical social thinking and by the new science of psychology. One influential source of progressive thought on kibbutz education derived from several earlier experimental schools in Palestine, whose progenitors were influenced by the activity school associated, *inter alia*, with Kerschensteiner (Kerschensteiner, 1929). The educational philosophy of John Dewey (Dewey, 1963) was another influence (Segal, 1979). Progressive educational thought was mirrored in kibbutz education in its paedocentric accent, its belief in the developmental capacity of education, the centrality of experience in the educational process, the multifaceted school, the integrated curriculum, and the merging of school and community. Dewey's attempt to reconcile the unabated growth of the individual with societal needs, not by restricting the individual but by allowing him or her to participate freely in socially relevant tasks, strongly appealed to educators whose commitments were always divided between the individual and the group.

Finally, the reliance on psychoanalysis exemplifies a co-option of science to justify ideology (Berman, 1988). On the one hand, psychoanalysis increased sensitivity to the personal needs of the child. On the other hand, by emphasizing pathogenic potentials in traditional parent-child relations, it provided arguments for educational arrangements which went against the commonly perceived human nature. For instance, the claim that Oedipal conflict might be moderated by the child's sleeping outside the family home (Golan, 1959) served to calm anxious mothers who feared they were not fulfilling their maternal roles. Similarly, the notion of the prosocial sublimation of the libido (Yitzhaki, 1982) helped foster a near puritanical sexual code among coeducated and cohabitant adolescents living in dormitories geographically removed from parental supervision.

CONTRADICTIONS WITHIN THE NORMATIVE MODEL

This gathering of social, educational, and psychological ideas helped, paradoxically, both to mitigate and to accent the tensions of collectivistic-individualistic dualism inherent in kibbutz ideology. The child-centered pedagogy and personality-centered psychology counterbalanced the socially centered ideas of the educational group and youth culture. In retrospect, the present observer can discern at least two potential contradictions that were hardly apparent at the time to the progenitors of kibbutz education.

The first is the potential contradiction between social and cognitive openness and closeness: an effort to preserve what has already been accomplished as opposed to social renovation and change. This is coupled with an unintentional ideological indoctrination side by side with a genuine belief in the autonomous individual.

The second is the potential contradiction between the elevation of group, or the collective, as an educational goal while exalting the individual. The children's society was perceived not only as a "miniature kibbutz, a kibbutz to be and a framework which educates toward the kibbutz," but also as "a way of life which guarantees a beneficial and creative balance between the education of the individual and an education whose focus is society and society's objectives; which gives every individual opportunity for activity and creativity, inculcates a sense of responsibility toward society, and fills one with the joy that comes from serving society" (Golan, 1961, 178–179). At the same time, "education will attain its full potential if it will ally itself with the full development of the individual. An individual who has a rich and independent spiritual life and is highly articulate in matters which are dear to him will enrich society. It is important that the individual attain fulfillment and discover within himself a veritable fountainhead of creative powers" (Golan, 1961, 81).

Faith in the harmony between the individual and society and insensitivity to the constraints the group may impose on personal freedom are striking. It may be explained by a strong belief in the veracity of the kibbutz way of life and its social mission, which accords a moral meaning to the subordination of self-interest to the common goal. This collectivist perception of self-realization (or individual perception of the innately moral quality of the group) alleviated, though it did not eliminate, tensions between the individual and society.

CONTENT AND STRUCTURE

The way these values were transmitted from the founders' generation to the younger generation added to the potential for conflict because socialization did not have strong enough cognitive components to back up emotional components. Idealistic fervor helped to base education on structural messages, and only a little attention was paid to messages of content. "Our youth is not exposed to any intentional inculcation of the doctrines upon which the kibbutz is based: its fundamentals are manifest to them as a living reality, but not as a theoretical doctrine" (Golan, 1961, 292).

The transmission of values and behavioral norms through formal, verbal, or textual instruction (as, for instance, in religious indoctrination) was restricted. Kibbutz education here functioned primarily through a hidden curriculum. Orientations and value commitments were acquired by studying role models, experiencing relations, solving problems, coping with moral dilemmas, and implementing tasks, all of which formed part of the life-routine in the social structures of the kibbutz community as well as in its groups of young students. Life within the commune, experience within the educational group, and the example older members set for the young were all regarded as efficient educational devices.

This view of learning by doing fitted the progressive educational philosophy and the idea of the educational community in which primacy was given to practical experience over theoretical study. This resulted in a paucity of articulated ideological conceptualization along with a strong, almost instinctive, commitment to the kibbutz way of life, sometimes classified as "pragmatic value commitments" (Kahane 1975) or as "light on Socialism, heavy on Kibbutzism" (Quarter, 1984).[3] These never-to-be-solved dualisms contributed later to the transformative propensity of the educational system.

ATTITUDINAL AND BEHAVIORAL OUTCOMES

Voluminous research on children, adolescents, and young adults has not managed to locate any uniqueness in personality traits among kibbutz-born (Liegle, 1980; Rabin and Beit-Hallahmi, 1982). However, behavioral characteristics of kibbutz-born (while living in the kibbutz) do tend to differ from those of other youth. Some of these characteristics are clearly traceable to the structural characteristics of kibbutz education.

The first attitudinal set—an apparent outcome of life in close and egalitarian groups—is a cluster of pro-social traits founded on the development of a *basic trust* and dependent not only on experience in the immediate family but also on the emotional security given by the protective educators, the supportive age group, and the sheltering milieu of the commune (Bettelheim, 1969). This cluster includes relatively high levels of *tolerance* (Pirojnikoff, Hadar, and Hadar, 1971), *altruism* (Nadler, Romek, and Shapira-Friedman, 1979), *social responsibility* (Nevo, 1977), *cooperation* (Eiferman, 1970; Shapira and Madsen, 1974; Hertz-Lazarowitz, et al., 1989), *sharing* (Faigin, 1958), belief in egalitarian *social justice* (Nisan 1984, 1989), and the accelerated development of *moral judgment* that is articulated at an early age (Snarey, 1987; Eisenberg, Hertz-Lazarowitz, and Fuchs, 1990). A preference for social *solidarity* and expressive *self-actualization* over personal achievement also characterizes kibbutz children (Levy and Guttman, 1974; Sohlberg, 1985).[4]

The second attitudinal set is a tendency to *moderate emotional responses and to diffuse affect* (mostly negative) among many significant others—as opposed to concentrating it among a few. This tendency can be attributed to the communal sleeping arrangement, which involves "multiple mothering" (attachment to the mother and several caregivers at the same time) and intensive interaction within groups (Rabin, 1965; Regev, Beit-Hallahmi, and Sharabany, 1980). By enduring the pressures of togetherness, the individual may move toward a more effective functioning within different groups. Moderation of negative affect may also have contributed to the success of kibbutz youth in the army, especially in the tight social network of the small, elite, combat unit (Amir, 1969; Agin, 1970), and to the relative stability of the family unit among second-generation kibbutz members as it was revealed in the 1960s and 1970s (Gerson, 1978).

The third attitudinal set is reflected in the fact that kibbutz youth seem to share a strong *sense of affiliation*, accompanied by a strong commitment to the place, the commune, and the peer group. This sense of affiliation is strengthened by a firm feeling of *status security* regarding one's personal future.[5] Both the family—immediate and extended—and the age group play a central role in shaping this sense of belonging and security.

On the negative side, the norms of equality and life within groups may lead one to downplay one's ego and to curb ambition for personal accomplishment and excellence (Spiro, 1965; Sohlberg, 1985). This may be caused by: (1) deep concern with one's status within the peer group that may enhance the fear of failure (Handel, 1971); (2) strong pressure from a peer group that may depress norms of achievement; and (3) the security that the kibbutz offers its offspring, discouraging investment in high-level achievement. Such arguments may also be derived from the noninstrumental, egalitarian, and collectivist accents of the school.

Then, too, the intensive togetherness may restrain *self-disclosure and spontaneity* (Biran, 1983), inhibit display of *creativity* (Eddelist and Nevo, 1983), and enhance *compliance with group norms* (Tal, 1982). Note, however, that at least one carefully designed study (Shouval et al., 1975) failed to reveal greater conformity among kibbutz youth than among urban youth.

Consistent with the tendency for emotional diffusion and moderation, the supportive group may have also reduced the need and, perhaps, the willingness, but not necessarily the ability, to form *intimate friendships* in preadolescence and adolescence (Sharabany and Weisman, 1993).[6]

Next, strong commitment to the peer group, to parents, and to the kibbutz, along with moderation of conflicts with parents in the adolescent years, may lead to problems of individuation and separation (Berman, 1988) and may delay their onset from the time of adolescence to young adulthood (Weiseman and Lieblich, 1992). In the same vein, the strong support of the group, the sheltering caregivers, the generous provision for one's needs, and the security of a material future, all coupled with a strong dependence on the group, on the caregiver, and later on the collective decisions and institutions, may hinder development of the *individual's sense of responsibility* for his or her fate (Shner, 1986). These factors also seem to have reduced the clarity of personal *future orientation*, particularly occupational expectations and planning (Seginer, 1988).

Finally, the moratorial, noninstrumental significance of multifaceted education is well suited for a late assignment to a permanent job (Talmon-Garber, 1972) and helps fashion identity around the role of kibbutz member rather than a specific occupation. However, this moratorial significance has been hindered by an adamant demand made by the founding generation that the young generation view the kibbutz as a perfect entity in no need of change. Coupled with the relative confinement of the kibbutz within its social and conceptual boundaries, this demand has had the potential of encouraging among the first generation of kibbutz children a *premature psychological closing* (Marcia, 1980), leading to early and conformist assumption of adult roles.

In the shadow for a long time, these potential constraints of educational collectivism have been progressively illuminated with the decreasing communalism of the kibbutz.

SOCIAL AND EDUCATIONAL CHANGES

The economic crisis that began in the mid-1980s merely served as a catalyst for the kibbutz's gradual social transformation starting years before. A detailed analysis of this transformation, and its association with the comprehensive change of Israeli society, is covered in more detail in other chapters of this volume. The following is a brief list of these changes experienced by kibbutz communities which have most directly affected the educational system.

The transformation of the kibbutzim from farming communities to industrial communities during the last thirty years was accompanied by an academic revolution, introducing more formalization to the organizational structures and principles of conduct in the kibbutzim as well as more social differentiation and a greater diversity of personal careers. At the same time, kibbutzim experienced an appreciable increase in material standards of living. The general effect of these changes was toward more individuality and less collectivity as the guiding principle of personal and kibbutz conduct.

The structural changes have been accompanied by changes in values and sentiments. The utopian emphasis of the kibbutz has waned, as has its self-image as a social elite. Equality and communalism are no longer so central in motivating the kibbutz member and in giving meaning to kibbutz life. Consequently, the sense of togetherness and the commitment to the collective have lessened, and legitimization has been given to the fulfillment of individual needs, even when these needs stand apart from the needs of the collective.

THE EDUCATIONAL EMPOWERMENT OF THE FAMILY

A major change came about in the relationships between community and family. The role and status of the family within the community have been enhanced. The family household (and residence) have grown in size, function, and scope of resource control, helping the family to become the most important center for both adults and children. It may have also prompted the increasing demand that children sleep in the family home rather than in children-houses.

The process of bringing children into the family home began in the late 1950s, accelerated in the 1960s and 1970s, and was eventually accomplished by the time of the Gulf War in 1989 (see the chapter by Plotnik). Although the dual pattern of education (communal institution and family) has been retained, the family is now preeminently responsible for its children, and parents spend much more time with their children. Simultaneously, greater flexibility is evident in educational practices (Kaffman, Elizur, and Rabinowitz, 1990; Raviv and Palgi, 1985).

With the change in sleeping arrangements, the children-house has lost its significance as a real home for the children and is now becoming more and more a day-care center (Sagi and Koren-Karie, 1993). This is most apparent when the child reaches elementary school (especially if that school is regional rather than local); at this stage the educational role of institutions and caregivers has been significantly undermined (Gilad, 1990).

The family-based sleeping arrangement reduces participation in communal activities but helps the family to fortify its internal cohesion and enhance its influence on children. With parents having more say about raising their children, their views about education in kibbutz schools has assumed more importance. However, these views are expressions of the average parent rather than the community and its leaders, and the two views are not necessarily compatible. Parents tend to attach less importance to socialization for kibbutz life, to educational goals that promote kibbutz values, and to the investment of school time in preparation for work roles. What matters to them are creativity and academic achievement, as well as general Jewish and humanistic values, good manners, and individual independence (Avrahami and Getz, 1994).

THE SCHOOL: FROM MULTIFACETED EDUCATION TO ACADEMIC ACCENT

At the same time, prompted by technological and organizational advances and the increasing demand for higher education, the school had been pushed already in the 1960s to raise its academic profile (Dar, 1968) and this trend was accelerated later on. However, this has not been accomplished without cost to the previous structure. In order to offer a variety of high-level programs and to take account of economic considerations which favor size, the local, community-integrated school is fast disappearing. The formation of regional schools, at first high schools but now elementary schools as well, has led to the demise of the multifaceted, comprehensive nature of the school and resulted in academic teaching and learning as the most important educational goal.

This change was facilitated by the regional status of the school, which allowed reduced communal control and increased school autonomy in setting objectives and establishing its organizational procedures. These are now generally decided according to such criteria as institutional considerations, the interests of the teachers, the needs of the students, and the wishes of the families rather than ideological imperatives and needs of the kibbutz community. The separation of school from community has further increased through integration of schools into the state educational system, where they must adopt the national curriculum and become subject to state supervision, and through selective acceptance into the school of nonkibbutz students from the vicinity (Liberman, 1994).

Whereas, previously, emphasis had been placed on the accomplishment of varied educational tasks ("education"), the focus in schooling has shifted to achieving specific academic results ("studying"). The former multi-role house of education has now dwindled into a (mere) school. Teaching has become more professional, with teachers specializing in academic disciplines and no longer so concerned about affecting the personality and the moral and social attitudes of the students. Even the evaluation of students (based on grades and exams) is now increasingly meritocratic.

Another manifestation of the changes that kibbutz schools have experienced— though only after several years of heated debate—has been the incorporation of the state matriculation exams in their curriculum. As a result, the school curriculum has become subordinated to achieving the greatest number of matriculation certificates. Although the examinations have strengthened the academic dimension of the school, they differentiate between a majority of students who take exams and a minority who do not, thus impairing the school's nonselectivity (Shoham, 1990).

The decline of kibbutz-oriented education and the shift of emphasis to academic disciplines resulted not only from social change within and without the kibbutzim but also from a growing uncertainty among educators about aims. The generation of teachers who were committed to the social vision of the kibbutz has been replaced by those whose attitude toward the kibbutz is more skeptical and ambivalent. "Today we don't know what or how to teach the kibbutz subject. We are perplexed because no one knows where the kibbutz is heading. It is difficult to . . . transfer commitment to kibbutz life to your students when one is not sure what one wants it to be" (a teacher cited in Avrahami and Getz, 1994). Consequently, many teachers retreat to the haven of seemingly value-free academic disciplines where they feel themselves liberated from the need to articulate an unclear educational message.

Along with the changes in orientation and organization, the previously diffuse roles of educator and educand, with their emotional and moral connotations, have been gradually replaced by the more specific, neutral, and hierarchically related roles of teacher and student. The change in nomenclature signifies diminishing reciprocity within this relationship and a change in its content. The student-teacher relationship has become less personal, and teachers are much less involved in the lives of their students. There has been a consequent change in the control system of the school: The reliance on normative power (based on a moral affinity between educator and educand and sometimes on the public opinion of the class) is reduced to control by manipulating grades and inflicting sanctions. Control is made less intrinsic and more extrinsic, less charismatic and more bureaucratic.

THE WEAKENING INFLUENCE OF THE PEER GROUP

Another major change has had to do with the shift of the child's home from the children-house to the parents' apartment, thereby weakening the peer group as a potent socializing agent. Dependence on the original local age group is further reduced when the child joins new groups in the regional school.

In most kibbutzim, adolescents at age fifteen or sixteen still return to the framework of communal sleeping arrangements, but they are coming to a rather weaker adolescent society. The attenuation of collective ideological emphases reduces the willingness of individuals, especially the young, to work in groups for the achievement of collective objectives. This willingness is further weakened by the identification of adolescents with the hedonistic youth culture, allowing free expression of pop and hippie life-styles, increased sexual freedom, and experimentation with alcohol and even hashish (Kaffman, 1993). Increasing academic demands of the school, greater engagement in individual enrichment activities such as sports and the arts, and the exposure to television also reduce student willingness to invest time and energy in collective social, cultural, and political activities.

Recently, erosion of the sanctified place of children's work in the kibbutz has become apparent. Schools dedicate more time to academic teaching at the expense of working time, especially prior to examinations. This trend has been supported by structural changes in the kibbutz economic domain—the increased specialization in agriculture and industry and the introduction of hired workers into the service branches—which have reduced the need for children's work.

THE PROLONGED TRANSITION TO ADULTHOOD

Yet another change is evident in the pattern of transition to adulthood. Since the 1970s, there has been a tendency to prolong the years of adolescence into the late twenties and early thirties, reflecting the enhancement of individualist orientations (Alon, 1976; Avrahami and Dar, 1993).

With growing doubts about the kibbutz, yet enjoying the social and economic security afforded them by the kibbutz, youth prefer to keep their options open and not to commit themselves either to ideology and lifestyle or to family and profession. Uncommitted, they are engaged in identity formation, personal development and individuation, and exploration of alternative personal paths and are encouraged to do so by several sequential experiences outside the kibbutz: a year of voluntary social service, several years in the military, years of leave off the kibbutz (mostly for a trip to explore the world), and college years. Together with interim periods within the kibbutz, these experiences coalesce into a distinct stage of youth between adolescence and adulthood which spans the ages from twenty to thirty (Dar, 1993).

CONCLUSION

As described, major structural changes have occurred in the normative system of kibbutz education. The educational role of the family has been strengthened at the expense of the commune; the school has assumed greater autonomy and concentrates on academic achievement; the role of the age group in the child's and adolescent's life has been restricted; child and adolescent societies no more exert the same socializing influence; and the once short transition to adulthood has been extended into the early thirties.

Earlier educational patterns still exist, but changing concepts have neutralized their former socializing strength. Specifically, the system's ability to socialize via structural messages—the most profound socializing power of this education—has been impaired. At the same time, an ideological anomie precludes the substitution of eroded real-life messages by articulated ideological, more theoretical messages. These developments have diminished the ability of the kibbutz to ensure its continuity—in its traditional form—through its offspring.

Several developments of the last decade have further contributed to weakening the present ability of the kibbutzim to hold on to their youth. First, youth today represent the third sociological (though not necessarily biological) generation in the kibbutz. Their parents succeeded in maintaining a direct, though sometimes strained, dialogue with the founders, who transmitted a clear and obligatory message of "kibbutz." The third generation is experiencing a more relaxed dialogue with their parents of the second generation, who pass confused and equivocal messages on to them. In a recent investigation, only one-third of the eighteen-year-olds perceived their parents as presenting to them the kibbutz as a preferred way of life. It is, therefore, no wonder that only 52 percent of them favored the kibbutz over other ways of life and that 73 percent were uncertain whether they would opt to remain on the kibbutz. In their connection to the kibbutz, most of them weighed individualistic and utilitarian considerations as more important than ideological considerations, though the latter were not abandoned (Avrahami, 1993).

Second, the ambiguity of the educational message of the family in the present-day kibbutz is further accentuated by the high rate of young adults permanently leaving kibbutz life for the city. Between two-thirds to three-quarters of each age cohort of the young leave the kibbutz today, as against one-third to one-half in the early 1980s. Many of them offer a model of material success to their younger sisters and brothers still in the kibbutz (Leviatan and Orchan, 1982). As a result, the commitments of the typical kibbutz family are split between kibbutz and children who opt for another way of life.

Third, the relatively strong commitment of the second generation to the kibbutz was largely mediated by the past organizational (and mostly economic) development—agricultural modernization in the 1950s and industrialization in the 1960s and 1970s. Organizational and industrial entrepreneurship provided an importnt source of self-fulfillment and status. This integrating force is losing importance in the present economic recession and shortage of investment capital in the kibbutzim.

Finally, college education, which is now afforded to all youth, increases differentiation of peronal pathways, decreases dependence on the kibbutz, and furnishes young people with resources for successful adaptation to life outside the kibbutz.

Thus, a profound social change is eroding the distinctive characteristics of kibbutz education which, in the past, made it a highly effective system of socialization for communal life. The conceptual dualisms which were inherent in this educational system from its beginning played an important role in the process of change.

The growing individualism within and outside the kibbutz are clearly opposed to the initial educational aims of the traditional kibbutz community and are more compatible with the personal needs of the majority of youth who leave the kibbutz. If present trends toward privatization (Helman, 1994) continue, these changes will also better fit the needs of those who opt to stay on the kibbutz, now with much less emphasis on a communal life-style than there used to be.

NOTES

1. In formulating this normative structure, I lean heavily on three leading educators of the three secular kibbutz movements—Golan (1961) of the Kibbutz Artzi, Segal (1955) of the Kibbutz Meuchad, and Messinger (1973) of Ichud Hakvutzot ve'Hakibbutzim—and on an external observer—Spiro (1968). In outlining the ideal type of kibbutz education, I gloss over some important differences between the various kibbutz movements. That presented here is closest to the educational pattern of the Kibbutz Artzi, the most left-wing kibbutz federation, because its stronger ideological emphases resulted in a more consistent educational system than that of the other two federations.

2. The group extends over the years. The child starts group life from his or her birth within a group of four to six toddlers. At the age of three, two groups of toddlers are combined into a prekindergarten group of up to a dozen children. In the kindergarten the group is extended to about fifteen to twenty children. Usually this group also comprises the class, or the educational group, in the local school. In regional kibbutz schools, classes may accommodate about twenty to thirty students coming from kibbutzim in the vicinity.

3. The scarce use of ideological content in education may also explain the apprehension about movement-wide activity among kibbutz young adults and the weakness of intellectually innovative elites among them (Zamir, 1991).

4. In this cluster of prosocial characteristics, there may be observed the characteristics of a foundation for the leftist social and political attitudes of kibbutz youth, including their stand with regard to the Israeli-Arab peace process.

5. Following their military service, kibbutz young adults are allowed to take a leave from the kibbutz for several years. During this time they may confidently expect their kibbutz to receive them with open arms at any time they decide to return to the fold (Dar, 1993).

6. The tendency to restrain communication of emotions was found to be more marked among kibbutz-born who were raised in communal sleeping arrangements, while no signifi-

cant difference was found between city youth and kibbutz adolescents raised in familial sleeping arrangements. This restraint was explained as protection for the individual from the potential intrusion of the group, and shielding the daily intense interactions from the upheavals of emotional expression (Sharabany and Weisman, 1993, 689).

6
Attitudes of Parents toward Their Own Role and That of the Caregiver in Two Sleeping Arrangements for Kibbutz Children

Ronit Plotnik

January 1991, the onset of the Persian Gulf War, signified the end of an era in the kibbutz educational system. By that time, almost all kibbutzim had changed the sleeping pattern of their children from the communal arrangement (sleeping in their children-houses [see Dar's chapter]) to the family arrangement (sleeping in their parents' homes). This chapter reports on how the change has affected parent-child relationships.

COMMUNAL AND FAMILY SLEEPING ARRANGEMENTS

In the family sleeping arrangement, children spend the night and their off-school hours with their parents and in their parents' homes—similar to the way most children are raised elsewhere in the industrial world. In the communal sleeping arrangement, children spend most of their time (including sleeping) around the children-house rather than the family home. This communal arrangement was the original and the most common sleeping arrangement in kibbutzim until the early 1990s. Indeed, with the exception of a few kibbutzim from one of the federations, this was the way children were raised in all kibbutzim until the late 1970s, when a growing number started the move toward a family sleeping arrangement.

The communal sleeping arrangement, divided by age cohorts, created a unified educational frame for all children. Each age cohort resided in a children-house of its own, where the children spent most hours of the day and all hours of the night. The team of educators working in this children-house was responsible for many functions that are usually regarded as the responsibility of parents—health, food, clothing, mental problems, and socialization to various roles. The parents' interaction with their

This chapter is a summary, translated from Hebrew by Uriel Leviatan, of the author's Ph.D. dissertation (University of Tel Aviv, 1992).

child was restricted to feeding (only at infancy), expressive-emotional education, and leisure activities after working hours. The communal sleeping arrangement aimed to minimize the parents' role in the instrumental aspects of educating their children and to strengthen community involvement. As the founders saw it, this educational model best expressed the kibbutz ideology and its values. It stressed group processes, collectivism, and solidarity among the children; equality; and social responsibility. In short, it represented kibbutz community life in miniature.

The family sleeping arrangement differs from the communal sleeping arrangement first in the division of time spent by the child between family and school. While the communal arrangement has the child in the children-house most hours of the day and all the night hours, the family arrangement has the time divided more equally. Less than half the day is spent in school (usually from 7 A.M. to 4 P.M.) and the rest in the parents' homes.

Changes in time distribution between the two socialization foci (parents and caregivers) developed gradually over several decades. At first, the children spent with their parents only about one or two hours a day—in the late afternoons from 5 P.M. to about 7 P.M.—after which they would return to their children-houses for supper, followed by an educational activity (a story, a game, a discussion, a party, reading, or homework) and bed time. Subsequently, this time with the family was extended to include supper and also the activity of putting the child to bed (in the children-house). The next stage was marked by the children staying at their parents' homes during the afternoons of the Shabbat (Saturday) and later throughout the entire weekend. The last stage was a full transfer of the children to their parents' homes, with the children-house serving as a day school.

This change of sleeping arrangement involved more than a redistribution of time. It has also led to a redistribution of responsibilities and even of material possessions between the two foci of education. For example, beds have been transferred from the children-house to the parents' home, clothing the children has become a parental responsibility, and parents are also responsible for their children's physical welfare, for their health, and for their extracurricular activities.

Since the 1950s, hundreds of studies have appeared on the topic of kibbutz education, most of them dealing with the effects of the sleeping arrangement from the perspective of the children. Very few studies, however, have focused upon the parents' point of view and the impact on them of their children's sleeping arrangement.

CHANGES WITHIN THE FAMILY

How does such a change—from one sleeping arrangement to another—affect relations and emotional expressions between children and their parents? Previous studies (e.g., Regev, 1977) found that children from communal sleeping arrangements were less expressive with their emotions (both positive and negative) compared to children from kibbutzim with the family sleeping arrangement or to children from cities. Children in the communal sleeping arrangement also tended to spread their negative emotions among more individuals (both within and outside of their families) and to express such emotions less intensively (in a "shallower" way). By contrast, children in kibbutzim with the family sleeping arrangement tended to focus their negative emotions only on one or two figures and in a much more intensive way.

Other research into sleeping arrangements tested how they influenced the role-taking characteristics of father and mother toward their child. This direction of research was of interest because findings from similar studies in the industrial world showed major differences between father and mother in this regard, and the question in kibbutz research was on whether, given the greater intrafamily similarity of responsibilities and other community roles, mother and father roles would be more similar. The common finding of research in industrial society showed that fathers were less involved in raising their children during the early ages and that their interaction with their children was usually characterized by play that stressed some combination of motor and intellectual stimulation. Most of the interaction between the fathers and their children was of a challenging type, seeking to develop the ability of the children to take on new tasks. Mothers, by contrast, took prime responsibility for caregiving and emotional education, with a stress on comfort and calm. Kibbutz research confirmed the expectation of greater similarity between father and mother in expressing their parenthood roles.

Studying the impact of changes in sleeping arrangement, Palgi (1982) found that fathers in the family sleeping arrangement described themselves as standing higher on the dimension of family cohesiveness and emotional expression, while fathers in the communal sleeping arrangement described themselves as more central on such dimensions as organization of family life, responsibility for the leisure activities of the family, and the transfer of ideology to their children.

Children from the two sleeping arrangements also differed in the way they perceived their parents. Those from the family sleeping arrangement described their parents more as givers of support and their mothers as offering more warmth, and caregiving, while children from the communal arrangement described both parents as demanding more achievement, adding that their fathers emphasized autonomy and instrumentalty.

At the beginning of the transition period between the two sleeping arrangements, parents in the newly established family sleeping arrangement tended to cling to their original role as expressive socialization agents who offered mostly warmth and love. Meanwhile, parents still in the communal arrangement tended to take on roles previously the sole responsibility of the education team—as if to emphasize that they (the parents) were also instrumental socialization agents. Such trends were already a prelude to conflict between parents and educators, conflict that would develop later on. It is also important to note that at the beginning of the transition between the sleeping arrangements, the roles of both parents in the family arrangement were similar. As will be shown later, this was to change. Other research found that fathers in the family sleeping arrangement reported greater involvement in the upbringing of their children.

The type of sleeping arrangement adopted also affected the relationships of the family with the educational institutions of the kibbutz. In the family sleeping arrangement, the family gained more authority in its dealing with the educational institutions, thereby creating conflict and communication problems between parent and caregiver. One study (Shes, 1977), for instance, compared two federations—one with family and the other with communal sleeping arrangements—as to the division of educational roles between parents and caregivers (*metaplot*, in Hebrew). In the federation with the communal arrangement, the caregiver's role was characterized as instrumental caregiving—taking care of the child's needs and the structuring of his or her personal and social habits. The caregivers carried out their duties in a task-oriented style, setting examples, explaining, and placing emphasis on verbal rewards.

Some examples of the socialization strategies in the children-house were preventing a child from going to play before finishing his or her meal; rewarding with a sweet a child who led others in cleaning and tidying the children-house; taking away privileges from children who failed to perform tasks or to meet deadlines; and expressing esteem and publicly congratulating children who helped or collaborated with other children in some mutual endeavor.

Both parents in the federation of the communal sleeping arrangement were perceived as emphasizing the expressive socialization role to complement the instrumental role expressed by the educators. They displayed this expressive role mostly during the "children hours" in the afternoon, when both parents dedicated themselves solely to their children. During this time, they showed love to their children, played with them, and gave freely of themselves in unconditional personal interaction. Yet the emotional relationship between child and parent that developed in the communal arrangement was shallower because it was divided between two socialization agents (father and mother) at the same time.

Whereas both parents in the other federation (with the family sleeping arrangement) also emphasized the expressive role, mothers took upon themselves the major responsibility for fulfillment of physical needs of their children, using extrinsic (mostly positive) rewards for reinforcing desired behavior. At the same time, mothers tended to use the fathers as negative socialization agents whose tools were punishment and the invocation of authority. As a result, a major difference developed between the roles of father and mother.Furthermore, the entry of mothers into the instrumental caregiving domain caused conflicts with the assigned professional caregivers, who saw that sphere as their responsibility. Lakin and Constantz (Lakin and Constantz, 1979) found that caregivers of toddlers in kibbutzim with communal sleeping arrangements believed that they had the sole responsibility for basic training for toddlers, while caregivers in kibbutzim with family sleeping arrangements thought that this training was the joint responsibility of both the parents and themselves. Other researchers reported similar findings (for example, Feldman et al., 1983).

A recent study (see below) has followed in the same direction. Its purpose was to investigate how a particular sleeping arrangement (communal or family) affected the attitudes of parents in two domains: (1) the roles of mother and father within the family and (2) their roles vis-à-vis the caregiver of their child.

THE STUDY

The study involved 160 pairs of parents with children of kindergarten age (four to six years). Half the families were from four kibbutzim with a communal sleeping arrangement and the other half were from four kibbutzim with a family sleeping arrangement. About half of the parents from each group were themselves kibbutz-born and were raised within the communal sleeping arrangement. The data (collected in 1989) aimed at establishing each parent's behavior on each of two orthogonal dimensions of attitudes toward their children: autonomy in contrast to control and love in contrast to resentment.

Autonomy refers to the readiness and ability of the parent to allow the child free action appropriate for his or her age—for instance, allowing the child to visit friends of his or her choice, to choose entertainment inside or outside the house, or to visit different places.

Control expresses the parent's concern to limit the child's activities and to have the child conform to the parent's wishes—preventing the child from expressing aggression, limiting the places and times of the child's activities, demanding a report on the child's whereabouts, or being strict about the child's orderliness and cleanliness.

Love refers to expressing care and deep emotional attachment to the child—for instance, offering the child encouragement, liking to play with the child, hugging the child, including the child in family activities, buying the child presents, and supporting him or her in times of difficulty.

Resentment refers to the expression of a negative attitude toward the child—for instance, not recognizing the child's legitimate needs, expressing rage without a specific reason, always giving preference to the parent's wishes and needs, and viewing the child as someone who impinges on the parent's time and resources.In addition, data were also collected about the demographic and biographic profiles of the parents and about parents' expectations for the caregivers of their children.

The following are some major findings.

First, the type of sleeping arrangement proved to be the most important variable to explain the difference in parental attitudes toward the children. Parents in kibbutzim with a family sleeping arrangement expressed less love and more resentment toward their children compared to parents with a communal sleeping arrangement.

Second, whereas mothers and fathers differed in their position on the dimension of love versus resentment in the way traditionally expected—mothers were higher on expression of love and lower on expression of resentment—that difference was more pronounced between fathers and mothers in kibbutzim with a family sleeping arrangement. Thus, fathers in kibbutzim with a family sleeping arrangement showed the strongest evidence of resentment and were also higher in their expectations of autonomy from their children. Furthermore, parents who were from kibbutzim with a family sleeping arrangement and who themselves were kibbutz-born and products of a communal sleeping arrangement displayed the least adjustment to their new roles as parents in the new (family) sleeping arrangement. Of all groups of parents, they also displayed the strongest levels of combined resentment and autonomy. This last finding is of significance for two reasons:

1. Past research on fathers in kibbutzim did not show such a tendency. Although fathers displayed less involvement in their children's education and an involvement in a more instrumental direction, their interaction never included an emotional component of resentment.

2. When used in studies in other parts of the industrial world, the same research instruments have shown that fathers attitudes toward their children in which there is evidence of strong combined resentment and autonomy characteristically produce children who develop criminal personality and behavior. This finding should therefore serve as a warning for action to be taken with parents in the new (family sleeping) arrangement.

Third, few differences were recorded among the four defined groups of parents (mothers and fathers in the two sleeping arrangements) about their expectations for the role of the caregiver. One finding, however, was of interest: Fathers in the communal sleeping arrangement expected the caregivers to use punishment and expressions of resentment in their job as educator and socialization agent—in other words, the same role that fathers of the family sleeping arrangement took upon themselves.

These findings lead to several conclusions. They support a claim for the importance of inter-generational transfer as a major mechanism in training people for their parental roles. The most serious role-identity crisis occurred among parents who were kibbutz-born, who grew up in a communal sleeping arrangement, and who then had to raise their own children in a family sleeping arrangement. Apparently, their personal experience as children raised in a communal sleeping arrangement, with socialization models such as their own parents and their caregivers, was not helpful in training them for their own parenthood roles. Thus, when they became parents in a family sleeping arrangement, they lacked appropriate parental training and reacted with more "negative" emotions as expressed in attitudes of resentment, control, and punishment toward their children.

A major finding in the study was the widening difference between fathers and mothers in the expression of emotions and attitudes toward their children. Fathers were found to express more negative emotions than mothers, and this difference was stronger in families with a family sleeping arrangement and strongest in families where the parents were kibbutz-born and raised in a communal sleeping arrangement. Of significance, the transfer from one to the other sleeping arrangement occurred concurrently with an ideological change as regards intergender relationships: from an ideology of equality between mother and father in their parental roles into a more traditional family model of differentiated roles. Mothers became the focus for expression of love, while fathers were assigned the role of authority in the family.

The findings I report here cast a bleak shadow on the results of the transformation from a communal sleeping arrangement to a family sleeping arrangement in the education of kibbutz children. Although I believe that the negative attitudes of fathers who experience this change are an internal component of the transformation process, that these attitudes stem from their own background as products of a communal sleeping arrangement and from the confusion that occurs in role definitions when such a transformation takes place, I would point out that several time-related and immediate external conditions may have also contributed to the results.

The transfer from a communal sleeping arrangement to family sleeping arrangement occurred in the kibbutzim during a time of dire economic stress. Because of this economic crisis, many kibbutzim could not offer appropriate housing to families who had to bring their child or children to sleep in their homes. Families with small children were forced to live without enough room to allow privacy for the parents. Parents had to give up important aspects of their private lives (such as entertaining guests and fostering their spousal relationships) in order to house their children. This hardship added to the fact that in many kibbutzim, the transfer occurred without proper time for preparation—because often it happened during the Gulf War when all children were moved to their parents' homes for fear of chemical or biological bombing by the Iraqis. Some resentful emotions of parents toward their children (as observed in my study) could be a reaction to these unfavorable circumstances for the transfer.

It should also be noted that the debate about the mode of sleeping arrangement was to some extent inter generational: Young members tended to support the family sleeping arrangement, while the veterans supported the communal arrangement. The change of the sleeping arrangement led to the enlargement of apartments, and this, in turn, led to conflict among generations—because construction started with needy families (young families with small children) instead of abiding by the common pattern in such matters, which was based on seniority rights. In some families, the result was a rift and feelings of guilt among the generations—feelings that created emotional difficulties and resulted, among other things, in young parents refraining from asking their parents to help in their family life (for example, in such matters as baby-sitting or helping with a sick child).

A final thought: It seems that the breakdown of the educational system based on the communal sleeping arrangement together with the changes to family life and to the whole community environment has been accompanied by attitudes and emotions that are resentful. And this indeed should be anticipated—as an expression of mourning following any major community change. It is, therefore, possible that what has been reported here is a temporary situation that will change when the new model of child upbringing is stabilized both as a social institution and as a normal pattern in the minds of parents.

7

Second and Third Generations in Kibbutzim—Is the Survival of the Kibbutz Society Threatened?

Uriel Leviatan

Survival beyond that of their founders' life cycle is of concern for all societies and organizations, but particularly for ideologically centered social organizations (social utopias) that aim to be alternatives to their surrounding communities. This is because social utopias are constantly threatened by absorption.

At the time of their emergence, most social utopias consist of ideologically committed young people and are homogeneous in their composition. These characteristics help utopias withstand surrounding pressures. Moreover, being young and strongly motivated, founders of such communities do not pay serious attention to potential threats to their communities' survival: They trust themselves to be able to carry on against outside adversaries and believe their own youth and commitment will endure forever. Concern for survival and continuity becomes more acute later in the life of such communities—when the second generation joins as adults, thereby transforming the community into a more heterogeneous body that is not so young as before. Kibbutz history demonstrates this pattern of a utopian society dealing with its future beyond the life of the founding generation.

The first kibbutzim were the creation of ideologically committed, homogeneous groups of youth in their late teens or early twenties. They separated from their parents in Europe to create a new society, one which would differ in all its characteristics from what they had left behind. Similar to other founders of utopias, they believed their society to represent the future of the world, to be a pillar for the creation of a Jewish state (still nonexistent at the time), and to be more just and better than most other human societies. Indeed, they regarded kibbutz society as the only worthy choice for any young person who wished to leave his or her mark on human history. Deep in their hearts, the founders trusted themselves to stay young and, therefore, always to be there to secure a future for their society. Unfortunately for the founders, life proved stronger than utopian imagination: They got older and had families. But even then, it never occurred to them that their children, being products of kibbutz life, might not choose to remain on the kibbutz and to continue building this best of all possible worlds.

APPEARANCE OF THE SECOND GENERATION

Because of the slow growth in the number of kibbutzim during the first several decades of the kibbutz, the question of natural continuation by the second generation did not concern the founders. Although the first kibbutz was settled in 1910, it was not until ten to fifteen years later that another dozen kibbutzim joined it. Therefore, it was the late 1950s before the membership of second-generation, kibbutz-born adults reached any significant number. In 1956, for instance, there were less than nine hundred members who were kibbutz-born (i.e., whose parents were also kibbutz members), while the total membership was about forty thousand.

At that time, young kibbutz-born members leaving a kibbutz was an infrequent occurrence: about 7 percent versus a population growth of 35 percent. To illustrate, in 1958 the number of kibbutz-born members had grown by more than 600 to about 1,500, while only 140 kibbutz-born members left their kibbutzim.

However, by the 1960s, the numbers of kibbutz-born members had begun increasing at an ever faster rate and were becoming sizable (about 2,100 in 1960, 3,000 in 1962, 4,400 in 1964, 5,600 in 1966, 7,600 in 1968, 9,100 in 1970, and 17,800 in 1973). In 1968, kibbutz-born members accounted for about 20 percent of kibbutz membership and, five years later, for 32.3 percent. Moreover, among the newly joining, the kibbutz-born accounted for about half. (Others came from the ranks of graduates of kibbutz youth movements in Israeli cities and abroad and from individuals who joined kibbutzim for personal reasons, mostly marriage to kibbutz members.) Thus, this source of membership—the kibbutz-born—became significant for kibbutz survival, and its retention within the kibbutz was central in kibbutz discussions and in the members' concerns.

The founders eventually realized that they would not stay young forever and that the future of their dream depended on its continuation by their offspring. Reaching old age, they became concerned about the survival of the kibbutz idea not only as an abstract concept but also as the continuation of their life investment. As one female veteran member put it (Leviatan, 1982, 19): "Here I am at an age where I feel that we [the founders] have done all we can. . . . We are walls of a large building. Yet I do not feel that our business is finished. It seems to me that in a natural way, the second generation should become additional bricks to our unfinished building." Another member stated: "The reason for our anxiety about the second generation is the anxiety of the founders and their concern about the future of the kibbutz creation." And, of course, there was the plain human familial perspective— a wish to have one's children at one's side as one grew old.

Earlier I mentioned that the founders did not believe that any of their children would leave their utopian society. They conceived of leaving almost as treason and even felt betrayed when two kibbutz-born members from two different kibbutzim got married and one of them moved to live with the other. I recall a case on my own kibbutz in the late 1950s. A young woman, twenty years of age, from the first class of our kibbutz-born members, announced that she was marrying a youth from another kibbutz, where they were intending to live. The matter was brought to the general assembly of our kibbutz. A line of founders came one after the other to the podium, denouncing the poor woman (some directing their criticism at her "mourning" parents) as a traitor to the most sacred goals. The central line of argument was that: "Not only is she leaving our kibbutz, but she dares to join a kibbutz of another political affiliation!"

Nevertheless, reality began to force itself upon the kibbutz members. The numbers of kibbutz-born opting for life outside kibbutzim increased, and the founders' concerns about the kibbutz's future, joined by the concerns of the kibbutz leadership, became very real. The two years following the Six-Days War of 1967 saw a major increase in the accumulated rates of leaving by the kibbutz-born to about 34 percent. This increase translated into an expressed need to learn more about the kibbutz-born's commitment to kibbutz life and about the factors that determined the probability of their leaving or of staying as members.

Since then, examination of commitment to kibbutz life by kibbutz-born members and the search for determinants of leaving or staying have become central in many studies of the kibbutzim. I have been involved in most of these studies, and the present chapter summarizes the knowledge that has been accumulated; it also presents recent findings influenced by the changes that kibbutzim have undergone during the last decade.

Two goals have given direction to the research that I report here. The first was to accomplish what its title promised—discovering the determinants of commitment to kibbutz life together with reasons for staying or leaving. The second was to find an answer to a more theoretical question: What type of social organization is a kibbutz community? This second goal needs elaboration.

TWO TYPES OF SOCIAL ORGANIZATION

One way to categorize social organizations is by the type of interaction that members have with their organization and how this interaction translates into members' commitment. The most prevalent type of social organization is one that develops exchange relationships: The organization promises opportunities for the satisfaction of its members' needs and expects, in return, a demonstration of commitment in both attitude and behavior. The needs for which such organizations promise satisfaction may cover a wide range.

Further subdivision among such social organizations leads to narrower exchange relationships. Thus business or work organizations create commitment in, and make themselves attractive to, their members by promising need satisfaction in such domains as material benefits, economic security, self-realization, achievement, status, esteem, and prestige. Neighborhood communities (another type of social organization) offer satisfaction mostly in such domains as ecology, convenience, children's education, security, personal prestige, and social interaction. Face-to-face primary groups offer satisfaction mostly with social support and, sometimes, prestige and status.

Although the three types of social organization described here may seem very different from each other, they all have exchange relationships with their members, and they all stand apart from another type of social organization. That other type appears in its purest form in ideologically driven political movements or in evangelistic religious groups. Here the kind of relationship that prevails between members and their social organization is not one of *exchange* but rather of *identification*. Members' commitment to their organization arises out of their identification with its values—not out of their expectations of need satisfaction as a reward for their commitment (as in the exchange relationship).

Kibbutzim are clearly complex social organizations that include ingredients of both exchange and identification relationships. All four types of social organization referred to above (neighborhood community, business or work organization, face-to-face primary group, and ideological movement) are present in kibbutz life. Nevertheless, the question that needs to be answered is which type of social organization is most strongly represented. Is it mostly an exchange relationship or of identification relationship? How is the kibbutz composition perceived by its youth? What is the relative importance of its four major components (as a neighborhood community; as a work and economic organization; as an intimate, primary, face-to-face social grouping; and as an ideological movement) for its young, kibbutz-born members? As will become clearer later in this chapter, answers to such questions could decide the extent of its members' commitment and the kind of individuals it attracts or repels.

RESEARCH FINDINGS OF STUDIES CONDUCTED DURING THE LATE 1960s AND THE 1970s

The first study (Leviatan, 1975a; Rosner, Ben David et al., 1990), in 1969, covered fifty-four kibbutzim, eighteen from each of the three large movements of the time. As part of the study, more than nine hundred kibbutz-born members (aged twenty to thirty-five) were interviewed about their level of commitment toward life on a kibbutz and about its determinants. In 1971, a follow-up study of the same kibbutz-born sample registered their whereabouts since the first data collection. (About 10 percent of the sample had left kibbutz life by that time.) The follow-up focused upon the determinants of staying or leaving and upon factors differentiating kibbutzim in their retention of kibbutz-born members. Analyses included demographic data for the years preceding and coinciding with the time of the studies. The central findings from the 1969–1971 studies are summarized below.

1. A comparison between rates of leaving kibbutz life by kibbutz-born and rates of leaving other rural settlements in Israel (or abroad) by native-born showed that kibbutz-born left in much smaller numbers. Their leaving rates were also lower than those of other groups of kibbutz membership— graduates of Zionist youth movements or individual joiners.

2. Demographic characteristics indicated some variation in probability of leaving by kibbutz-born. The retention rates of male members at different ages were higher than those of female members at the same ages. For instance, by 1971, 68 percent of all kibbutz-born males were still members of their kibbutz of origin and 76 percent were members of kibbutzim. Only 51 percent of the kibbutz-born females were still members of their kibbutz of origin and 66 percent were members of kibbutzim. Findings of the 1969–1971 study illustrated the same intergender difference. Out of the 917 kibbutz-born respondents included in the study of 1969, 12.3 percent of the women, as compared to 9.0 percent of the men, had left their original kibbutz by mid-1971, and 9.2 percent of the women, as compared to 8.4 percent of the men, had left the kibbutz movement.

Age was also important in affecting probability of leaving, and it also differed among men and women. The critical five-year age group among the women was between nineteen and twenty-four years (78 percent of the women who left the kibbutz did so while in that age group). Among the men, the most probable age for leaving was between twenty-two and twenty-seven (67 percent of the men who left the kibbutz did so while in that age group). In the 1969 study, one other biographic characteristic differentiated the leavers from the stayers: The stayers tended to be more active in social functions and more likely to hold public office in their kibbutz.

3. External events had a stronger impact upon kibbutz-born males than upon the kibbutz-born female members in deciding their probability of staying or leaving. For instance, the period immediately following the Six-Day War had a major impact upon all age groups of kibbutz-born males, and the years 1967–1969 registered their highest rates of leaving. This was not true of female kibbutz-born.

4. Kibbutzim varied in their rates of retention among kibbutz-born members. In some kibbutzim, the retention rate in the kibbutz of origin was above 80 percent, while in others it was between 30 and 50 percent. (Retention rates of staying in any kibbutz ranged between 50 percent and 90 percent.) In one federation (based on data from forty-one kibbutzim), the mean retention rate within the kibbutz of origin was 63.5 percent, with a standard deviation of 10.5 percent (as against a mean of 77.2 percent and a standard deviation of 8.6 percent retention rate within the kibbutz movement). Since this distribution was similar to a normal-curve distribution, it suggested that several independent factors contributed to its explanation.

5. Permanent characteristics of kibbutzim could not account for differences among them in retention rates of their kibbutz-born members—for example, geographical position of the kibbutz, its proximity to large cities, country of origin of its founders, and years since settlement. Neither were differences in retention rates explained by numbers of the young membership. Finally, the study found no correlation between the rates of retention in two periods: 1968–1971 and 1964–1968.

6. Yet variability in retention rates of young members at a given time was not a spurious finding. This was evidenced by the correlation between the retention rates of kibbutz-born males and females ($r = .37, p < .05$; for the thirty-five kibbutzim with available data), signifying that kibbutz characteristics, be they what they may, were important determinants of leaving or staying.

7. Adherence of a kibbutz to traditional kibbutz values (such as the principles of self-labor, equality and solidarity among members in all domains, support of the movement's goals, and service to Israeli society) was the most important factor in explaining why commitment to kibbutz life of kibbutz-born members was lower (or higher) in some kibbutzim than in others. This factor rated much more important (almost three times in magnitude) than factors expressing the level of members' satisfaction with their welfare (such as standard of living, probability of acquiring higher education, and economic success).

In total, 31 percent of the variance in level of commitment to kibbutz life among young kibbutz-born members was due to characteristics of how the kibbutz functioned. Out of this statistically explained variance, the level of a kibbutz's adherence to its distinct ideology accounted for almost three-quarters (73.8 percent), while level of functioning in other domains (such as social interaction, career development, satisfaction with work, and standard of material living) accounted for only a quarter (26.2 percent) of the variance.

Therefore, the results of this study strongly suggest that kibbutz communities are social organizations of the kind where the primary relationship of members is that of *identification* and not of *exchange.*

8. Expression of commitment to kibbutz life at one time constituted an important predictor of the probability of subsequent staying or leaving by young members: In 1969, 20 percent of those expressing a low level of commitment to kibbutz life had left by mid-1971; only 4.6 percent of those expressing a high level of commitment had left by that time, together with 9.6 percent of those expressing an intermediate level of commitment.

Another important finding was that the socialization system offered by a kibbutz was central in shaping commitment to kibbutz life. The more a community promoted the socialization of its offspring along communal lines, the higher was the probability of their becoming committed to kibbutz life. An immediate conclusion suggested by this finding was that increasing the community-values emphasis in education would increase retention rates of kibbutz-born within the kibbutz movement.

∽

Although the study was supported by the kibbutz movement's leadership, the recommendations it came up with failed to register with most kibbutzim and were ignored by the movement institutions. Recommendations by the movement's departments responsible for youth counseling emphasized the importance of satisfying the young members' personal needs (material, social, achievement, and self-realization). Likewise, the kibbutz educational system did not follow the direction suggested by the findings, and education oriented toward values and social goals was replaced by emphasis on academic achievement and neutrality in dealing with social values. This lack of response to the findings of the study was later to have negative repercussions for the kibbutzim.

SEVEN YEARS LATER

In 1976, another study (Leviatan, Orchan, and Ovnat, 1984) focused on commitment to kibbutz life among kibbutz-born young members. This time, young respondents (aged twenty to thirty-five), including both members (about 300) and ex-members (about 150) from nine kibbutzim, were compared on a variety of measurements: biographical, demographical, attitudinal, reflections on their own life, perceptions of life on their kibbutz, and personal values. In addition, we (the researchers) obtained economic and social information about each of the nine kibbutzim. These data were collected through interviews with informants and from analysis of documents. Central to the study design was a comparison of six kibbutzim known to be more successful in retaining their young kibbutz-born members with three kibbutzim which were less successful—namely, which had higher rates of leaving during the years preceding the study.

Results from this study supported and corroborated those from the 1969–1971 study. While the ex-members and the members were of similar age and gender composition, some differences were apparent in their kibbutz-related biography. Thus, when age at the time of membership was held constant, a higher percentage of those who had remained members had held public office in their kibbutzim and had enjoyed more intensive social ties within the kibbutz. The two groups did not differ in aptitudes, talents, and skills.

Major differences between the two groups appeared in their personal beliefs and in their expressed values. Ex-members attached more importance to having a high standard of living, while members attached more importance to realization of ideals, to an active life with the possibility of influencing events, and to equality and other ideals of kibbutz society.

A comparison between the two groups of kibbutzim—those with higher and those with lower levels of retention among their kibbutz-born members—showed that the extent of adherence by a kibbutz to its distinct values (democracy, equality, communal principles, solidarity, and self-labor) was the most important differentiating factor between the two. The extent of adherence differentiated between the two groups to about the same degree as all other factors combined—and twice to four times as strongly as any other single factor (such as economic success, opportunities offered for higher education, possibilities for self-realization, and current standard of living).

The two most important conclusions from this study were the same as those from seven years earlier. Successful retention of kibbutz-born youth as members depends (1) primarily on the kibbutz being true to its declared distinctive values and (2) on education that results in individuals for whom those values are of prime importance.

THE 1990s

For the next fifteen years, no intensive studies focused on kibbutz-born commitment to kibbutz life or on retention of kibbutz-born as members. But the topic received renewed attention in the early 1990s, which was prompted by young kibbutz-born members leaving in alarming rates (more than 50 percent of each age cohort, sometimes up to 90 percent) and which led to another study.

This study was part of large-scale diagnostic surveys that began in many kibbutzim in 1992. The part of the study relevant to this chapter concerns data from thirty-three kibbutzim surveyed to mid-1995. In these kibbutzim, more than five thousand members responded to questionnaires. About seven hundred of the respondents were kibbutz-born between the ages of twenty to thirty-five and constituted more than half of that age group across all kibbutzim in the study. The seven hundred kibbutz-born members had an additional factor differentiating them from those in the previous studies: By the 1990s, many older kibbutzim now harbored members of the third generation (that is, with at least one of their parents born to kibbutz members). Thus, this study had about four hundred kibbutz-born members of the second generation and about three hundred kibbutz-born members of the third generation.

Two central foci of the diagnostic surveys were the same as in the studies reported earlier in this chapter: (1) the commitment members had to their kibbutz life and the factors that affected such commitment and (2) finding what type of social organization, in the members' view, their kibbutz represented—based on importance attached to factors that determined commitment to kibbutz life.

The researchers also extended their focus with a third question: how answers to the first two questions would be affected by the current changes in kibbutzim. Or, more specifically, how would the answers be affected (if at all) when a kibbutz transformed from a social organization emphasizing identification relationships to a social organization emphasizing exchange relationships? This third question arose because in some kibbutzim (see the chapter by Getz) exchange relationships between member and community became the central type of relationship.

The first important research finding from the diagnostic surveys shows that the changes occurring in the kibbutzim were strongly affecting the value system and worldview of their young members. Kibbutzim that emphasized the material needs of their members, together with a reduced emphasis upon the distinct values of kibbutz life, had a larger percentage of young members (kibbutz-born and non-kibbutz-born) who held to a worldview or a value system that was materialistic; achieving a high standard of living was for them of prime importance, while molding their life according to social ideals was of less consequence. To illustrate: about 60 percent of the young members from the five kibbutzim with the highest emphasis on satisfying their members' material needs expressed a materialistic worldview, whereas only 46 percent of the young members from the five kibbutzim with the lowest emphasis on satisfying their members' material needs expressed a materialistic worldview.

Thus, it is clear that the current social atmosphere or Zeitgeist in a kibbutz decides, at least to some extent, how its young members shape their view of life and their value system. It is important to note, however, that no such relationship between emphasis and expressed values was found among members of a somewhat older age (thirty-four to forty-five). Apparently, the value systems of young people in their twenties are more likely to be influenced by outside events.

The changes currently occurring in some kibbutzim and the attendant individu-alistically oriented value system of many young members found expression in the relative importance of forces that determined their commitment to kibbutz life. In this study, rank order of importance leaned more in the direction of the kibbutz as a social organization able to satisfy individual welfare needs and less as an ideological social movement whose attraction for its members was the offering of values and goals with which they could identify. However, the distinct values of the kibbutz and the ideological concerns of the young members continued to be the most important factors influencing commitment to kibbutz life. These factors were more important than any one of the other factors, in particular, the three factors which emerged from analysis of the data as having significant impact (namely, self-reali-zation, material standard of living, and personal home-feeling), all of which were concerned with individual welfare needs.

Table 7.1 illustrates the relative importance of each factor in influencing com-mitment to kibbutz life among the second and third generations of kibbutz-born members aged twenty to thirty-five, and differentiated according to gender (the first four columns from the left). The right-hand column shows the result of a similar analysis (adapted from Leviatan, 1994) for the entire group of young members—about 1200 aged twenty to thirty-three—from the thirty-three kibbut-zim included in this study.

The results show how satisfaction with the functioning of a kibbutz (community factors) and the importance attached by an individual to ideological-social values (personal factors) determine the level of commitment to kibbutz life. Each number in the table represents an estimate of explained variance (as a percentage) of the level of commitment to kibbutz life. These estimates (as they resulted from multi-ple-regression analyses) are separate for each subgroup.

The findings from Table 7.1 lead to several conclusions. First, the structural components of a kibbutz—namely, the way it functions in various domains—are still central in deciding its young members' commitment to kibbutz life. Struc-tural components in this study explained about half the variability in level of commitment. This was true for all four subgroups (males and females of both the second and the third generations), although to different degrees. The struc-tural factors were slightly more important for the kibbutz-born members of the second generation than for the third generations, explaining 52 percent and 48 percent, respectively, of the variance for the second and third generations of female, kibbutz-born members and 61 percent and 48 percent, respectively, of

Table 7.1

Contribution to the Explained Variance in Personal Commitment to Kibbutz Life Based on Community (Kibbutz) Factors (Satisfaction with Kibbutz Characteristics) and Personal Factors (Expressed Personal Values) (Percentages)

Factors	Second Generation		Third Generation		All Young Members
	Females	*Males*	*Females*	*Males*	
1. Ideology	25	23	22	16	18
(Kibbutz)	(24)	(15)	(20)	(16)	(13)
(Personal)	(1)	(8)	(2)	—	(5)
2. Standard of Living	14	13	6	10	9
(Kibbutz)	(14)	(13)	(6)	(10)	(8)
(Personal)				(1)	(1)
3. Home-feeling	13	15	—	—	12
(Kibbutz)	(13)	(15)	—	—	(12)
4. Self-realizaion	—	10	20	—	11
(Kibbutz)	—	(10)	(20)	—	(11)
Total Variance Explained	52	61	48	48	50
Number	190	220	160	140	1200

Results based on multiple regression analyses. Young kibbutz members are aged 20–33.

the variance for the males in the same two groups. Apparently, personal characteristics (which were not part of the analysis) played a more important role in determining commitment to kibbutz life among kibbutz-born members of the third generation.

Second, the realization by a kibbutz of kibbutz-distinct values differed in its importance as a determinant of commitment for members of each of the two generations of kibbutz-born—as did their ideological identity. It was the single most important determining factor for both males and females of the second generation (accounting for 23 percent and 25 percent, respectively, of the variance), while for the third generation it contributed 22 percent of the explained variance in commitment among female members.

Third, for the third generation of kibbutz-born members (particularly the males), the potential of individual self-realization (utilization of skills, knowledge, and experience) was the most important determinant of commitment to kibbutz life (accounting for 22 percent of the variance for the males). This generation differed from the same-age second generation of kibbutz-born, for whom the realization of kibbutz-distinct values in their kibbutz counted as the most important determinant of their commitment to kibbutz life.

The intergeneration difference poses several questions. Is it illustrative of a historical trend (common to many utopian communities) where the greater the generation gap from the founders, the lesser the emphasis given to the founders' values and to the community's ideological foundations? But if so, why is there a difference between generations rather than between age groups or historical periods? Is it (the intergeneration difference) related to the socialization messages given by kibbutz-born members who did not have to make a choice for kibbutz life? Is it a delayed reaction (one generation removed) to the strict ideological commitment of the grandparents (i.e., the founders) transmitted, perhaps, via the parents (kibbutz-born members of the second generation)? Is it a reaction to the covert message in education emphasizing practical components of kibbutz life and neglecting the theoretical-ideological components—as argued by Dar in another chapter of this volume? Answers to these questions will have to remain in abeyance for some time as no research is yet available.

Finally, in the right-hand column of Table 7.1, similar data are shown for young kibbutz members (aged twenty to thirty-three) irrespective of gender or of origin of joining—whether kibbutz-born or not. Fifty percent of the variance in commitment is explained by the functioning of kibbutzim in four domains: realization of distinct values, feeling of home, self-realization and standard of living. The domain of realization of distinct values accounted for 18 percent of the total variance (36 percent of the explained variance); followed by home-feeling, which accounted for 12 percent (24 percent of the explained variance); followed by satisfaction with opportunities for self-realization, which accounted for 11 percent (22 percent of the explained variance); and finally standard of living, which accounted for 9 percent (18 percent of the explained variance).

Thus, from the perspective of the current (1992–1995) young members in kibbutzim, the kibbutz is first of all a social organization that attracts commitment from its young members through an identification relationship with them: It offers its distinct ideology as the model for identification. More than a third of the commitment forces for which kibbutz functioning (and not individual characteristics) is the source originate from the kibbutz's realization of ideological promises (its distinct values). Next in importance are the opportunities for satisfaction of individual welfare needs (home-feeling, self-realization, and standard of living). In short, little has changed. However, a difference from the past is that, in combination, these three personal welfare criteria account for about two-thirds of the total explained variance, while the ideological criterion accounts for only one-third.

The findings are, therefore, both similar to, and dissimilar from, those of a generation ago. While the kibbutz, as yet, has not changed its basic characteristics, the data for the third generation of kibbutz-born members in Table 7.1 reveal a marked change in the way that the characteristics of the kibbutz are perceived. Kibbutzim appear to be moving closer to a social organization that attracts members through exchange relationships and further from a relationship based on members' identification with kibbutz goals and values. They are being transformed into social organizations that secure their members' commitment mostly by offering personal rewards and satisfying welfare needs rather than the realization of social values and the pursuit of national and human goals beyond the immediate needs of the individual members. As I will show, such a transformation may adversely affect the commitment of young members to kibbutz life.

KIBBUTZ LEADERSHIP AND PRIORITIES IN KIBBUTZ FUNCTIONING

The findings reported on the preceding pages make it clear that young members' commitment to kibbutz life is affected largely by how the kibbutz functions. This raises a new question: Who is responsible for how a kibbutz functions? Two recent studies (Leviatan, 1994; Belzer-Zur, 1996) show conclusively that it is the local leadership in each kibbutz community that is responsible for satisfaction in those domains that determine commitment to kibbutz life. The way this leadership acts, the commitment of this leadership to kibbutz ideals, the level of trust that the leadership emanates, and the homogeneity among members in their basic beliefs— all these factors in combination strongly influence members' perceptions of and reactions to the important domains of kibbutz life, the same domains that later (as I have shown) determine levels of commitment to, attraction for, or repulsion from kibbutz life.

The first study on the topic of youth commitment to kibbutz life found no consistency, across the years, in percentages of leaving. I interpreted that finding to suggest that important determinants of commitment were not permanent characteristics of the kibbutzim. I argued that there must have been some changing characteristics in kibbutzim to explain the finding. A full generation of research effort—from 1969 to 1996—showed these changing characteristics to be the ideological, social, and economic domains of kibbutz functioning. The connection— how local leadership affects functioning—gives the anchoring answer to our whole investigation: namely, that individuals in leadership positions are bound by kibbutz norms to be replaced by other individuals every two to five years (Leviatan, 1992). As a result, a kibbutz has a totally new leadership every several years. Since there is nothing to ensure that the new group of leaders has the same characteristics and the same guiding goals as the previous group, no correlation in a kibbutz's expressed priorities of functioning should be expected between any two periods. Therefore, no correlation should be expected in the outcomes of their functioning—namely, the level of commitment of members to their life on the kibbutz.

It is possible now to summarize the causal chain of factors that lead to commitment to kibbutz life: Local leadership determines the level of functioning of a kibbutz in several important domains. To some extent, it also determines the kind of value system held by the young members. These two factors in combination decide the level of commitment to kibbutz life among the young members. Finally, level of commitment at any given time influences the probability of these members staying or leaving their kibbutz.

NEGATIVE SELF-SELECTION

The research reviewed in this chapter dealt with the factors that determine commitment of kibbutz youth to kibbutz life and what influences the probability of their remaining kibbutz members. However, a question no less important is which youth, in the process of self-selection, decide to leave: Are they the better ones of their age group, therefore representing negative self-selection? Or are they the lesser ones, therefore representing positive self-selection? Or, perhaps, is personal potential unrelated to the probability of leaving?

Past research on this question (e.g., Natan, Shnabel-Brandeis, and Peskin, 1982; Helman, 1982; Leviatan and Orchan, 1982) did not support speculations of negative self-selection among kibbutz-born young members. However, the hypothesis tested in those studies was crude and anticipated negative self-selection within all kibbutzim. A more refined hypothesis suggested by myself and my coresearchers (1984) and by Rosner, Ben David et al., (1990) anticipated negative self-selection of young members only in kibbutzim that possessed the following combination of characteristics: a materialistic emphasis so that the satisfaction of material needs of the members had a higher priority for them than the realization of distinctive kibbutz values; and presence in those kibbutzim of young members who held a worldview or a personal value system that was materialistic.

The opportunity to test this hypothesis did not arise until the late 1980s because no negative self-selection was observed in kibbutzim. This is no longer true. Since the late 1980s, several examples of this phenomenon have appeared which enabled me to undertake a study (using data from the diagnostic surveys described earlier) to look for characteristics leading to negative self-selection among young members of kibbutzim (Leviatan, 1996).

I should note, though, that I could not study actual negative self-selection because the young members who participated in the study were all, at the time, kibbutz members. Nevertheless, I could measure their level of commitment to kibbutz life as a predictor of their staying or leaving at a later time, thereby providing an estimate of the tendency for negative self-selection.

The young members (twenty to thirty-three years of age) were differentiated according to their personal resources: level of formal education, level of managerial office held on the kibbutz and at work, and self-estimates of personal talents—intellectual, creative, managerial—in comparison to others in their age group. Tendency for negative self-selection within a group (such as members of one kibbutz), or a subgroup (either within a given kibbutz or among members of a group of kibbutzim) was inferred if the individuals with higher personal resources showed a lower level of commitment to kibbutz life. Conversely, positive self-selection was inferred if the reverse was true. No relationship between personal resources and commitment to kibbutz life would mean that commitment could not be graded according to personal resources.

The results of the study supported expectations but not very strongly. Overall, there was no indication of a tendency for negative self-selection among young members of kibbutzim. Such tendencies were found only among young members of a small number of kibbutzim which were extreme in their materialistic emphasis. But even in those kibbutzim, the tendency for negative self-selection was to be found only among the younger members (twenty to thirty-three and not thirty-four to forty-five) and only among those for whom the achievement of a high material standard of living was the most important goal in their life. Within these conditions, the youth with more personal resources expressed lesser commitment to, and lower identification with, kibbutz life than the ones with less personal resources.

But an additional result from this study came a surprise: The very kibbutzim (six that emphasized welfare needs) that recorded negative self-selection also displayed, for another group, a tendency for positive self-selection. This tendency for positive self-selection was among young members of the same age as the first group but who differed in their personal value system. They gave priority to social values and to ideological considerations over a high standard of living.

Table 7.2 illustrates both findings with one measure of personal resources and one measure of identification with kibbutz life. Among young members with a materialistic value system, 31 percent with higher education expressed identification with their kibbutzim (agreed with the statement "the kibbutz is me"), while 53 percent of the youth with only secondary schooling agreed to the same statement. Among young members with a ideological or social value system, 59 percent with higher education expressed identification with their kibbutzim, compared to only 30 percent with secondary schooling.

The results about the tendency for negative self-selection are ironic and even paradoxical: The best intentions seem to lead to the worst outcomes. Kibbutzim that put the satisfaction of their members' personal welfare as their first priority ("because this is what is important") and neglect kibbutz-distinct values ("because this is unimportant") might expect a tendency for negative self-selection among their young members. Some of the most talented from among the youth in those kibbutzim might be expected to say to themselves: "If the most important criterion for deciding to stay on a kibbutz is the satisfaction of my personal welfare needs, why do I need all those partners to share the fruits of my personal resources? I could get for myself much more elsewhere with no need to share and with my rewards congruent with my talents."

Table 7.2
The Expression by Young Members of Identification with Their Kibbutz

Level of Formal Education	Materialistic Values	Social Values	Total
Higher Education	31% (N = 49)	59% (N = 27)	41% (N = 76)
Secondary School	53% (N = 51)	30% (N = 40)	43% (N = 91)
Total	42% (N = 100)	42% (N = 67)	42% (N = 167)

The sample consists of members in six kibbutzim that emphasize welfare needs.
The four groups resulted from a cross-tabulation of personal values and level of personal resources.
The four groups are as follows: (1) individuals with higher education who are guided by materialistic values; (2) individuals with higher education who are guided by social values; (3) individuals with secondary schooling who are guided by materialistic values; and (4) individuals with secondary schooling who are guided by social values.

Source: Adapted from Leviatan (1996).

The strong emphasis by a kibbutz on the satisfaction of welfare needs creates, paradoxically, an effect opposite to that desired because of two unplanned outcomes. First, when the only criterion for an individual deciding whether or not to become a member is the promise by the kibbutz to fulfill his or her welfare needs, the higher the personal resources of that individual the wider the range of alternative organizations that would offer him or her the same (or higher) level of satisfying those welfare needs. Thus, such a kibbutz stands in danger of losing those individuals with the highest potential to contribute. Second, negative self-selection among youth of a kibbutz diminishes the ability of that kibbutz to satisfy the personal welfare needs of those remaining, leading to negative self-selection among individuals with lower and lower personal resources, and ending when the only members remaining are those who have no need to elaborate on what such a kibbutz would look like and what its chances of survival would be.

The finding, however, about the tendency for positive self-selection leads to more optimistic conclusions: Young members who have high personal resources and who also identify with kibbutz ideology seem to be committed to their kibbutz even when it supports priorities contrary to their own value system. It seems that they are willing to fight to change their kibbutz. Their reaction contrasts with that of their colleagues who enjoy the same personal resources but who hold a different value system. One could not have a better "fighting squad" for kibbutz survival than the former group.

But how did that group acquire their worldview? How did they establish their value system? Since it could not have been the result of the current priorities of their kibbutzim (whose priorities are opposite), it must have resulted from their socialization during their school years—a strong recommendation for investment in directed education.

CONCLUSION AND SUMMARY

This chapter has reviewed research and findings that pertain to kibbutz survival as a social phenomenon. It has dealt with what determines kibbutz continuation by a second and a third generation of kibbutz-born members. There are lessons to be drawn from this review—for kibbutz society and perhaps for others as well. Here are the most important.

First, any social organization whose claims to uniqueness are its ideologies (be it as good to its members as it may) cannot assume automatic commitment of its native-born future generations. Furthermore, it should not assume automatic absorption of its ideologies by its future generations. Ideological foundations should be purposefully erected and intentionally transferred to the prospective members who grow up within the organization.

Second, kibbutz characteristics strongly determine the degree of commitment of kibbutz-born. They are much more important as determinants of commitment than demographic, biographic, or personal characteristics of the individual kibbutz-born. In short, kibbutzim need to be active in creating conditions that attract their kibbutz-born to become members.

Third, the characteristics of kibbutzim that are responsible for deciding the level of commitment of their young members are complex. They represent a configuration that appears in a purer form in four types of social organizations: ideological movements, business and formal organizations, neighborhood communities, and face-to-face intimate groups.

The research reported in this chapter shows that, for the kibbutz-born population, the ideological component is the most important of the four. This last assertion, however, needs to be treated with reservation. In my recent studies, I have detected a trend across the generations that suggests a transformation of the kibbutz into a different type of social organization, in which other characteristics are taking precedence over the realization of ideology in determining commitment to kibbutz life. The current changes that kibbutzim are undergoing are making them similar to other organizations that aim at attracting members only by offering satisfaction of their welfare needs. Yet this change of emphasis in the kibbutz is shaping members whose expectations are like those of members in other organizations. This is a battle which kibbutzim cannot win. Therefore, it will result in diminished commitment of members, more members leaving, and what is worse, a trend to negative self-selection so that the ones with more personal resources leave first.

Fourth, the history of research in kibbutzim on the subject of youth commitment shows clearly that it is strongly affected by the way the kibbutzim express their priorities. Yet it is also clear that these priorities result from actions and decisions taken by local leadership. Therefore, a change of leadership or a change in the directions taken by leadership affects commitment to and future survival of kibbutzim.

Fifth, this research teaches us a more general lesson of importance beyond the kibbutz society. Under certain conditions and with certain populations, social organizations may build motivation for commitment among their members based not only on a promise of satisfaction of welfare needs, but also on identification of the members with the values and goals expressed by their organizations. Kibbutz research shows that identification operates not only in organizations that are purely ideological or purely religious, but also in social organizations which embrace the whole spectrum of human activity.

8
The Governmental System of the Kibbutz

Avraham Pavin

INTRODUCTION

In its early days, the kibbutz was characterized by the absence of a formal organizational structure. In the first kibbutzim, the yearning for independence and self-administration was no less strong than the desire for equality, and it was expressed in the general, rather vague principle of community sovereignty over all. Decisions were reached through free discussion among the members. Later, during the first decades of kibbutz existence, institutional arrangements were formed that would characterize the kibbutz political system for years to come. These arrangements were based on three principles: direct decision making by all the members on all important matters—through the organ of the general assembly; the distribution of authority among a large number of officeholders and public committees; and rotation of administrative positions, thereby preventing the accumulation of power by the few.

In the atmosphere of crisis in which kibbutzim have found themselves since the mid-1980s, these three arrangements have come under attack, and there has even been a demand for their abolition. The participation of all members in decision making has been reduced to a number of issues considered important. At the same time, a complementary but converse demand has arisen in many kibbutzim for a monitoring institution to supervise the behavior of functionaries, to ensure proper management and implementation of public decisions, and to protect the members from the establishment. In this chapter, I analyze the organizational changes that have taken place over the years.

The uniqueness of the kibbutz governance structure stems from the complexity of the functions the kibbutz, both as a residential municipality and a social unit, fulfills for its members. As a municipal unit, the kibbutz is responsible for public order and is obliged to provide services for its residents. As a social unit, the kibbutz must generate income for the livelihood of its members, guarantee their welfare, distribute rewards among them, and act in accordance with their worldview. Outside the kibbutz, these functions embrace most areas of the lives of individuals and are performed by a variety of organizations: the market (labor, money, etc.), formal organizations, affiliative groups, and voluntary associations or social movements. These social formations vary in their characteristics and are based on different structural foundations. In each, different rules and regulations apply, and different mechanisms of control are employed. By contrast, the kibbutz is subject to a single governing system.

The form of management specific to each of the four types of social formations mentioned above is based on different assumptions about the nature of the organization. Two parameters enable us to distinguish the basic assumptions related to the exchange existing in the various organizational patterns. The first parameter emphasizes the sovereignty of the individual as opposed to the sovereignty of the community; the second parameter emphasizes the shared or compatible interests of the participants as opposed to conflicting or rival interests. The combination of parameters describes four cells in a table in which structural forms can be placed according to their chief characteristics (see Figure 8.1). Each cell expresses the principles according to which members are obliged by the normative system to weigh their behavior and according to which they justify their behavior and/or demands from the system.

In *affiliative* groups, membership itself is the basis for interaction among the individuals and the principle according to which rights and obligations are defined. Membership in the kibbutz framework, for example, simultaneously determines and is determined by collective ownership of land and of means of production. In such groups, commitment is a central force, and the effect an action has upon the good of the group is the standard by which behavior is evaluated.

The basic assumption of the affiliative structure is the shared interests of the partners in the group. Accordingly, attraction to the group is based upon solidarity; motivation is based on responsibility toward others; and the general expectation is that individuals will comply with the needs of the whole system, with control based on informal social pressure.

In *hierarchical* organizations, activity derives from the contract principle (tasks in exchange for wages or other benefits), and authority is accorded to those in charge. In a hierarchical organization, there is no expectation of compatibility between the objectives and interests of the organization and the objectives and interests of individuals. Obedience is expected, and the activity of workers is coordinated by a hierarchy of authority. Motivation is based on incentives and penalties, and control is based on supervision by the managers.

Through the price mechanism, the *market* organization integrates the activities of individuals motivated by their own self-interest. Here, competition is the predominant principle, and considerations of profitability are legitimate and acceptable. The relationship with other participants is one of expedience, and motivation is prompted by egotistical interests. Opportunistic behavior is thus expected. The market mechanism coordinates activities, but not those who execute the activities;

Figure 8.1
Expected Behavior and Control Mechanisms in Various Types of Social Formations

Perception of Interests	Degree of Individual Freedom	
	Centrality of Collective	Centrality of Individual
CONFLICTING OR COMPETITIVE	HIERARCHY	MARKET
Expected behavior:	obedience	opportunism
Motivating factors:	incentives and penalties	egotistical interests
Control:	managerial control	price mechanism
SHARED OR COMPATIBLE	AFFILIATIVE GROUP	SOCIAL MOVEMENT
	kibbutz as home	kibbutz as movement
	solidarity, affinity	normative affinity
Expected behavior:	responsiveness	volunteering
Motivating factors:	shared responsibility	worldview/vision
Control:	social pressure	self-discipline

and so it does not require agreement on policy and does not necessarily lead to achievement of shared objectives.

A *social movement* draws its strength from a public characterized by a similar worldview and similar objectives. In a social movement, achievement of a goal or of a shared vision is the main driving force of action, and agreement is the basis for joint action. An individual's affinity with the organization is ideological; but in addition to the common idea, individual motivation is derived from individual commitment to decisions (and the execution thereof) taken collectively by the participating individuals, and the principal mechanism of control is self-discipline. We can therefore define the activity of members and the coordination among them as self-management.

As a social entity, the kibbutz is an integrated unit: a combination of an affiliative group, a formal hierarchical organization, a marketplace, and a social movement. The kibbutz, therefore, represents a unique combination of fundamentally opposing systems. Because of the comprehensive nature of the partnership involved, the kibbutz—as a commune—cannot be an organization, movement, home, or business alone: It must be all of these. Over the years, changes have taken place that can be seen either as changes in the balances among the components or as a shift of the center of gravity from one type of affinity to another. These changes have affected the organizational structure of the kibbutz.

HISTORICAL DEVELOPMENT OF THE ORGANIZATIONAL STRUCTURE

This section describes the general trends that led to the "classical" normative model of kibbutz organization (which, with some changes, was the basis for the organizational structure of kibbutzim from the 1950s) and thence to the wave of organizational modifications that took place in the late 1980s.

In the beginning was "the table." The table is all-powerful. The power of the table stems from the conception of the kibbutz as a family communion. Some twelve to seventeen young men and women sit together in the evening after work and exchange opinions and impressions. In the course of the conversation—and with the participation of all members of the kibbutz—all questions of life are decided. And if you will, you can (together with sixteen pairs of arms) embrace matters of eternity and redemption of the world and the nation, all at once (Likver, 1947).

These were spontaneous gatherings, with no fixed agenda, times, or convening body. The discussions dealt with daily matters of work and economy, society and culture, politics and Zionist and socialist ideology. Decisions grew out of the search for broad agreement and were accepted without a vote, often with one of the members summarizing the spirit of the discussion along the lines of "the table decided. . . . " During this period, the modular component of social movement dominated the member's concept of the kibbutz. Kibbutz members viewed themselves as realizing their shared vision and believed that the kibbutz could manage its affairs without recourse to formal institutions and administration.

The evolution of comradely discussion into an intricate decision making structure is illustrated in Derekh's story (1970) of one kibbutz. The first period encompassed the first decade of the kibbutz's existence (1927–1940) and was characterized by spontaneous democracy, charismatic leadership, and sporadic, loosely formed institutions. The general assembly was nothing more than a gathering of members—or rather, members remaining in the dining room after the evening meal to settle work-related matters for the next day. This meeting took the form of free discussion without a coordinator and, apparently, no formal decisions were arrived at through a vote. To resolve specific issues, a committee was sometimes elected that dissolved on completion of its task (if not sooner). The only formal officeholders were the kibbutz-authorized representative and treasurer, the kitchen manager, and the clothing manager (Derekh, 1970). This period emphasized the voluntary component of the kibbutz.

In the second period (the second decade of the kibbutz's existence, 1940–1950), the secretariat (central committee) which had appeared at the end of the previous period became a fixed institution of increasing importance and size. In this period, a new office was created: economic coordinator. This had the effect of separating economic from social coordination (which remained in the hands of the secretary). The secretary's office became a job performed during work hours, and committees were elected for different functional areas. Although these official positions placed greater responsibility on their incumbents, they did not provide greater authority over other members. In the absence of any institutionalization, the work process was based on familiarity and spontaneous understanding among members. There was a high turnover of members in the various branches, frequent changes in office holders, and a general feeling of impermanence. The success of such an informal structure depended on the members' deep identification with the values of the kibbutz, a high level of social solidarity, the simplicity of kibbutz life (particularly work), and an emphasis on voluntary participation.

The third period covered two substantially similar decades—from 1950 to 1970. In theory, the general assembly preserved its character, although in fact more weight was shifted to the committees, particularly the secretariat. A trend emerged in which the office of committee chairperson (coordinator in kibbutz lingo) became a job performed during work hours, and the authority of the committee was in effect concentrated in the hands of its chairperson. Depending on the conditions in each kibbutz, the office of committee chairperson evolved from "coordinator" to "executive"—a clear manifestation of a shift in balance from the kibbutz's founding principles. Economic performance became central, and emphasis was placed on the organizational component, with a corresponding weakening in kibbutz solidarity and the voluntary component.

Size became a determinant of these changes. Larger kibbutzim (more than four hundred members) led the search for organizational efficiency. Having more people in the community necessarily involved greater complexity in function and communication. Thus new offices had to be created: cosecretaries who shared responsibility for social matters, a secretary for business enterprises (in addition to the economic coordinator) who supervised activity in industry, and a secretary for services (responsible for consumption). In some kibbutzim, a secondary parliamentary level was established—a council or expanded secretariat—to reduce pressure on the general assembly and to legitimate the activity of the secretariat (Lanir, 1985).

Such changes related to the development of kibbutz economy. During the first stage, the economy was characterized by many small branches which were not so much organizational frameworks as divisions of occupation based on crops and the like. No clear internal professional or administrative distinctions had yet been made. At that time, the economy needed few institutions and administrative functions (the office of economic coordinator did not yet exist). In the second stage, larger, more clearly defined branches evolved, each of which constituted a semi-independent unit. Internal supervision was informal, and coordinating the branch was regarded simply as an additional job activity imposed on one of the regular workers. These units competed for resources, and the main job of the economic coordinator was to distribute the resources (such as tractors and equipment) among the various branches—or, more precisely, to mediate among branches and try to create a unified economic layout. In the third stage, the structure of the economy became centralized. It was built on the organizational integration of a number of branches in an inclusive and complex economic system. The office of economic coordinator took shape as a clear-cut managerial role with far-reaching authority over the branches and their managers (Cohen, 1963).

The federation to which a kibbutz belonged also had a bearing on its structural makeup. Kibbutzim of the Kibbutz Artzi, which believed in the importance of interpersonal relations in an "organic" community, maintained a greater degree of informality. The Kibbutz Hameuchad (a federation existing until 1982, when it merged with another federation to form the United Kibbutz Movement TAKAM) saw the kibbutz movement first and foremost as an instrument for building the national homeland on a socialistic foundation, and the federation tended to favor a more clearly defined and centralized structure (Rosner and Cohen, 1980). By opposing any form of institutionalization, the Hever Hakvutzot (a federation of kibbutzim with small memberships) sought to maintain the intimate nature of their kibbutz. For years, the kibbutzim prevented any new members from joining, and if a kibbutz did grow, it was divided. In the small kibbutzim, there were no regular places of work and no institutions, and the only offices were those dictated by outside expediency, such as the *mukhtar* (responsible for contact with the British Mandatory regime) and a representative to institutions responsible for settlement.

Institutionalization was widely seen as a devaluation of the kibbutz way of life because it was considered to be a "routinization" of the revolution—as in the transition from commune to community (Talmon-Garber, 1970). Yet it is important to distinguish between institutionalization per se and the nature of the institutions that developed. An appropriate criterion for our evaluation of institutionalization is the degree to which it contributed to the democracy of the system.

Frequently, the tendency to form fixed patterns of organizational structure emerged because of pressure from below. The table of the pioneer period is a good example to illustrate this point. We do not know how round—in terms of equality—the table really was. From letters and documentary excerpts, Derekh (1970) reconstructs those early days: "It is apparently an organizational structure sufficient for a small group of people, who meet not only in the evening around the table in the dining room but are together at work most of the day (and in the common shower after work). It seems that the picture was not so idyllic and raised criticism even then. Not all the members of the kibbutz were present or actually participated in the discussions of the meeting. Their knowledge of matters that determined the fate of the kibbutz then—budgets, loans, investments, financial problems, ties with settlement institutions—was limited, and the talking was done by a few informal leaders, who performed all the central functions on a more or less regular basis and who actually made the decisions."

In the wake of criticism, a permanent committee was set up, as opposed to the ad hoc committees elected from time to time to resolve specific issues. In time, with varying names and responsibilities (central committee, extended secretariat, economic committee plus skeleton [reduced] secretariat, synthetic secretariat), this committee became the central governing body of the kibbutz.

The initial institutionalization of the kibbutz settlement began when additional groups of members ("supplements") joined the kibbutz (Derekh, 1970; Topel, 1992). These were young people who had formed pioneering youth movements in Eretz Israel and overseas for the purpose of settling Eretz Israel ("Land of Israel," as Jews referred to what was then Palestine). They arrived at the kibbutzim as unified groups with their own identities and leadership. Their encounter with the existing kibbutz leadership sometimes generated friction, because the young people did not always accept the "natural" leadership of the more senior members. The arrival of a new social body, experienced in public and political struggle, exerted pressure to implement formal democratic procedures, rotation in work and administrative positions, and the establishment of standard forms of organization.

The formalization of the decision making system, then, may contribute to the democratization of the governmental system—but not under all circumstances. In many instances, the institutionalization of the decision making system has brought with it increasing centralization. This is in part the unforeseen result of adopting directive institutionalization—that is, placing responsibility for various activities on individuals without prescribing rules—and in part a shift in the balance of power that has led to preference for hierarchy over other components of the kibbutz entity. A consequence of the changes has been poor attendance at and reduced influence of the general assembly.

ORGANIZATIONAL MODELS TAKE SHAPE

The shift in the balance of power among the structural elements of the kibbutz system is also reflected in the relative importance attached to work and economic management as opposed to the other two subsystems—the social and the educational. Shepher (1977) argues that the most common structure is dual: economic committee and members' committee, with the secretariat above them creating a synthesis of the two. Since the economic committee must weigh professional, organizational, and economic factors, and since the members' committee is burdened with an excess of urgent "little" (mostly personal) problems, Shepher believes there is a danger that problems of social ideology will be transferred to the secretariat. This situation may jeopardize the organizational primacy of the secretariat and place it on the same level as the economic committee. In such a secretariat, no synthesis can take place, leading to one of two possible results: dominance of economic factors in determining policy or bringing unsolved problems before the general assembly and thereby generating endless unsolved arguments and depleting the assembly's ability to deal with major issues (Shepher, 1977). Another possible model of dual structure is the parallel existence of both institutions. As early as the 1950s, Etzioni found a number of kibbutzim in which, instead of the usual single central organizational unit, there were two upper institutions—the economic committee and the "social secretariat" (Etzioni, 1980).

A third model stems from the growing influence of the economic committee and heralds, perhaps, the possible triumph of the economic sector. The supremacy of the economic committee arises from its control of the budgets and the dependence of the social institutions on work performance and allotment of budgets (both controlled by the economic officeholders).

According to historical analysis, the three models described above represent three principal conditions of balance of influence between holders of economic and holders of social office: (1) supremacy of the secretariat, with emphasis on the social sector and the ideological aspect—that is, a combination of affiliative and voluntary components of structure; (2) division into areas of authority (dual structure) with balance between the power of the secretariat and that of the economic committee; and (3) supremacy of the economic committee, with emphasis on the economic sector—that is, the hierarchical component. Industry has, in effect, swung the balance in favor of the economic system. The industrialized kibbutz can be considered a fourth stage of development—not only in the realm of work but also in the organizational structure of the kibbutz as a whole.

Integration of industry into the economic order of the kibbutz has been problematic from the outset: "The kibbutz is threatened with the possibility that the center of gravity will shift from the central institutions of the kibbutz to the management of the factory, which will become in effect the nerve center of the kibbutz" (Cohen, 1963). In kibbutz humor, this situation is described as "a factory that has a kibbutz."

According to the formal structure, the office of economic coordinator should be at the apex of the pyramid of economic management (in today's terminology, a sort of general manager of the kibbutz). In the distribution of political power in the kibbutz, his or her authority is considerably less. An examination of the typical professional career of economic functionaries shows that, in many kibbutzim, the position of economic coordinator is held by a recent graduate of economics or business administration whose previous experience consists of no more than coordinating a branch or an industrial department.

By contrast, the managerial positions in the factory are held by people who, following a term as economic coordinator, have already held a variety of other financial or business management offices in the kibbutz, in the kibbutz federation system, or in other large external economic organizations. The economic coordinator is, in effect, a novice who must confront more experienced and established senior functionaries. Such organizational contradictions have influenced the organizational changes that have occurred in recent years.

CHANGES OVER THE PAST DECADE

The General Assembly

According to kibbutz regulations, the general assembly is the highest institution for reaching binding decisions on ideological problems and important public matters. Over the years, however, its power in most kibbutzim has declined—and this despite the fact that great effort is invested in ensuring the assembly's proper functioning. In 83 percent of kibbutzim, there is regular distribution of information on matters that are to be discussed at the assembly, and in 90 percent of kibbutzim, decisions are widely publicized. Furthermore, over half the kibbutzim broadcast the meeting live over the internal video channel to members' residences.

The significance of the assembly in the public life of the kibbutz movement varies greatly among kibbutzim. The frequency with which the general assembly is held serves as an indicator: In 5 percent of kibbutzim, the general assembly is called once or twice a year; in 20 percent, approximately five times a year; in 40 percent, once a month; and in 35 percent of kibbutzim, on a weekly or biweekly basis. Differences among the kibbutzim as to the authority still invested in the general assembly are clear and statistically significant. Those kibbutzim in which the general meeting is called once or twice a year are those in which its responsibilities have been reduced to a minimum—generally to dealing with ideological issues; in those kibbutzim where the assembly has retained all its responsibilities, meetings are held with much greater frequency.

It should be noted, however, that in some of the kibbutzim reporting a restricted definition of the role of the assembly, the number of meetings is too many to be confined only to fundamental issues (or matters of principle), while in some of the kibbutzim claiming comprehensive authority for the general assembly, the number of meetings is too few to cover all areas of kibbutz life. These contradictions between the principle proclaimed and the situation in reality can be explained in a number of ways. Even in kibbutzim where, in theory, the assembly discusses and reaches a decision on every matter, most of the decisions, even those very important to kibbutz life, are actually made by other bodies. The difference is that, in principle, no subject raised for discussion is rejected on grounds that the subject does not fall within the realm of responsibility of the assembly. By contrast, the frequency with which assembly meetings are called in kibbutzim that have, in principle, abolished most of its functions is an indication of conflict and disagreement in the community, raising the need for public discussion and decision making in the assembly.

We can learn more about the position of the general assembly in the government system of the kibbutz from the way in which its agenda is determined and from the nature of its debates. In most kibbutzim (77 percent), the secretariat determines which matters will be brought before the general assembly. On most subjects, furthermore, a single proposal is presented for approval; or, if there is disagreement, a number of alternatives are presented, with a recommendation that reflects the preference of the secretariat. In almost 10 percent of kibbutzim, subjects are presented as announcements on behalf of the secretariat, and whether the floor is opened up for debate depends on the wishes of those present. In only 15 percent of kibbutzim is the public given a choice of open alternatives. One kibbutz is noteworthy for its unique practice of testing public opinion in discussion groups before bringing proposals to its governing institutions.

The survey enables us to divide most kibbutzim into three major groups, according to the degree of authority exercised by the general assembly and to the scope of subjects deliberated there: (1) kibbutzim in which most functions of the general assembly have been transferred to a council or to other intermediary bodies (21 percent); (2) kibbutzim in which routine management is in the hands of elected bodies and the general assembly discusses only issues considered central or fundamental (43 percent); and (3) kibbutzim in which the meeting discusses and decides every issue (32 percent).

Voting by Ballot

Among changes that have taken place in recent years, voting by ballot on important issues has grown to the extent that in some kibbutzim, this has become the main instrument for reaching public decisions and determining policy. Our survey shows that although in 10 percent of kibbutzim there is no voting by ballot and in 13 percent this method is used only for election of committee members and officeholders and for voting in new members, in most kibbutzim (56 percent) vote by ballot supplements the general assembly on subjects considered matters of principle, most of which involve fundamental changes to the kibbutz way of life or are points of contention that have proved difficult to resolve. In other kibbutzim (22 percent), vote by ballot has become an integral part of the assembly. The discussion takes place at the meeting and is broadcast on the internal channel; votes are cast in the polling booth within a week.

Supporting the use of the ballot as an instrument of decision making is the view that decisions made in the poorly attended assembly do not represent the will of the public. However, its drawbacks for democracy are numerous. It dramatically reduces the number of issues decided by the public. In a small number of kibbutzim, public participation (in the assembly or in the polling booth) is already limited to election of institutions and officeholders. For the most part, vote by ballot is not a way of influencing policy making but rather a formal endorsement. Furthermore, a ballot enables various interest groups to coordinate their vote, and thus it defies the pursuit of community goals. Finally, although the ballot provides legitimacy for decisions that have been made, it does not create agreement about policy—because there is no room for dialogue and compromise. Vote by ballot, then, has a polarizing effect on the life of the community and thereby prejudices one of the fundamental assumptions of kibbutz administration—namely, that there exists an identity or sharing of interests (see Fig. 8.1) among different groups and between the establishment and rank-and-file members.

Representative Council

A different direction proposed as a solution to functional problems of the general assembly is an intermediate framework—the council. Councils have been established in two forms: a single central council and separate councils for economic and social areas. These councils, existing in 43 percent of kibbutzim, are mediators between the executive bodies and the general assembly. Among kibbutzim with councils, sixty have a single council—in forty of which there is a central council, in five a social council, and in fifteen an economic council. The place of councils in the government structure of the kibbutz is not clear. On the one hand, some kibbutzim have transferred most areas of jurisdiction from the general assembly to the council. On the other hand, the power of the secretariat over the agenda of the council makes clear that the council is dependent on the executive bodies. In many kibbutzim the council seems to suffer from the same problems that beset the general assembly, and the nickname "mini-assembly" is a reflection of its limitations.

Board of Directors

The board of directors has assumed considerable strength in many kibbutzim: in industrial enterprises (73 percent), in other branches (25 percent), and even in agriculture (18 percent). Establishment of a board of directors in effect separates the business enterprise from the community. Furthermore, in many kibbutzim, the management of the factory has been freed from control of the economic management of the kibbutz. An independent treasury for the factory represents a wider gap: detachment of the factory from the economy of the kibbutz and therefore a restriction of the control exercised by the central economic institutions over the kibbutz's principal asset. Although the separation is not necessarily claimed as an objective, the establishment of a board of directors is associated with many features of the dissociation of business from community.

Changes in Officeholders' Titles

The change in the conception of the organizational system of the kibbutz—from participatory democracy and self-management to a hierarchical system—is expressed symbolically in the changes in the names of institutions and offices: management and manager have superseded committee and coordinator.

Committees were part of the self-management system of kibbutz members and handled issues which, because of their technical complexity or detailed nature, could not be debated at the general assembly. The role of committee head was to coordinate various activities and to prepare for meetings, emphasizing teamwork and equality among committee members. The change of name—turning coordinators into executives or managers—is an expression of the change that has taken place in the balance of power between the establishment and the general membership. The term manager contrasts with the transitory nature of officeholder in the early days of the kibbutz and with the former strength of the general assembly. In a number of kibbutzim, this change has spread to the social sphere, but for the most part it is restricted to the economic sphere with the introduction of economic management and boards of directors. The disappearance of the economic committee in many kibbutzim (40 percent) and its replacement by economic management are an indication of far-reaching changes in the conception of the economic sphere and in the organization of work.

Changes in Management Culture

Much of the organizational change is an attempt to address the difficulties that institutions and officeholders face when trying to impose the authority invested in them by the collective on the individuals who make up that collective. In kibbutz discourse, these difficulties are termed *poor work ethic* or lack of motivation. It would seem that in addition to the economic, social, and ideological crises the kibbutzim are undergoing, they are also experiencing a crisis of governability (see Binder et al., 1971). Traditionally, the public authority of the kibbutz has been based on the ideological identification of members with the kibbutz and on the pressure of public opinion as the principal means of enforcing suitable behavior. The authority of officeholders is based on imposition of obligation. Imposition of obligation is, by its very nature, dependent on the internalization of values by the individual and on broad public agreement serving as a basis for social pressure. Because public criticism constitutes the principal control mechanism of the kibbutz, in the event that the flow of communication (information on the one hand and evaluation on the other) is halted for some reason, those who have infringed the norm may not have to pay the price in terms of public evaluation.

Whereas accentuating the financial-economic aspect of the kibbutz has weakened the commitment of members to the system and their identification with its values and goals (Ben-Rafael, 1988), so has diversification of the kibbutz population reduced accord among the groups. And both changes have undermined the ability of the community to impose its will on individuals. To this must be added the unexpected results of historical changes that have taken place in the organizational structure as part of the industrialization process: the bureaucratization of the system and the distancing of members from foci of decision making. Public expression (in newspapers and individual statements) points to a growing alienation among kibbutz members, between members and the establishment, and between the individual member and his or her kibbutz. Loss of identification with the kibbutz and alienation of members, leading to problems of work motivation, make it difficult for the production system to function. These problems have led to a search for other ways to activate members. Alongside the structural changes I have discussed, two other changes need to be mentioned: the separation of business from community and the turning of branches into profit centers or responsibility centers (see the chapters by Rosner, Palgi, and Getz).

In terms of the governance structure, centers of responsibility are only one example of a much wider and more consequential phenomenon of change in the mechanisms of social control in the kibbutz: namely, financial control or control through the budget, rather than direct supervision of officeholders. Although there is not necessarily a connection between centers of responsibility and the separation of business from community, the establishment of centers of responsibility in kibbutzim that have separated business from community is four times that in other kibbutz. It would seem that the connection between the two organizational solutions stems from management philosophy which was not formerly accepted in the kibbutz and which points to a cultural change in the kibbutz.

SUMMARY

Over the years the kibbutz has experienced a number of changes, as it has moved from an emphasis on the social movement component to an emphasis on the component of group belonging (the kibbutz as home). This was followed by a process of hierarchical structuring of the system (emphasis on the organizational component), which tended to have an alienating effect.

The changes that have taken place over the last decade can be represented by two dimensions:

1. Members' involvement in decision making has been reduced to the point where the government is indirect and representative—that is, an elected government rather than self-management. The change is characterized by

the establishment of intermediate bodies (such as councils) and centralist institutions (such as the active secretariat) and by the abolition of public committees, their areas of jurisdiction passing to career officeholders.

2. Conceptions of management not formerly accepted in the kibbutz have been adopted. Institutionally, the change is evident in the division of the decision making system in various ways—for example, separation of business from community, departmentalization according to function, and turning branches into autonomous profit centers.

The organizational structures that have recently been introduced into the kibbutz political system reflect various degrees of division between different spheres (usually between economy and society, but also within them) and reduced participation by the general membership in decision making. For example, the establishment of a representative council constitutes a weakening of the direct and participatory character of the kibbutz system of government. Establishment of a board of directors constitutes a de facto separation of business from community, with power concentrated in the hands of a small group. A general board of directors for all the kibbutz, relying on centers of responsibility, is in effect both an election of government (instead of participatory decision making) and an essential change in the method of management. The changes that have taken place recently represent a transition from viewing the interests of the general membership as shared to viewing them as conflictual or competitive. This change in basic assumptions about the interaction among the members has given rise, in turn, to changes in the nature of the commitment of individuals to the kibbutz framework, the type of motivations to action, and the preference given to the various mechanisms of social supervision and control. In some kibbutzim, these changes have undermined the minimal basis of agreement necessary for the proper functioning of the system.

9
Women in the Changing Kibbutz

Gila Adar

Outcomes of the current kibbutz crisis are expressed in the adoption of values of the surrounding society, which uses market, rather than communal, principles. Consequently, women's status in the kibbutz should reflect that of women in the industrialized society, and changes happening in the kibbutz should enhance intergender inequality.

Studies conducted during the 1970s and the 1980s showed that the intergender division of labor in the kibbutz located women in domestic jobs (such as services or education) while men took on the breadwinners' roles (working in farming, industry, or administration). Thus, by being excluded from the economic and political domains, women were made to feel inferior (Tiger and Shepher, 1975; Palgi et al., 1983; Adar, 1981; Leviatan, 1983a; Ben-Rafael and Weitman, 1984).

In an attempt to enhance the status of women, the kibbutz federations (in 1981) founded gender equality departments (GEDs) to counter the traditional view about the division of labor. Exemplifying the traditional view was that women had sole responsibility for child care on the kibbutz. As a result, women were confined to the children-houses and prevented from exploring other occupational opportunities.

The gender equality departments also aspired to abolish the powerlessness that accompanied the political and economic status of women. They initiated such diverse activities as consciousness-raising workshops, assertiveness and leadership training, and involvement of women in the federation's central decision-making bodies, actively encouraging women to seek high-level office. Although the GEDs succeeded in introducing feminist issues to public discourse and in reshaping the structure of work in kibbutzim by legitimating, for instance, work for men in children-houses and work for women according to their choice, they failed to convince kibbutz members (both men and women) that gender equality should be of high priority on the kibbutz social agenda. With the onset of the economic crisis in the mid-1980s and the downsizing of the federations' headquarters, it became clear that the gender equality departments were doomed for closure. They ceased to function in 1990.

CHANGING THE MEANING OF EQUALITY

How do kibbutz members presently perceive the term equality? Equality, as well as gender equality, was a cornerstone of kibbutz ideology. During the kibbutz's first sixty years, equality meant that every member had the same access to economic benefits. Ownership of kibbutz property was collective/communal, and expense money was divided according to rules combining equal rights with the individual needs. All this is changing (see Getz's chapter).

While Shur (1984) found that only 2 percent of respondents supported allocating the budget according to distributive justice (allocation of rewards according to level of contribution), Palgi and Sharir (1995) found that already 63 percent from the TAKAM membership and 53 percent from the Kibbutz Artzi membership supported curtailing the expense budget of members who failed to fulfill their quota of work hours. In short, the criterion of equality was being transformed into the criterion of equity, and the egalitarian principle for allocation of resources was being converted to norms of distributive justice.

Palgi and Rosner (1983) used the phrase "different but equal" to describe their perception of intergender equality in kibbutzim. Hebrew has the same word for "equal," "alike," and "egalitarian." In debates held during the early 1980s, many kibbutz members argued that "there is no equality between men and women." (They meant "equality" in the sense of "likeness" or "similarity.") Despite the feminists' efforts to explain the difference between "equality" and "likeness," most people preferred to ignore the first meaning (equality). People would argue that "genders are different, and therefore no equality between them can be achieved." Indeed, in one study that I conducted in 1987, most women thought that intergender equality was best expressed by the statement "Everyone should choose his/her work according to his/her will." Yet, when asked what they thought was the most popular view among members, their response was "Men and women should have their typical jobs and offices, but the prestige and esteem accorded to them should be equal."

WOMEN AND THE PRESENT STRUCTURAL CHANGES

Failure to shape a model of egalitarian society induced kibbutz members to believe that gender equality was no longer a realistic target. However, the change in the perception of equality is nowadays accompanied by a movement to adopt individualistic values and principles of the market. Three of the main changes that the kibbutzim are currently experiencing may have a major impact on women members. These are privatization, separation of business from community, and differential material rewards. In the following sections I analyze the impact of these trends on intergender equality in the kibbutzim.

The World of Work

In the past, work segregation has been very marked in the kibbutz (Tiger and Shepher, 1975), and it still is. Most women work in education and public services, while most men work in agriculture, industry, and production services. Industry, which is the main income producer in kibbutz economy, is also gender segregated: Of the few women in industry, most work in office jobs. Kibbutz administration is also segregated: Men work in the higher levels and women in the lower levels.

Table 9.1 indicates some changes in the occupational structure. The increased number of women in industry is mostly because of the inclusion in this category of female crafts and tourism, which are new additions to the general category of industry in kibbutzim and which employ mostly women. Conversely, the decreased number of women working in education is because many kibbutz women have been replaced by hired workers from the outside and because of the diminishing need for child caregivers (*metaplot*), stemming from both the unification of smaller elementary kibbutz schools into larger regional schools and the transformation from communal to family sleeping arrangements (see Plotnik's chapter).

One outcome of the changes in the kibbutzim is the abolition of the axiom of self-labor. As a result, women feel free to choose their place of work, even when this has resulted in the need to employ outside workers to replace them. Greater personal freedom accompanied by an urgent need for larger incomes has allowed kibbutz members greater access to the job market—both inside and outside the kibbutz. More kibbutz members, men and women, currently have jobs outside their kibbutzim. Estimates indicate that about 8 percent of men and women (not including those in the inter-kibbutz organizations) work in jobs which are not part of the kibbutz milieu, and another ten per cent plan to do so in the future. Although no significant intergender differences exist in this trend, women experience more

Table 9.1
Women and Men in Work Branches, 1978, 1986, and 1994 (Percentages)

	1978		1986		1994	
	Women	*Men*	*Women*	*Men*	*Women*	*Men*
Agriculture	1.0	31.0	3.0	22.0	5.0	23.0
Industry, crafts, and tourism	8.0	30.0	6.0	38.0	21.0	34.0
Public services	37.0	10.0	30.0	6.0	26.0	16.0
Education	39.0	5.0	38.0	4.0	26.0	5.0
Administration	8.0	8.0	12.0	14.0	12.0	15.5
Other	7.0	16.0	11.0	16.0	10.0	6.5
Total	100.0	100.0	100.0	100.0	100.0	100.0

Source: Unpublished data files from the Institute for Social Research of the Kibbutz.

difficulty finding well-paid jobs in the Israeli job market (outside the kibbutz). As a result, only professional women (such as teachers or professionals in the health services) find appropriate jobs outside.

Although legitimization of outside work has increased kibbutz women's job opportunities in nontraditional occupations, the intrusion of hired workers into the kibbutz work structure has not changed the basic intergender segregation of jobs—because women (hired) replace women (members) and men (hired) replace men (members). The current job structure of men and women continues to differ in some other characteristics: More men's jobs have an aspect of management associated with them. Leviatan (1995), for instance, found in his survey that 43 percent of the women described their jobs as having a managerial component, compared to 57 percent of the men. Forty percent of the women defined their work as low in training needs while only 31 percent of the men said so. When teaching is excluded, most women's jobs are lower in their required level of education. Thus, although more women than men attain higher education, they have less opportunities to implement it. Along with outside salaried jobs, a number of new jobs inside the kibbutz have also become income-producing jobs—for example, small businesses such as cosmetics services for outside clients, gift and craft shops, health clinics, and jobs in the tourism branch.

As a result of both these trends (work outside the kibbutz and the new range of jobs inside the kibbutz), a larger percentage of women contribute to kibbutz income. Palgi (1994b) found that 33 percent of women defined their jobs as income producing—a jump of 8 percent from 1985. Furthermore, the need for more income and the removal of limitations on women's choice of work have increased their economic power in the kibbutz, and their position in the occupational market may well become an important negotiating lever should differential economic rewards become a norm in kibbutzim.

However, another change that kibbutzim have experienced—the separation between business and community (see Getz's chapter)—has had an opposite impact upon intergender equality. Where it has been implemented, this change has weakened members' control over the economic activity of their kibbutz, but especially the ability of women to exercise political power; for whereas the separation of business activity from community activity has brought more autonomy to the production branches, the voice of the service branches is less heard, and women (as said before) are the major occupiers of the service branches.

Women in the Public-Political Elite

Rosner, Ben David et al. (1990) and Adar (1981) showed public-political office to be the best predictor of social status in the community, helping to explain the perceived influence that men and women enjoy in the kibbutz. Men and women differ in their involvement in public-political activities. While the number of female officeholders in the low levels tends to be equal or even higher than that of men, the higher the level of office, the lower the proportion of women (Rosner, Ben David et al., 1990; Leviatan, 1983a). Tiger and Shepher (1975), for instance, found that while 51.4 percent from the rank-and-file membership in committees were women, they constituted only 36.5 percent of coordinators and only 8.4 percent of the central public officeholders. This has changed somewhat over the years. In my own study (Adar, 1992) I found that women constituted 41.5 percent of committee coordinators and 21 percent of central officeholders. As an illustration, the proportion of women in the highest-ranking committee (kibbutz secretariat) was about a third. This higher proportion of women in public office is due mostly to the increase in complexity of kibbutz life, which demands more institutionalization and specialization and thus more public officeholders. As a result, kibbutzim have been forced to recruit more women (Adar and Louis, 1988).

Another trend that has become apparent in recent years (Adar, 1992) is the gender polarization of the public-political sphere. The domains of education and health have been dominated by women: 80 percent and 77 percent of the coordinators of these two committees were females, whereas only 3 percent of the committees of economics and finance were headed by women. We (Adar and Louis, 1988) located 3,481 women who were known to be active within their kibbutz in the public-political sphere. Among them we found only ninety-two women who had been economic coordinators or treasurers or general managers of a kibbutz factory. This topic was investigated ten years later with similar results, except that the proportion of women in the central social office (kibbutz general secretary) had grown appreciably (Getz, 1994).

The separation of business from community has increased the importance of economic committees, and because positions in these committees are mostly held by men, there has been a further widening of the intergender gap of political power.

Women's Education

During the past twenty-five years, higher education has become commonplace for both men and women in the kibbutz. At the beginning of the 1970s, academic education was sanctioned only for teachers and engineers; today anyone can study in any field and institute of higher education. Consequently, 32 percent of the men and 37 percent of the women have thirteen or more years of schooling (Maron, 1995), and 21.4 percent of the men and 23.7 percent of the women have academic degrees (Palgi and Sharir, 1995). However, men and women study different subjects. Women comprise the majority of students in the arts, education, and the humanities, while men comprise the majority in economics, engineering, and the natural sciences. This difference is illustrated in Table 9.2.

Although intergender polarization is very marked in the fields of study shown in Table 9.2, it is less obvious in the social sciences. Moreover, with the younger groups, intergender differences (at least for the domain of economics) decrease dramatically. In the age group of forty to forty-nine years, 28 percent of the students who study economics are women; this percentage increases to 33 percent in the age group of thirty to thirty-nine years and to 47 percent in the age group of twenty to twenty-nine years. Thus, although no structural changes may have occurred, small changes like this may signal a future direction.

Table 9.2
Graduates of Various Domains of Study by Gender, 1993

	Women	Men
Economics, Engineering, and Natural Sciences		
Percent	25.0	75.0
Number	1,389	4,252
Arts, Education, and Humanities		
Percent	76.5	23.5
Number	4,736	1,475

Source: Dept. of Statistics, TAKAM, 1994. TAKAM data only.

The sex-typed division of disciplines has a long-range effect on gender segregation in the world of work and in public-political central office. It limits the scope for women to become involved in high-status professions and if differential remuneration were ever to take hold in kibbutzim, might have a significant impact on their reward potential.

The Family

The kibbutz family is also undergoing change (Maron's and Plotnick's chapters). Although the family is still the most important social cell of kibbutz society, some indicators suggest that familism is no longer the main characteristic of kibbutz life: Kibbutz-born men and women establish a family only after a long period of travel and study (Orchan, 1991). The divorce rate of married men in 1990 was 2.9 out of 1,000, and this figure increased to 4.1 in 1994 (Israeli Statistical Department Bulletin, 1995). By contrast, the marriage rate of men decreased from 13 in 1990 to 12.6 in 1994. (Among the Jewish population in Israel, the corresponding figures were 17.2 and 17.4, respectively.) Postponement of marriage has increased the percentage of never married persons in the kibbutz.

The privatization of public budgets and the transfer of functions (children's health care and other physical needs, looking after the clothing of all family members, and food preparation) from the public to the family domain are contributing to intergender differences in time allocation. Palgi (1994b) reported that women now invested more time on home tasks: 47 percent of the female interviewees stated they were spending more time on home duties today compared to the past, while only 30 percent of the men reported an increase in time allocated to house duties. Although most family tasks and decisions, including the management of the increased family budget, were shared by both wife and husband (Orchan, 1990), 59 percent of the women respondents reported that they did all or almost all of the house chores.

Interviews with women that I and my associates conducted recently (Adar, Tornianski, and Rosner, 1993) showed that women felt disillusioned. Although women originally supported privatization to gain more personal freedom as consumers (and particularly freedom from dependence on the discretion of officeholders), they discovered that the enlarged budget became the easiest target for cutbacks when hardship hit their kibbutz. Thus, families with children at home have more expenses but less money to cover them.

Legal Issues

Women become kibbutz members as individuals (and not as part of a family). They are treated as individuals concerning their rights and obligations. The standard of living of men and women is independent of their marital status, and (contrary to the situation outside the kibbutz) it remains so in the event of divorce. Pension money also relates to each member as an individual, irrespective of his or her marital status. Today, there is a debate about the principle of individual membership. Over the last twenty years, divorce rates in the kibbutz have increased, and during the crisis, more men than women have been leaving the kibbutz. The social committee of TAKAM federation has held several discussions about the status of membership of those who remain on the kibbutz after their mate or ex-spouse has left, struggling with the problem of whether to ask a member to leave because his or her spouse is leaving. Such a resolution may force some women to leave the kibbutz against their wishes.

THEORETICAL APPLICATIONS AND CONCLUSIONS

Blumberg (1984, 1989) claims that economic power is the most important independent variable affecting gender inequality. If women were to increase their access to, and control of, economic resources, they might gain control of other resources and thus improve their standing in other domains. However, while control of economic resources may play an important role in enhancing women's social status, it is not the only determining force.

Are the current changes in kibbutzim extending (unintentionally) women's opportunities for more personal and social growth (Chafetz, 1988)? The answer is unclear. On the one hand, we observe that the kibbutz's need for a larger income from outside, the opening up of the job market, and the reduction of social control inside the kibbutz have all increased the proportion of women who bring money into the kibbutz. The diversification of occupational opportunities in the outside job market has also broadened the experience and performance of some women and, together with growing access to economic resources, may change the traditional division of work between the genders. On the other hand, women without occupational skills are doomed to stay where they are—in the unskilled service jobs which are located at the lowest level of the rewards scale. Analysis of trends in occupational education and training does not promise any fundamental change to the structure of women's jobs in the near future.

The proposals for change raise two questions about intergender equality in the kibbutz. First, how will the change affect the position of women in the kibbutz elite strata? As Chafetz (1992, 220) demonstrates, "Equal representation for women among society's elites constitutes the single most important change required to produce a system of gender equality." Second, because intentional change is not targeted toward gender equality, how can change be expected to ensure its realization?

As to women joining the kibbutz elite and becoming more powerful, there is some prospect because of the need for more individuals to fill the various managerial positions. This new need resulting from the many qualified persons leaving the kibbutz or taking jobs outside should offer women the opportunity to gain more powerful positions. The need for officeholders together with the improving image of successful women may strengthen women's influence in public decision-making bodies. At the same time, past experience demonstrates that kibbutzim may recruit candidates for important office from the outside, while blaming women for being unqualified. The failed experience of the gender equality departments shows that the realization of this opportunity may have much to do with women's willingness to express themselves in leading their kibbutzim through intentional change toward more intergender equality. As stated by Chafetz (1990, 175): "The larger the proportion of women who experience role expansion, the greater the public acceptance of the goals and ideology of women's movements." Translated into the kibbutz situation, this means the election of more women into the offices of management, economic coordination, and treasurer.

For some women, the structural changes have consequences which are in accord with the process described by Chafetz. The expanding role experience, the acquaintance with outside influential ideas, the sense of their inferior status in the Israeli labor market and society—all these may generate a group of women prepared to take measures for structural change that favors gender equality.

Fortunately, kibbutz attributes support the development of intentional activity because the kibbutz is an ideologically committed community and is open to its surroundings and the ideas expressed there. However, it is up to the women themselves, by becoming more involved in the economic and political domains, to win the struggle for their equal standing.

10
Individual Needs and
Public Distribution in the Kibbutz

Yaakov Gluck

The kibbutz combines in one socioeconomic system two (usually separate) major social domains: the production domain (expressed in the contribution members make to society) and the consumption domain (expressed in what society offers to its members). Combining these two domains differentiates the kibbutz from other forms of cooperative organization, which generally relate only to the one or to the other. In short, a kibbutz represents a *total*, or a *whole*, society.

This uniqueness of the kibbutz is illuminated by the Marxist dictum "to each according to his or her needs; from each according to his or her ability," which serves as a central guide for the relationship between kibbutz members and their community ("needs" relate to the consumption domain in kibbutz life, and "ability" relates to the production domain). Although the phrasing of this dictum means that no relationship is expected between the contribution of individuals to their kibbutz and the satisfaction of their needs as offered by their kibbutz, the two are united to emphasize the *wholeness* or *totality* of the kibbutz phenomenon.

This chapter focuses upon the consumption domain of the kibbutz and its changes over the years. Yet it is important to locate these changes within the full framework of kibbutz life, including contribution—because, as will be described and analyzed later, recent developments in the kibbutzim have led the two previously separate domains to form a closer relationship.

The kibbutz commitment to satisfy its members' needs embraces their whole lifespan—including all those needs which, in other societies, are provided by the family, the community, or the welfare state. (Even state services are provided to kibbutz institutions, and individual members obtain their services through them.)

During the eight decades of kibbutz history since 1910, the organizational concepts of the consumption system have undergone a dynamic process of institutional crystallization; this process is still going on—and, from the mid-1980s, at an accelerated pace. An interesting feature of this system is that there has never existed an ideological code or a blueprint from which all norms stem. The absence of such a code has enabled the kibbutz to develop a normative system of needs provision that is free from dogmatism, is based on a dialectical relation between ideology and practice, and is constantly evolving through adaptation to changing economic, structural, and environmental situations. Recently, however, due to the worsening economy in most kibbutzim on the one hand, and the demand to introduce new value concepts on the other, the delicate balance between members' wants and institutional constraints has been upset.

As mentioned, a basic tenet of kibbutz ideology is the struggle to realize the Marxist utopian principle that commits the community to satisfying all needs of all members and to ensuring that all members contribute all their abilities to the community. This principle, despite its simplicity and apparent clarity, has resulted in endless discussions and arguments about the problems of its practical implementation and about contradictions between fundamental kibbutz values and operative norms of kibbutz conduct.

Both parts of the Marxist principle offer an optimistic view of human nature. It assumes people can create a world where every need is provided by the society (which must be very affluent to achieve that objective). It also assumes people will contribute to their society to the best of their ability, and this will be done because of their identification with their society and not because of their wish to have their personal needs satisfied as reward for their contribution.

Faced by the constraints of reality, the kibbutz, in its early days, adopted an additional principle: that society may dictate what human needs are normatively legitimate and may socialize its members to seek gratification only within a restricted range of personal needs.

The kibbutz value system demanded a dissociation between contribution and remuneration as expressed in the form of need satisfaction. Kibbutzim assumed that as their economic status improved, they would get nearer to the goal of full free provision of goods and services to meet new needs of their members. However, through a long part of its history the kibbutz has faced economic hardship and sometimes lacked even the most basic provisions. Therefore, only through the surrender of individual needs to the communal good could the society survive.

IDEOLOGY AND PRACTICE: CONFRONTATION OF CHANGE AND BALANCE

The first systematic research of the kibbutz was conducted by the late Yonina Talmon-Garber in the mid-1950s. At that time, thanks to the improvement of the kibbutz economy, the collective consumption standard had shown some improvement over ideologically supported frugality. Talmon described the early kibbutz ideology as "voluntary-secular asceticism," which enabled collective implementation of the ideal "to each according to his needs."

However, collective satisfaction of needs has its social cost because it demands members' compliance with restricted, humble, and standardized provision of basic needs. Talmon described the dangers that would threaten collective consumption if the value of voluntary asceticism were replaced by demands for a higher living standard: "As consumer demands increase, they also tend to become more diversified, and threaten to throw the collective consumption pattern out of gear, since a wide and varied range of consumer demands obviously makes it more difficult for the community to enforce a standard distribution pattern" (Talmon, 1972, 207).

Furthermore, as consumption becomes more central in members' lives, the rigid pattern of curbing expenditure breaks down, giving rise to ever new demands. In Talmon's words: "The sense of inequality becomes more acute: kibbutz institutions are subjected to pressure and can no longer perform their function properly" (1972, 208). Thus, the ideology of asceticism—the voluntary acceptance of restrictions on living standards—helps achieve congruence between individual desires and collective policy imperatives.

The years which have passed from the time of Talmon's research have, on the one hand, been years of reinterpretation of values and, on the other, seen the introduction of new needs accompanied by the constant struggle to keep a balance between individual desires and collective demands. The years that followed the mid-1950s were characterized by a constant effort to put into practice the vague ideological imperatives contained in the Marxist dictum.

Initially, there was the reality of deficiency—because the kibbutzim were formed as poor communes. This required the "first amendment" to the dictum, a clause of restriction: "To each according to his or her needs, but within the limits set by the capability of the collective." But then, after economic conditions in the kibbutzim had improved, three new questions emerged:

1. The first question touched the very basics of kibbutz responsibility for satisfying its members' needs: What should be the definition of human needs based on "to each according to her or his needs"? Should the kibbutz meet all the needs of its members or should it restrict needs to a standard set recognized and legitimated by the community?

2. The second question related to limits of collective capability: What should determine allocation of resources between immediate consumption and investment in the production system? Should it be according to collective preference or to some average calculation across individual demands?

3. The third question was that of practice: What method of distribution of collectively approved needs would meet value dictums of equality and social justice on the one hand and the satisfaction of members on the other?

Constant struggle with these questions has generated changing methods for distributing consumer goods to satisfy individual needs.

The answer to the first question—what should be considered a legitimate need?—led initially to a definition of needs either by local institutions (committees or the general assembly) or by experts at the federation level. After ratification by federation decision-making bodies, the suggested consumer-goods basket of each federation became the yardstick to which each of their kibbutzim fitted its local consumer-goods basket. Thus, as Table 10.1 illustrates, the standardized basket suggested by the federation generated a substantially equal standard of living across all kibbutzim irrespective of their economic performance or accumulated wealth.

Research in a sample of twenty kibbutzim (Rosner, Gluck, and Ovnat, 1979; Gluck, Goldemberg, and Helman, 1988) showed that nineteen of the twenty kibbutzim accepted, within 17 percent, their federation's consumption proposal. This was despite the fact that income level differences between the kibbutzim in the study exceeded 450 percent.

This homogeneity brought with it an unintended result: The consumption level of each kibbutz became dissociated from its level of economic functioning—since consumption level was more or less constant across kibbutzim but economic performance was not. Some kibbutzim were consuming below their economic potential, some above it, thereby upsetting their income expenditure balance (see Helman, 1994). Until the mid-1980s, the number of kibbutzim consuming above their potential was small. Most kibbutzim consumed below their potential and this contributed to the creation of surpluses. Federations counterbalanced the inequities by making transfers from the wealthier kibbutzim to the kibbutzim consuming above their potential resources. (These transfers were an expression of mutual help among kibbutzim as expressed through a progressive intrafederation taxing mechanism.) However, the economic crisis of the last decade forced many kibbutzim to lower their living standards, and at the same time, it curtailed the ability of federations to help the needy. As a result, budget proposals by the federations ceased to have much influence on local consumption policy, and diversity in standard of living among kibbutzim replaced the former homogeneity.

Table 10.1
A Summary of the Consumption Budget Proposal for a Single Adult

Total expenditure (1993) for one adult in NIS (New Israeli Shekel):	12,150
Total expenditure for one child (63.3% of an adult budget):	7,691

Suggested allocation to different domains of consumption expressed as a percentage of the total:

Food Services	18.0
Health budget	7.3
Water and energy	4.0
Committees (social, culture, education, etc.)	9.8
Taxes	12.6
Personal (comprehensive) budget	48.3
Total per member	100.0

REDEFINITION OF NEEDS: THE PROCESS OF INSTITUTIONALIZATION

More recently the policy on needs has been modified. Collective provisioning of needs was divided into functional subunits: the kitchen and the dining hall, the laundry and the clothing department, the health clinic, kindergarten, and so on. Growth and maturation demanded the formalization of the guiding principles of need provision too.

Two seemingly contradictory principles have been accepted as the bases of collective consumption:

1. Human needs—material or otherwise—are not equal; therefore, the provision of needs cannot be based on a principle of *mechanical equality*. Members and children have a host of individual needs. Examples are health care, cultural and educational preferences, assistance to family members, or old age care. To this group of needs, the application of the principle of to each according to her or his needs is the correct one; it also does not provoke the envy of fellow members.

2. For other needs, the Marxist dictum has been replaced by the principle *of qualitative and quantitative equality.* Equality may contradict the original dictum because equal distribution is not always in accord with personal needs. However, where individual differences cannot be objectively justified, or where differentiated distribution would cause social stress or envy, equal distribution may be the only justifiable system. Within this distribution are housing and furniture, casual clothing, holiday expenditure, and cash allowance. (A good example of the application of the principle of need versus the principle of equal distribution is the provision of eyeglasses for members. There may be an equal budget for the frames while lenses are given according to need—as prescribed by the optometrist.)

Different methods of consumer-goods distribution evolved from the interpretation of these two principles. From time to time, the definition of needs has been revised to bring it in accord with changes in taste, economic conditions, individual wants, and technological innovations.

If, during the pioneering period of material hardship, it was easy to define needs (which, en passant, hardly exceeded survival necessity), economic affluence widely extended the list of needs and demands. Even so, there have always been needs requiring preferential treatment—for example, children's education and housing, health of community members, and the physical security of the collective. Children-houses were built of stone or concrete, while adults dwelt in tents. In border areas, security expenses have always demanded significant allocation of resources, even today.

The whole spectrum of consumption has been divided into such functional units as the communal kitchen and the dining hall, the clothing department, the general store, education, health services, and the like. For most of these units, a coordinator is elected; some others are controlled by committees (elected by the kibbutz assembly) which have the authority to define needs. Usually, a long and often movement-wide dispute precedes the legitimation of a new need.

The introduction of previously unaccepted needs tended to follow a common pattern. When deviant members privately obtained items that until then were considered illegitimate, there would be protests from the community and from its social institutions; but when other members followed suit, the new items became legitimate, after which they were provided to all members by the kibbutz as an integral part of the consumption basket. Many such innovations were introduced because of members' demands and regardless of economic conditions.

Women's cosmetics and higher education are prime examples of this pattern. Both were once disregarded, yet today both are considered part of the basic needs of members. Previously, culture and values dictated indifference to clothing styles, cosmetics, and all other symbols of conspicuous consumption. Members of both sexes were proud of their distinct kibbutz-style appearance. Objection to higher education was part of this culture: The *ideal* member was to be the self-made person who gained knowledge by studying on his or her own. Changes of attitude came with an altered cultural climate; currently, for instance, kibbutzim even supply cosmetics to their women members and in such a high level of service that many customers for this service come from outside.

One expression of the dynamic processes in the consumption domain is the changing meaning of equality. In the early years, equality meant to be alike or to have the same; today equality is expressed in the equal right to be different. Members may equip their homes according to their taste and use their free time for hobbies; many of them collect books, records, and stamps, and in some kibbutzim, these activities are financially supported by the community. Improved economic conditions have enhanced the ability of kibbutzim to cater to individual needs, and the list of socially legitimated needs is constantly expanding. Still, the overall size of the kibbutz budget restricts full implementation of the principle of "to each according to his or her needs."

THE DISTRIBUTION SYSTEM: ECONOMY VERSUS VALUE STRUCTURE

Scarcity of resources has always had a decisive impact on the extent to which needs can be provided for. Kibbutzim have had to find methods of distribution which regulate or limit individual wants by fitting them to the economic capability of the collective and to its order of priorities. While it was easy to satisfy the humble needs of members in the pioneering days, the growing affluence and the possible decline of the ascetic spirit have put great strain on the system. Two questions need to be answered:

1. How can the kibbutz combine all of the divergent consumption preferences of individual members into one satisfying policy? Is it possible to create a mutually agreed upon communal basket of needs?

2. How can the kibbutz respond institutionally to the widening spectrum of individual wants?

Diverse methods for goods and services distribution and for budget allocation have been suggested and experimented with in an attempt to answer these questions. These methods may be classified into four categories: (1) distribution according to needs; (2) distribution of free goods; (3) distribution according to ascribed criteria (e.g., seniority, age, size of family, etc.); and (4) rationed or budgeted items. Table 10.2 illustrates how consumption budgets in a typical kibbutz are represented by each of these four methods.

Distribution According to Needs

If the basic value to each according to his or her needs cannot be fully implemented, constant effort (within the constraints of reality and of policy) is made to approximate it. Expenditure for food, for example, is budgeted by the economic committee. Within this budget, the kitchen coordinator sets the standard, but once food has been prepared, there is no restriction as far as quantity is concerned; everyone can eat according to needs. Special dishes are prepared for those who suffer from ill health, for those on special diets, or for vegetarians. Self-service was introduced in the 1970s, offering a choice of dishes and catering even more to individual tastes.

One of the best illustrations of the transformation of needs from the communal domain to the family is the *four o'clock tea*. This was once served in the communal dining hall, but later it became a sort of family rite, and this change, in turn, introduced the kitchenette and (since the 1960s) the kitchen into the family home. Food items to be consumed at home are provided by the communal kitchen or become budgeted items which are at the discretion of the family. (A recent innovation in about a third of the kibbutzim is the transfer of all food costs to the budgeted system—see the Getz chapter. Members pay for meals consumed in the dining hall or purchase them elsewhere.)

Health and education needs are fully catered to: Health services are provided for all without restriction of budget; and if parents or educators so request, children may get additional tutoring in any academic subject. Other expressions of individual-need satisfaction lie in the personal domain. The members committee, for instance, has at its discretion a budget allocation to respond to exceptional and unforeseen needs of members—requests for money to support relatives outside the kibbutz or expenses due to family festivities or to bereavements. Another expression is the care given to older members. With the number of aged or disabled members growing in most kibbutzim, attention to their special needs involves substantial investment and maintenance costs.

Distribution of Free Goods

The choice and quality of consumer goods which fall under this category are limited and are determined by the amount of budget allocated by the community.

Table 10.2
A Sample of Consumption Fields and the Most Common Systems of Distribution
Applied to Them

Area of Consumption	Institution in Charge	System of Distribution
Food	Kitchen coordinator	Free quantity, choice of dishes
Education	Education committee	Free for every child
Clothing	Clothing store coordinator	Free work clothes, rationed after-work clothes
Kibbutz store	Store coordinator	Home maintenance, toilet articles, sweets and drinks, etc; some free, others rationed
Cultural needs	Cultural committee	Festivities, cultural activities, newspapers free; theater and concert tickets rationed
Housing	Housing committee	Allocation of new homes by seniority preferences or point scale system; rationed budget
Furniture & appliances	Housing or members' committee	Point scale system, rationed budget
Health services	Health committee, nurses	Free without restriction
Tobacco	Kibbutz store	Very different systems, from free to rationed
Vacations	Members' committee	Usually fourteen days, six days in a holiday resort
Travel abroad	Members' committee	Seniority preference list
Higher education	Higher education committee	Free to everyone but on a waiting list
Arts and hobbies	Cultural committee	Public facilities, individual needs supported
Special individual needs	Members' committee	Each case dealt with individually

The range of articles varies from kibbutz to kibbutz. It may include food items for home consumption (e.g., sugar, tea, eggs, fruit, milk, etc.); home maintenance items; and toilet articles. Postage, telephone service, and bus tickets are also free in most kibbutzim. Generally, this category includes articles for which free distribution will not increase demand (for example, toothpaste or even the dentist's services—no one would want his or her teeth repaired more than needed just because it was free). However, since the onset of the economic crisis (mid-1980s), many kibbutzim have moved items of this kind to the budgeted list.

Distribution According to Ascribed Criteria

Distribution according to ascribed criteria was introduced only because of economic constraints: No kibbutz could afford to provide all its members at once with, for example, houses or apartments of equal standard nor to furnish them with all the modern appliances of an affluent society. Usually, when a new standard of apartment or a new appliance was approved, within a few years, the kibbutz made provision of it to all the members. Priority was based either on seniority of membership or on a priority scale in which such factors as seniority, family size, health considerations, and age were weighted.

During the years of economic scarcity, the priority allocation method (based mainly on membership seniority) was generally adopted for determining distribution of major consumer goods, but its use diminished in the 1970s due to the relative affluence experienced by the kibbutzim. Durable goods (television sets, refrigera tors, airconditioners, furniture, etc.) became available without a need for gradual distribution; and new houses were built for younger families concurrently with the renovation of veterans' apartments to bring them up to new standards.

The introduction of a new need may be illustrated by the allocation of a budget for overseas tourism and visits abroad. At first, visiting or traveling abroad was an unrecognized consumer item; hence no budget was allocated for it. A special decision was needed when a member had to visit an overseas relative or travel to fulfill kibbutz duties. Starting in the late 1960s, however, mostly as a result of the intensive introduction of industry into kibbutzim and its dependence on markets and suppliers abroad, more and more members were required to make overseas business trips. This created a feeling of inequality among members who were not in a position to travel. To deal with this inequality, a new need was legitimated: the recognition of vacations and touring overseas. Due to economic constraints, this need was given a low budget by the federation, and waiting lists based on some criteria had to be introduced. The long (sometimes lifetime-long) lists caused dissatisfaction and social tension. New methods of budget allocation for overseas visits had to be found. The problem was considerably alleviated when the waiting list was replaced by a relatively small yearly allowance introduced into the family budget, enabling the family to decide upon its expense preferences within the limits of its budget. The family now has a substantial yearly budget at its disposal.

Rationed or Budgeted Items

If equality is defined as sameness or similarity and the yardstick of needs is used, no distinctive treatment of an individual member or for goods considered a luxury can be justified. Examples of goods in this category are cash, casual clothing, cosmetics, home appliances, furniture, and the annual vacation budget. Despite the fact that all the needs included in this category accounted in the 1970s for no more than 20 to 25 percent of the overall consumption budget, most of the debates and ideological disputes have been focused here. The principle of rationed distribution for consumer goods has, over the years, been achieved through a variety of methods, reflecting changing views of what is equality and what are legitimate individual needs of members.

Normative Distribution. Historically, the first method of distribution within this category was called *normative*. As mentioned, the original method in this category was that everyone got the same. However, once conditions allowed a recognition of a diversity of needs among members, another method became dominant: A basket of alternative consumer goods of the same kind (e.g., clothing, shoes, soft furniture, etc.), but costing a similar amount of money, was worked out by the community. This "basket" was provided to every member, and individuals could consume at the same cost yet express their individual tastes and preferences. This system prevailed till the late 1960s (for some items and in some kibbutzim much longer). The yearly allocated list might be two sets of bedclothes, four towels, two casual dresses, four socks, and underwear. Two arguments have been raised against this method:

1. It is wasteful, because members are provided with items they may not need, whereas they may be in need of other goods. If member A wanted books and member B wanted records, the principle of equality demanded that both members be given records as well as books.

2. It creates dependence on the judgment of the coordinator of the area and on his or her preferences; hence individual wants, tastes, and preferences are inadequately satisfied. A coordinator may purchase goods that satisfy his or her own taste and budget constraints but that do not appeal to the taste of another part of the membership.

Conversely, from the perspective of preserving kibbutz values of equality, this system has been considered as the best because it avoids the translation of needs into money; it also safeguards the collective nature of need provision. It is the duty of the collective to cater to members' needs; by replacing needs with money, the institution relieves itself of that responsibility.

Personal Budget. The next stage in the evolution of the category of budgeted goods was the *personal budget*. For items included in the normative distribution, an equal budget was allocated for the discretionary use of the family. Within that budget, family members were free to purchase goods—in the kibbutz or outside in the towns. The main feature of this system was its restriction: the budget allocated for a particular kind of goods could not be transferred to another kind (for example, vacation money could not be used for clothing, and everyone got vacation money). Only the cash allowance could be used in any way and for any item of consumption.

Most kibbutzim included the same four to six items in the *personal budget* allocated to the adult members of the family: casual clothing and shoes; home maintenance items; furnishings for the house; vacation expenses (this particular expense was included in only a few kibbutzim); and a cash allowance to enable visits outside the kibbutz.

The personal budget method, which prevailed in a large part of the kibbutz movement till the 1970s introduced three ideologically important changes over the previous method of *normative distribution*:

1. For the first time, the family—and not the member—became the unit of budget, and thus the family gained some economic functions while before it had none.

2. For the first time, needs were translated into money terms; thus—from a normative point of view—a mechanical equality replaced the previous principle of qualitative equality.

3. Money could be saved by families, enabling the purchase of consumer goods not included in the legitimate consumption basket.

At the same time, the personal budget granted much more freedom of choice (within the limitations of the budget), and unlike earlier methods, it freed members from dependence on kibbutz institutions and officeholders.

The Inclusive Budget. A new method of consumer-goods distribution—called the *inclusive budget*—was introduced in the late 1960s by one kibbutz federation (Ichud), and it penetrated into some kibbutzim of other federations as well. In this method the boundaries of the different areas of consumption were removed, and the family was credited with an annual budget covering clothing, purchases in kibbutz shops, cash, furniture, other housing items, and, in some kibbutzim, annual vacation expenses as well. Given the credit, the family might use it for any legitimate need—for example, lowering its clothing expenses and increasing its consumption of durable goods. About 20 to 25 percent of the overall consumption expenditure was thus transferred to the sole discretion of the family, while the rest of the consumption budget was still spent under the other categories of consumption distribution.

Long and harsh ideological disputes preceded and followed the introduction of the *inclusive budget*. Supporters of this method argued that it brought the family nearer to the original concept of according to needs by offering the family freedom of decision. They also claimed that the method helped improve relationships between members and formal kibbutz institutions. Opponents argued that the method (1) removed collective responsibility by replacing it with a semisalary system; (2) led to inequalities between members by granting advantages to those better able to manage their resources; and (3) replaced kibbutz responsibility for satisfying the "true needs" of members with the responsibility for satisfying their exchange value needs (to borrow another Marxist concept), thereby eradicating the unique consumption pattern of the kibbutz.

∼

In the debates over the merits and drawbacks of the various distribution methods, it was felt that research might come up with answers. However, research conducted in 1978 found no difference in the level of member satisfaction between kibbutzim which utilized the *personal budget* method and kibbutzim which utilized the *inclusive budget* method (Rosner et al., 1979). But whatever the argument, the *inclusive budget* became an expression of the growing emphasis on individualization of need satisfaction and on orientation to the family over the community in matters of consumption.

As the debate intensified, alternatives were sought. The Artzi federation, which had previously passed a resolution against the adoption of the *inclusive budget* method in its kibbutzim, chose to counter the trend of the enlarged budget by increasing dramatically the part of the consumption budget distributed under the category of *free distribution*. This alternative (free distribution rather than the comprehensive family budget) advocated gradual extension of freely distributed items by lifting restrictions on quality and quantity. Although during the 1970s and early 1980s, this was the alternative chiefly adopted by kibbutzim of the Artzi federation, the economic crisis of the late 1980s and the increasing individualistic trends among members worked decisively against it, and most kibbutzim abandoned it.

NEW TRENDS AND PRACTICES: THE COMPREHENSIVE FAMILY BUDGET

As discussed above, the introduction of new needs on the one hand and the greater amount of money that the family had at its disposal on the other raised the question: Is the kibbutz not moving in the direction of a salary system? It seems that, partly as a result of the economic crisis of the 1980s and partly as a result of the move toward the family, a new method—called the comprehensive budget—is being adopted by more and more kibbutzim. The comprehensive budget (*Takziv Makif*) permits about 50 percent of the annual consumption expense to be allocated to the family, and even more in some kibbutzim. Today, 75 percent of kibbutzim practice the new method; in another 13 percent of kibbutzim, proposals in this direction are being tabled in the general assembly.

The direction of change in consumption is toward privatization, the transferring of budgets to the family. By this transfer, the community relinquishes public responsibility for need satisfaction and instead grants the family increased spending freedom. At the same time, welfare remains within the domain of the collective. Child education, health services and expenses, care for the disabled and veteran members, municipal services, and cultural and festive activities are still public— that is, outside of the family budget.

Is the kibbutz collective consumption achieving now a new and more individualistic balance? Will the trend to privatization bring about the erosion of the kibbutz's uniqueness? Recent research (Getz, 1994) shows some slowing down in the introduction of changes. At present, collective consumption is in a state of flux, and there is no apparent agreement in ideology. Time will tell whether changes result in the crystallization of a new, more balanced consumption system or in the erosion of the kibbutz's basic principle: "To each according to his or her needs; from each according to his or her ability."

11
Aging—The Kibbutz Experience

Uriel Leviatan

SUDDEN AGING OF THE KIBBUTZ MEMBERSHIP

Currently, the aging phenomenon represents an important experience in all the older kibbutzim. In some of them, the percentage of members over the ages of sixty and seventy may reach 25 percent or even 30 percent of the adult membership, (while it is only about 17 percent of the total adult Jewish population in Israel). Nevertheless, despite the background of knowledge about aging, and despite awareness of the problems that accompany aging in the larger society, the kibbutzim were ill prepared when they were suddenly confronted by this phenomenon.

It happened suddenly because, twenty years earlier, the kibbutz society did not recognize the face of aging. It did not have any elderly among its members. The transformation is illustrated in Table 11.1.

Until the mid-1960s, only a small fraction of the kibbutz population had reached the age of sixty-five (0.3 percent), while in the general Jewish population there were already about 6.5 percent in this age group. The difference from the larger population diminished as the years passed, but it was not until 1980 that the percentage of aged kibbutz members became significant and started to approach that of the general Jewish population (5.3 percent compared to 9.7 percent). The difference between the two populations continued to diminish so that now they are almost the same. In fact, the very old group (seventy-five years or older) in kibbutzim comprises already a larger percentage of the population than the comparable group in the general Jewish population (in 1993, 5.3 percent compared to 4.3 percent).

These data underline the suddenness and the intensity of the recent aging of kibbutz society. However, inspecting the data of the total kibbutz population hinders one from seeing the even more significant aging process that has occurred in the older kibbutzim. For instance, consider in Table 11.2 the difference in

Table 11.1
Kibbutz Members and Israeli Jews Aged Sixty-Five Years or Older (Percentages in Selected Years)

	Age 65 and Older as Percent of Population	
Year	*Jews in Israel*	*Kibbutz Population**
1948	3.9%	NA
1960	5.2%	NA
1965 (census)	6.5%	0.3% (1.8%)
1970	7.2%	NA
1972 (census)	7.7%	1.7% (3.2%)
1975	8.7%	2.4% (3.9%)
1980	9.7%	5.3% (6.8%)
1985	10.0%	6.7% (8.2%)
1990	10.4%	10.2 % (11.7%)
1993	10.8%	10.4% (11.9%)

* The figures for the kibbutz population first appeared in the statistical abstracts after the census of 1965, supplement, 1967). These figures report all residents of kibbutzim (rather than the membership and their offspring). As a result, they include parents of members who are not members themselves and who came to the kibbutzim in their retirement. There are no annual figures about the numbers of those parents (who are usually of the aged sixty-five and older); but from the data available, we may estimate their numbers to be about 2.5 percent of the kibbutz membership population (Atar, 1983), which is roughly 1.5 percent of the total kibbutz population. The entries in parenthesis on the right give the total percentage of aged people in kibbutzim, while the smaller numbers of the kibbutz percentages are corrected, without the parents.

Sources: Central Bureau of Statistics, Annual Reports 1954, 1961, 1966, 1971, 1976, 1981, 1986, 1987, 1991, 1994; Supplement 1967, 18(5); Supplement 1975, 26(12).

Table 11.2
Percentages of Kibbutz Members Aged Sixty-Five Years and Older (in 1978) in Kibbutzim That Settled in Differing Periods

Group of Kibbutzim	Period of Settlement	Age 65 and Older as Percent of Kibbutz Members
A	1910–1929	12.6%
B	1930–1935	8.3%
C	1935–1944	2.8%
D	1945–1948	0.3%
E	1949–1978	0.0%

percentages of members aged 65 or older between kibbutzim that were established at different periods.

In kibbutzim that were established before 1929, the mean percentage of those aged sixty-five or older was already (in 1978) 12.6 percent as against 4.8 percent in the total kibbutz population. At the same time, kibbutzim that were established ten to twenty years later had only 2.8 percent of their membership in the sixty-five-or-older group. This grading of groups of kibbutzim according to their percentages of aged members represents the increase in percentages of aged members in individual kibbutzim along the progress of time from their establishment.

Are we then witnessing a demographic miracle? Is it not true that people get older every year by exactly one year only? What are the reasons for these demographic "jumps" in the kibbutz society? In point of fact, these jumps are the outcomes of historic events—some planned by the founders of the kibbutz movement, others beyond their control.

Most of the older kibbutzim were established during the 1920s and 1930s. The founding bodies were large groups of young people, all in their late teens or early twenties. Thus, as long as the founders themselves had not reached an advanced age, the only aged individuals in the kibbutzim were a few parents of members who came to live with their children (Talmon-Garber, 1972). This explains why the phenomenon of aging was not part of kibbutz demography until the late 1950s. It also explains why, to this date, aging is still unknown in the kibbutzim that settled since the 1950s.

Two additional factors, however, explain why the veterans of a kibbutz, upon reaching old age, suddenly form such a large, and what seems to be disproportionate, segment of their particular kibbutz population.

The first is the outcome of settlement policies of the kibbutz movement during the 1940s and the 1950s. The kibbutz movement adopted an approach that favored the placement of young recruits in new kibbutzim—rather than using them as reinforcements for the older. This policy created a lack of age continuity in the older kibbutzim because there were no age groups between the founders' cohort and the generation of their first children.

The second factor stemmed from the Holocaust of the Jewish people in World War ll. More than one hundred thousand graduates of the kibbutz youth movements were among the six million Jews annihilated during that period. These young people had been earmarked to join the kibbutzim in Israel (Palestine, at that time) and to serve as reinforcements for the older kibbutzim. Thus, the annihilation of this cohort formed a demographic void in each kibbutz—a void of twenty to twenty-five years that separates the founders from their children.

The phenomenon of the demographic void is so common in the age distribution of the kibbutzim that it has become one of their characteristics. It appears in kibbutzim of all ages, although its place on the age distribution in each kibbutz is a function of the years since each kibbutz's establishment. Currently, in the oldest kibbutzim the demographic void appears between the ages of fifty-five and seventy-five, while in the youngest kibbutzim it appears between the ages of twenty-five and forty-five.

"Sudden aging" in a kibbutz happens when the founders cross the particular age line that denotes the elderly, be it sixty, sixty-five, or any other age.

READINESS TO DEAL WITH AGING PROBLEMS

The growing numbers of aged members in each of the older kibbutzim generated major problems associated with aging. As discussed, the "sudden" appearance of aging was responsible for the lack of awareness about aging problems and for the lack of preparation in dealing with them. However, preparation was also hindered by a psychological impediment—denial by members of the possibility of becoming old. Consider the following: It was not until 1966 that the kibbutz federations institutionalized a department at a movement level to deal with the problem of aging. This action was tardy—because most older kibbutzim had been established bwtween 1910 and 1920, and their founders had reached the age of sixty-five in the 1950s. Moreover, many of the older kibbutzim did not start their own *committees for the elderly* until the late 1970s and early 1980s. Finally, the first large-scale research on aging commissioned by the kibbutz movement (upon which much of this chapter is based) dates back only to 1979–80.

No doubt, the demographics of the kibbutz population played an important role in fostering denial toward aging. However, other factors were also responsible. One of these had to do with the psychology of the founding generation of kibbutzim: their refusal to accept facts of life, their denying the marks of time. The following anecdote illustrates this attitude. One of the veteran kibbutzim whose aged members (sixty-five to seventy) were to participate in a study on aging wanted to discuss the study prior to its start. They invited the researchers to a meeting that took place in the cultural club, and most of the founding group were present. After the researchers described the objectives of the study and the way they planned to execute it, a discussion developed. The major discussion point among the members was an expression of wonder about the researchers' decision to study their particular kibbutz. "We do not have any aging problems," they argued. "In fact, we still have no aged members. We do, however, have other social problems, and you are welcome to study them. But why invent something that doesn't exist?"

Such an attitude of denial stems from two causes. First, the founding generation grew up far away from their parents (who stayed in Europe and most of whom perished during the Holocaust of World War II). As a result, the founders never had the opportunity to observe in any personal way aging itself or living models of aged individuals. The absence of such personal models prevented kibbutz members from developing realistic expectations about the process of aging and its results. It also prevented them from envisioning behaviors appropriate for the time of becoming old.

Second, then there was the ideology of youth idolization. This had served as a central educational theme when the youthful founders created their value system. And is it just a random occurrence that all the social movements which became the sources for kibbutz membership bore the adjective "young" in their titles—the Young Guard, the Young Pioneer, the Young Worker, the Young Maccabee, the

Young Judea? Individuals who steadfastly view themselves as young would have a hard time changing their self-image to the "old guards" or the "old pioneers."

UNIQUENESS OF PROBLEMS IN KIBBUTZ AGING

The kibbutz value system and its distinctive principles of organization created unique problems of aging that called for unique solutions, even when those problems were similar to those in the surrounding society. Here are some instances. The kibbutz elderly, like other elderly, experience significant deterioration in their sensory-motor systems and a proliferation of health problems. Intellectual functions change their patterns similar to the way they change for other aged. Major changes occur in the family, as the role of *parent* transforms into the role of *grandparent* and as the *family nest* becomes an *empty nest*. Older kibbutz members experience widowhood and bereavement with all its grave personal implications. Even the very status that they occupy within their communities is a topic of concern for the kibbutz elderly, as it is for those in other parts of industrial society.

Yet the seemingly strong similarity of the problems of the aged on the kibbutz with those of other aged is, in fact, superficial. In medical care, for example, sickness treatments would seem the same on the kibbutz as in the rest of industrial society. Yet even here, differences exist. Based on kibbutz principles of conduct, the responsibility for medical care is shifted from the individual (and his or her family) to the community. It is the responsibility of the local medical team to ensure that everyone gets the highest level of medical attention that the kibbutz can offer its members, including those who fail to seek medical advice on their own initiative.

Another example is the right of every member to a work activity within the economic framework of his or her kibbutz. This right endures throughout life and confronts the kibbutz with the need to create appropriate jobs for people over the age of sixty-five—a goal never addressed heretofore in the industrial world.

Likewise, the kibbutz holds it to be the right of every member of any age to participate in the cultural, social, and political domains of kibbutz life. This last obligation forces the kibbutz to find ways through which three, sometimes four, generations of adults can successfully function together within one community. Furthermore, the kibbutz community is committed to support its members in any way possible in times of need. To express such support, a kibbutz may take on roles that are traditionally regarded as the sole domain of the family—as, for example, in times of personal crisis such as bereavement and sickness.

Kibbutz society presents a unique combination of a modern industrial community mixed with traditional characteristics of family life. It is, perhaps, the only instance of an industrial society where three, sometimes four, adult generations of the same family reside in the same "home" (kibbutz). This provides opportunities for daily encounters and for intensive and frequent interactions in most realms of life: work, leisure, public life, personal treatment, and family.

All these examples illustrate that although the kibbutz setting offers many opportunities for successful aging, it also creates special challenges. Has it stood up to these challenges? The next sections of this chapter seek to answer this question.

Findings and conclusions reported here for the period of the 1980s result from a large-scale research project conducted by the author and his associates. Current findings come from more-recent studies.

LIFE EXPECTANCY AND MORTALITY RATES

Findings from studies on aging in kibbutzim strongly support the conclusion that kibbutz society has successfully stood up to the challenges of aging among its members. This is attested to first and foremost by the most robust indicators of survival: life expectancy (LE) and mortality rates at older ages.

But first, is longevity a true indicator of a successful life, of successful aging? Our cultural heritage is replete with expressions to the contrary. Take, for instance, the viewpoint of the *moth* as envisioned by Marquis. He asks a moth why they "pull this stunt" of trying to break into electric light bulbs or candle flames. "Have you no sense?" he demands. The moth replies: "We get bored with routine and crave beauty and excitement. Fire is beautiful. We know that if we get too close the heat will kill us, but what does it matter? It is better to be happy for a moment and to be burned up with beauty than to live a long time and be bored all the while" (cited in Bennis and Nanus, 1985, 53–55).

An anecdote from my personal experience, dating back to my high school years, also illustrates support for the opinion of the moth. My class was led by a youth counselor into a heated philosophical debate about which is a more desirable choice, a short but meaningful life or a long, boring, uninteresting life. Young as we were, most of us argued for the former opinion, because, like the moth in Marquis's poem, we wanted rather "to be burned up with beauty than to live a long time and be bored." Or, as suggested by Walter Scott's words: "One glorious hour of crowded life is worth an age without a name."

It was not until I became, as an academic, interested in questions of quality of life and health that I realized what was wrong in that educational episode. The question itself was fallacious. Longevity as a result of good health can never be a function of low or negative quality of life. True, some short lives may be rich and fulfilling, but no long life is dull, insignificant, and boring, because it is the accumulation of positive experiences in one's life that fosters longevity and pro-motes survival. Thus, a society that boasts extended life expectancy for its members is demonstrating some sort of positive quality of life over other populations. Kibbutz society fulfills this criterion.

Earlier I indicated that the proportion of the kibbutz population of seventy five years of age or older already exceeded that of the general Jewish population—5.1 percent versus 4.4 percent in 1990 and 5.3 percent versus 4.3 percent in 1993. These statistics are the first indicator of the relative longevity of the kibbutz population. But more direct evidence is available. Analyzing demographic data for the years 1974–1981, and calculating LE for the mean year of 1977, I and my coresearchers (Leviatan, Cohen, and Yafa-Katz, 1983, 1986) discovered that LE of the kibbutz population was considerably higher than that of the Jewish population in Israel (in 1977). Indeed, it was among the highest of the societies for which the United

Nations' demographic yearbook reports data. LE at birth was 79.0 years for kibbutz females and 74.4 years for kibbutz males (compared to 75.4 years for females and 71.9 years for males for the Jewish population in Israel). At age fifty, the LE was 31.0 years for kibbutz females and 28.3 years for kibbutz males, while for the general populations of Jews it was 31.0 years for females and 25.7 years for males. Similar numbers show in an updated study for the years 1981–1987: In 1984 LE at birth for the kibbutz population was 81.3 years for females and 76.7 years for males, while the comparable LE for the Jewish population for 1984 was 77.1 years for females and 73.5 years for males. At age fifty, the LE was 33.4 years for kibbutz females and 29.6 years for kibbutz males (compared to 29.2 and 26.5 years in the general population).

The significance of these comparisons should be considered against the historical pattern of LE trends. Since 1900, the LE at birth of most western societies has increased by about three months every year (thus raising it from about 40 years to about 78 years by 1990). This increase of LE over the years is a reflection of the improvement in life conditions and in quality of life in general. Applying this rate of progression in LE to the difference in LE between the kibbutz population and the Jewish population in Israel (i.e., more than three years) translates into twelve years of difference between the two populations in quality of life that contributes to this linear progression in LE. In other words, if whatever contributes to LE continues to develop favorably at the same rate as it did in previous years, the Jewish population of Israel would, about twelve years hence, reach the LE enjoyed now by the kibbutz population.

However, an index of LE by itself is too general. It does not show at what ages there occur the chief positive experiences that elevate the probability of survival of the kibbutz population. A remedy for this shortcoming is to be found in the gender-by-age specific mortality rates of the kibbutz population. I and my associates (Leviatan, Cohen, and Yafa-Katz, 1986) calculated these rates and compared them with those of the general population. Our conclusions follow.

First, infant mortality on the kibbutz is considerably lower than that in the general Jewish population. This sign of better medical services available to the kibbutz population is probably an important contributor to longevity. However, contribution to LE by the lower infant mortality was negligible—only three months.

Second, our data show that death rates of males aged fifteen to fifty were actually higher for the kibbutz population. Military service is a probable cause: Kibbutz men in the military serve in disproportionate numbers in combat units and in officer positions, the very positions which are most prone to danger in battle. This fact lowers the level of LE for kibbutz males.

Third, the most important conclusion relates to the age group fifty years and older. Starting at that age for males and earlier for females, the mortality rates of the kibbutz population are significantly lower than those of the general population. The kibbutz mortality rates are only two-thirds to one-half of those in the comparable age and gender groups of the general population. Our findings are for the year 1977. A more recent check of similar data for the year 1984 (seven years after the first collection of data) corroborates the former findings: The kibbutz mortality rates at the ages of fifty and older were again only two-thirds to one-half of the respective mortality rates of the comparable age and gender groups.

Fourth, another conclusion we reached was that these findings of successful aging on the kibbutz could not be attributed to self-selection or to personal characteristics of the kibbutz aged. Instead, environmental conditions and social arrangements on kibbutz communities were cited as major causes. Description and analyses of these conditions and arrangements form the focus of the next section.

ENVIRONMENTAL CONDITIONS AND SOCIAL ARRANGEMENTS THAT LEAD TO SUCCESSFUL AGING

I list first societal and environmental conditions and social arrangements of kibbutz life that appear to be responsible for the lower mortality rates among aged kibbutz members but for which no validating research is yet available. There is, however, strong support in general research on aging for the positive influence of these conditions and arrangements on the well-being of the elderly and on their survival.

First, the relative stability experienced by the kibbutz elderly in most central roles of life is one such influence. It differentiates aging on kibbutzim from the aging of most other populations in the industrial world. This stability exists in the domains of work, standard of living, social relationships, social involvement in the community, social composition of the neighborhood, housing, and family interaction. Other elderly usually experience major changes of their roles in these domains— changes that contribute to major deterioration in their well-being and in their physical and mental health. There follow several examples of the ways through which this stability in roles is achieved on the kibbutz.

While most aged members of industrial society cease to work on reaching a certain age (usually sixty-five), there is no compulsory retirement from work on the kibbutz. There exists, however, the provision for a gradual reduction in number of working hours per workday and number of workdays per year. As a result, all aged members continue to be part of the work force of the kibbutzim as long as they are physically and mentally fit to participate. Statistics show that in 1993, 79 percent of the kibbutz population aged sixty-five years or older (both males and females) held jobs in the kibbutz labor market, while this was true for only 18 percent of males and 6 percent of females in the Jewish population of Israel. (Differences for the thirty-five to fifty-four age group were much smaller: 97 percent for both males and females on the kibbutz and 90 percent for males and 71 percent for females in the general population.)

Once retired, many aged city people move to other neighborhoods. This may result from a decrease in income, a wish to be closer to family, or for other reasons. Kibbutz elderly, on the other hand, stay in the same community throughout their lives, thereby ensuring continuous relationships with their friends and involvement within a community that is both known to them and knowledgeable about them.

An adjunct of retirement and aging in industrial society is a substantial reduction in income and a subsequent decrease in standard of living. Again, this is not so for the kibbutz aged. Kibbutz society adheres to the principle of supplying the needs of individuals irrespective of their contributions. As a result, aged members enjoy the same standard of living as younger members.

Staying on the same kibbutz throughout their lives as full-fledged members in a self-governed community keeps the kibbutz elderly involved and in control of their lives. This is in contrast to many other elderly, who are, in their retirement, relegated to the status of second-class citizens in their community and in society at large.

Research (Am-Ad, 1985) shows that 65 percent of the kibbutz elderly have at least one adult son or daughter living in the same kibbutz with them—which means, in fact, within the same household. This ensures for the elderly almost daily contact with their children and their grandchildren. It ensures also the security of having the family nearby in case of need. It also allows for the experience of going through life's symbols and passages (holidays, celebrations, stations in the life cycle) in the presence of an extended family. Such experience is very different from the common lot of the elderly in the industrial world. For there, even if they talk to or meet their offspring on a regular basis, it is for visitations only and not as part of the regular, daily schedule.

Second, quality of medical care and the rural surroundings are other factors in kibbutz life that contribute to the lower mortality rates of its elderly members. Not only is the medical care among the best available in the country, but also the responsibility for members' health is at hand in the kibbutz medical institutions. The rural environment contributes to health by its positive ecology and by reducing risks to health and to life such as population density, congested traffic, and random violence against the aged.

Finally, an additional factor is the relative absence among kibbutz members of the stress and the strain experienced by members of most other industrial societies—from economic competition, lack of control over one's life, alienation at work, and the pressure to achieve. Kibbutz elderly also enjoy complete economic security for themselves and for their families.

SOME RESEARCH FINDINGS

The previous section presented hypotheses not yet substantiated by research findings. In what follows I present other factors that contribute to the well-being of the kibbutz elderly and that have been substantiated by research. The following reports bear on four topics: reduction of the intergender gap in life expectancy; centrality of work in determining life satisfaction; importance and availability of social support from the community; and the priority of social arrangements over personal characteristics in determining success in the aging experience.

Intergender Differences in LE

The same data that produced the findings about the LE of kibbutz members were analyzed for comparison between genders (Leviatan and Cohen-Mansfield, 1985). Results were quite different from those of similar analyses in other societies. The intergender difference in LE for the kibbutz population was much smaller than expected—the smallest (relative to the LE of the population) intergender gap compared to data from seventy-three different societies for which the United Nations' reports on age- and sex-specific death rates. Furthermore, the results showed that it was the kibbutz men who gained most from this reduction in the intergender difference in LE.

The reduction was even more singular at age fifty years and older. We interpreted these findings as resulting from the intergender similarity of roles in work and in the community among kibbutz members, similarity that is greater than in other populations. This similarity leads to stronger empathy between husband and wife —a higher probability of knowledge of, and identification with, one's spouse's roles and environment—which fosters more support for the spouse and, in turn, contributes to well-being and to survival. Recent focused research on this topic supports our interpretation: spouses whose jobs are similar exhibit greater empathy and stronger social support for each other.

Work as an Important Contributor to Life Satisfaction

In studies of industrial society, the recurrent finding is that work ceases to be important for the elderly (e.g., Larson, 1978). Health, family, socioeconomic status, and social activity become the domains that are most important. Our research on the kibbutz (Leviatan, 1981, 1985) confutes such conclusions. Work came out as the most important domain even for members who were older than sixty-five years. (This finding applied especially to men. Among elderly women, *family* was the most important domain, and *work* took second place.)

Because the work domain is of such importance, it exercises a strong influence upon the well-being and upon the general functioning of the aged on the kibbutz. In short, success in solving the work-related needs of the elderly represents an important contribution to success in the whole aging experience.

Research has also shown that kibbutz elderly experience frequent readjustment in their work role by moving to other occupations and activities more befitting their changing capabilities and sensory-motor functions. For instance, one research project found that the average member aged sixty-five years had experienced seven different occupations in his or her life on a kibbutz and three different central public offices. Such flexibility allows for better adjustment to the work role and assures the aged person of a work role that is fitting to his or her changing skills, aptitudes, and interests. Indeed, kibbutzim have created jobs and invested in industrial and service businesses that have as their major criterion appropriate jobs for their elderly.

Two other findings support the importance of a work role for the elderly. First, although kibbutz resolutions stipulate that, at age seventy, work becomes optional, none of a sample of about four hundred elderly members had chosen this option for himself or herself, and only a minority supported the idea as a desirable policy. Second, a follow-up in 1990 of the sample of elderly from the 1979–80 study demonstrated the importance of positive work experiences for aged individuals. It showed a more positive work experience (in the past) for the survivors than for those who had died during the eleven-year interval between the two points of data collection.

Community as a Compensating Support-Giver to the Single Elderly

Kibbutz data (Leviatan, 1988) do not show any difference in death rates between married and single aged individuals—in contrast to findings in the national statistics of industrial societies, where the single elderly have mortality rates up to twice as high as the married elderly. Research (House, Kessler, and Herzog, 1990) suggests that the reason for this difference between married and single elderly in mortality rates stems from the social support given to the married by their spouse.

Our explanation for the lack of difference in death rates between singles and married among kibbutz elderly is that, for singles, the community takes on the role of the missing spouse. Those who do not have a spouse (bachelors, the widowed, or the divorced) receive from members of their community support in all its expressions—direct help, acceptance, emotional support, and a source in which to confide. Various individuals in the kibbutz community offer social support; some are officers of the community, while others are friends and neighbors. As a result, the support for single elderly is similar to that enjoyed by the married elderly.

In general, kibbutz elderly report high levels of community support and positive social relationships. For instance, about 95 percent indicate there is always someone (not a family member) to help them in time of need. It is, therefore, likely that this social environment contributes to higher LE and lower mortality rates.

Priority of Social Arrangements over Personality Characteristics

Which factors are more important in contributing to the well-being of the aged on the kibbutz? Are they mostly expressions of personal characteristics or the results of the societal arrangements that the community offers to its elderly? An answer to this question is important because it also determines whether any of the social arrangements of the kibbutzim might usefully be transferred to other segments of the industrial world—which could perhaps emulate societal arrangements but could hardly emulate personality characteristics.

Research shows that benefits are mostly due to the societal arrangements. One research study (Leviatan, Adar, and Am-Ad, 1981) compared two groups of kibbutzim known a priori to differ in their success at solving aging problems. As anticipated, results showed that samples of aged members in these two groups of kibbutzim differed in their level of well-being. However, while the samples did not differ in any of the personal characteristics that the study investigated, they differed significantly in variables denoting social arrangements in their communities. The more successful kibbutzim had, for instance, institutionalized *gerontology committees*; they enjoyed better intergenerational relations; they had greater elderly involvement in the kibbutz public life; their members had more opportunities for "pleasant" meetings with other members. An analysis of time-use for the two groups revealed the more successful group to spend twice as much time as the other group in organized member activities. Members from the less successful group noted a lack of organized activity for the veteran members and reported having more leisure and more idle time.

EFFECTS OF THE CURRENT CHANGES IN KIBBUTZIM

Kibbutz social arrangements and ways of dealing with aging have traditionally been based on principles and values of solidarity and communality. As the research summarized and reported here suggests, these arrangements have proved to be successful both for the aged individuals themselves and for their communities.

Professed changes in kibbutz societal arrangements (see the chapter by Getz) are based, at least in part, upon individual and market values and principles (e.g., privatization of consumption budgets and services; overriding priority put on the profit principle in any economic activity; no restrictions on the use of hired workers; and differential remuneration according to contribution or position).

When such changes are added together and consolidated, they present the vision of a society becoming more similar to other parts of the industrial world and abandoning the uniqueness of kibbutz communities. We should, therefore, expect effects upon the kibbutz elderly resulting in their life experience and aging outcomes becoming more similar to the rest of industrial society—in short, less positive than hitherto. Given the validity of the research reported in this chapter, both well-being and physical survival (longevity) should be adversely affected.

One major direction of the changes suggested is the privatization of public consumption budgets and services, with individuals receiving money based on "sameness" rather than needs. Under such arrangements, we should expect many kibbutz elderly to lose out in welfare and health services, because these services would then be allocated on the basis of "sameness," whereas needs for the elderly would always be greater.

Privatization of public budgets also means that the community sheds part of its responsibility for individual members. In the case of the elderly, this might be reflected in reductions in social support originating from office-holders; in organized leisure activities for the aged; and in the investment of resources for creating appropriate jobs for the elderly. Privatization would also result in a sharper differentiation in gender roles in the domains of work, family, and public activity (see Adar in this volume), leading to less empathy and less social support within the families.

Another direction of possible change—emphasis on considerations of economic effectiveness as an overriding priority—would put aged members at a disadvantage in job allocation appropriate to their changing capabilities. The lifting of restrictions on the employment of hired labor would make it more difficult for elderly members to be allocated jobs because decision makers would see it as economically more effective to use hired workers than older members who may have physical or other handicaps.

Changes such as these would surely lead to feelings of insecurity and a deep sense of frustration of a dream, a vision, the work of a lifetime gone sour—and, in turn, to a diminishment of well-being and mental health. Although these and similar changes are already observed in a very few kibbutzim, there is no assurance that they will not catch up with many or most or all kibbutzim. Indicative outcomes of the changes suggested here are in the expected direction, but no solid research is yet available. In fact, it is much too early to pass definitive judgment. And although it is true that such changes would substantially affect outcomes for the aging population of the kibbutzim, it would take some years for them to come about (assuming they ever do), and therefore the effects would be most pronounced on the aged of ten years hence and not on the current generation.

Our data show the aged members tend to oppose most strongly the suggested changes enumerated above and are the most content with their kibbutz life. It is the fifty-to-sixty age group that shows the least contention with their present kibbutz life, although, paradoxically, they are also in opposition to the suggested changes when compared to the younger groups (ages twenty-five to fifty). Table 11.3 brings some illustrative findings from recent (1991–1995) surveys conducted in about thirty-five kibbutzim. The table summarizes attitudes of the population, broken into age groups of five-year intervals, toward more privatization, differential remuneration, use of hired labor, and satisfaction with kibbutz life. Age groups sixty years or older are in the strongest opposition to each of the suggested changes. Yet these groups are the most satisfied with their kibbutz life. The age groups of fifty to fifty-four and fifty-five to fifty-nine are next in the level of their opposition to the suggested changes; however, their satisfaction with kibbutz life is the lowest of all age groups (50.0 and 49.7).

RELEVANCE AND TRANSFERABILITY OF THE KIBBUTZ EXPERIENCE

In this last section, I enumerate lessons from the experience of kibbutz elderly that might be transferable to the larger industrial society and discuss how the kibbutz communities could serve as learning grounds for solutions to aging problems in the larger society.

- Rotation of jobs and of public office holding is promoted on a lifelong basis, in contrast to the practice outside the kibbutz, where it is assumed that an occupation or profession chosen by a person at the age of twenty will also be the most appropriate for that person on reaching the age of sixty. The arrangement of job rotation also ensures that society will get the most from its aged members, because it results in a better fit between the constantly changing needs and capabilities of a person and the demands of his or her job activities.

- The continuation of work by older members at ages beyond the current retirement years should help in studying job characteristics most appropriate for older workers—a study that is becoming more urgent as compulsory retirement is abolished in an increasing number of industrialized societies.

Table 11.3
Reactions to Suggested Changes in Kibbutz Normative Principles by Different Age
Group

Group	Age	%/No.	Oppose Privatization in Consumption	Oppose Differentiality in Remuneration	Oppose Use of Hired Labor	Satisfied with Kibbutz Life
1	20–24	5.3/277	64.5	43.9	26.4	50.5
2	25–29	7.6/399	61.2	36.6	22.3	58.9
3	30–34	10.3/539	61.8	37.4	19.6	55.3
4	35–39	12.1/630	64.9	36.1	18.4	56.0
5	40–44	13.5/707	64.5	39.5	20.2	52.9
6	45–49	3.1/682	68.2	43.7	30.1	53.1
7	50–54	8.9/466	76.0	49.0	33.8	50.0
8	55–59	7.5/390	71.2	58.1	33.7	49.7
9	60–65	6.3/328	82.7	69.6	43.5	59.0
10	66–69	5.6/291	82.2	76.4	46.7	65.6
11	70–74	4.6/239	85.0	75.3	56.0	69.9
12	75–79	3.4/177	85.2	80.1	62.6	73.4
13	80+	1.8/93	85.5	91.3	61.9	80.6
Total		100/5218	69.1	49.7	31.0	56.4

- In the domain of family life (as noted previously), the kibbutz society presents a unique combination of a modern industrial community and a traditional society. This fact may help answer questions about the importance of the family for the aging person and for the rest of the family members. It should also shed light upon the role of the extended family in the context of aging in modern society.

- Aged members of the kibbutz society continue to be fully integrated in the public, cultural, and social lives of their mixed-age kibbutz communities. This allows for research into the effects of such integration upon the functioning of their community and upon the well-being of the aged members themselves. Such research could provide answers to such questions as should we strive for a mixture of generations or is it better that each cohort develops its own life-style and activities? Should residential areas of the aged be interwoven with those of younger cohorts or should they be encouraged to reside separately?

- A rare opportunity for learning would arise should the suggested changes in societal arrangements and in redefinition of kibbutz values and principles take widespread hold in kibbutzim. We should then have the same members living in utterly changed social circumstances, a situation that would allow for testing of the central thesis of this chapter—namely, how important are societal arrangements compared to personal characteristics in determining quality of aging and survival?

12
Inter-Kibbutz Organizations and Cooperatives

Daniel Rosolio

The 270 kibbutzim in Israel, with their population of approximately 126,000 (Maron, 1995, 68), are organized in a web of inter-kibbutz organizations—political, ideological, municipal, economic, and educational—on national and regional levels. The first national inter-kibbutz organizations to emerge were the kibbutz federations, which date back to the beginning of the kibbutzim in Palestine (during the early decades of the twentieth century) and which were linked to political parties and to the Labor Federation. The kibbutzim with the moshavim (cooperative rural settlements) also established national cooperatives to meet the needs of their farms. The inter-kibbutz organizations enabled small (often very small) rural settlements to join together in such a way that would allow them to realize their power, their interests, and their mission in the wider Jewish society—both prior to and since the establishment of the state of Israel in 1948.

In this chapter, I will describe the major inter-kibbutz organizations on the national and regional levels and will analyze the sociological aspects of these organizations and their influence on the everyday life of the kibbutzim. This analysis will include the process of change—namely, the decline of the national organizations and the rise of the regional organizations. The point I wish to make is that the power structure of the inter-kibbutz organizations is linked to the power structure in the environment—that is, to the power structure in the state of Israel. The decentralization of the power structure in Israel has led, of necessity, to a similar process in the inter-kibbutz organizations—because, by definition, there must be congruency between the bases of power and the levels of organization of interest groups or political organizations which are active in the political life of the nation and are also the agencies through which government resources are distributed.

KIBBUTZ SUPRA-ORGANIZATIONS: THEORETICAL APPROACH

The inter-kibbutz organization is an integral part of the kibbutz entity, and in order to understand the kibbutz and the processes in it, one must take into account the fact that the kibbutz is not only a community but also a combination of a culture and a community and a part of a supra-organization (Rosolio, 1993). We can see this kind of integration in the cooperative movement in general (Valko, 1985, 186; Daniel and Szeskin, 1973; Dulfer, 1985).

The shift of influence of inter-kibbutz organizations from the national to the regional level demonstrates this point. It is a result of the decentralization of the political power structure in Israel. In a symposium in 1974, I described the relationship between the kibbutz and moshav federations[1] and the government, stressing the central structure of political power at that time and the weakness of the regional political power structure. Twenty years later, Schwartz and others (1994) described the process of decentralization and the accumulation of power by the regional municipal organizations. Gradus (1986) argued that the pattern of power centralization, dominant in Israel since the second decade of the twentieth century, resulted from the need to mobilize all the resources of the Jewish community in Palestine to establish a Jewish state and, since 1948, to cope with the challenges faced by the political leadership and government. According to Gradus, a trend toward pluralism began developing in Israeli society in the 1970s when the direct need for a mission-oriented society was diminishing. One of the expressions of this process was the decentralization of the political power structure, leading in turn to the creation of two levels of inter-kibbutz organizations—national and regional (Rosolio, 1975).[2] The decline of the national inter-kibbutz organizations and the growth of the regional and municipal organizations, starting in the 1970s, is continuing.

Horowitz and Lissak (1977, 47–50) explored the origins of the Israeli polity. They referred to the fact that the Jewish self-governing organizations played a role (which they defined as secondary centers) in the relationship between the Jewish political community in Palestine and the British mandatory government, thus creating also the pattern of power relations within the Jewish society. In other words, the political parties, the Labor Federation, and the kibbutz and moshav federations acted within the Jewish society as secondary centers between the individual kibbutzim and moshavim and the government. Through these organizations, the government distributed resources, thereby creating a corporate relationship between the government and the fedeations[3] and a paternalistic relationship between the federations and the individual kibbutzim.[4]

According to Panebianco's definition (1982), the inter-kibbutz organizations, and particularly the federations, can be defined as political organizations, because the kibbutz combines features of voluntary organizations with bureaucracies. In his words: "The representative character of many political parties depends on the fact that a party is, in a certain sense, a hybrid which combines features of bureaucratic organizations (and thus a system of interests) with those of voluntary associations (and thus a solidarity system). More socially, the party depends on the fact that selection of leaders at various levels involves two different requisites: that of *functionality* and that of *legitimation*" (1982, 224; emphasis in original).

The federations possessed the power of intervention in the individual kibbutz, while the regional inter-kibbutz organizations acted more as interest groups and economic conglomerates. I discussed (Rosolio, 1975) the interrelations between the inter-kibbutz national and regional organizations, showing that there are power struggles between the two levels of organization and that, in the course of time, the two levels gradually come to accept coexistence. The internal processes in the kibbutzim—organized as they are in inter-kibbutz organizations which have the power to intervene and to influence internal processes in the kibbutzim—can be understood only if the inter-kibbutz organizations on the two levels are not overlooked.

Another aspect of the inter-kibbutz organizations at the regional level is discussed by Bijaoui Fogiel (1988): the relations and activities of the kibbutzim within their nonkibbutz environment. She found alienation between the kibbutzim and their neighbors. This alienation worried the kibbutz leadership, especially after the political upheaval in 1977, when the Labor alignment lost its majority and a right-wing coalition took over for the first time since the creation of the state. Even in the pre-state period, the ruling bodies had been controlled by the Labor alignment (Harif, 1982).

Finally, I wish to emphasize the sociological, functional aspect of the inter-kibbutz organization as it affects the individual kibbutz. Cohen (1983, 99) described the development of the kibbutz from the "bund" type to the "association" type, arguing that: "The Association, unlike the Bund or the Commune, is to a large extent an 'urbanized' community, in the cultural sense of the term."[5]

In this connection, Cohen pointed out that the association type tends to create inter-kibbutz organizations both at the regional and national levels. In fact, the kibbutzim created inter-kibbutz organizations from their very beginnings in order to provide for their small communities a framework large enough to allow them to develop modern patterns of living, education, and culture. In addition (as already mentioned), the federations functioned as interest organizations in the economic and political sphere. The following sections discuss the various inter-kibbutz organizations. The kibbutzim are organized in two kinds of inter-kibbutz organizations at the national level: through kibbutz federations and through economic support organizations. Although the two forms of organization are linked, the federations have authority over the economic support organizations.

THE KIBBUTZ FEDERATIONS

The kibbutz federations are political, ideological, inter-kibbutz supra-organizations. All but one[6] of the 270 kibbutzim in Israel are organized in three major kibbutz federations and one minor federation. The three major federations are the United Kibbutz Federation or TAKAM[7]; the National Kibbutz or Kibutz Arzi[8]; and the Religious Kibbutz Federation or Hakibbutz HaDati.[9] The minor federation comprises kibbutzim affiliated to an extreme religious party—Poalei Agudat Yisrael.[10] Table 12.1 demonstrates the size of the different kibbutz federations.

Table 12.1
Kibbutz Federations, 1993

Kibbutz Federation	Number of Kibbutzim	Population
The United Kibbutz Federation	167	75,837
The National Kibbutz	84	40,622
The Religious Kibbutz	17	8,025
Poalei Agudat Yisrael	2	1,500

Source: Maron, 1995, 81–82.

The three main kibbutz federations play a significant role in major political parties in Israel. The UKM (United Kibbutz Federation) is affiliated with the Israeli Labor Party, in which it is the largest party district. The federation has two members in the current Israeli parliament (the Knesset) and, until the Labor Party lost its majority in 1996, had one cabinet minister (the minister of agriculture). There are another two members of the Knesset (MKs) from the UKM who represent two coalition nationalistic right-wing parties. The KAM (the National Kibbutz) is affiliated with the Mapam Party, a left-wing Zionist-socialist party which was a partner in the government coalition and a part of the ruling coalition in the Labor Federation (Histadruth) trade union movement in Israel. KAM is represented in the Knesset also with two MKs, one of them, until recently, the treasurer of the Labor Federation. The RKM (Religious Kibbutz Federation) is affiliated with the NRP (National Religious Party), which, since the elections in May 1996, has formed a part of the ruling right-wing nationalistic coalition. The NRP is represented in the Knesset with two MKs. The three federations[11] coordinate their activities of common interest through the Kibbutz Movement Federation.

The different kibbutz federations developed from different relational concepts among the individual kibbutzim: One of them was a centralist federation, with an almost unlimited power of intervention in the decisions of the individual kibbutz; the two others were more decentralized, with different degrees of autonomy vis-à-vis the individual kibbutz. In time, all the federations moved in the direction of centralism, which gained or preserved their power of intervention in the individual kibbutz—because (due to the centralist role the government played in resource allocation) they were the main agencies of resource allocation to the individual kibbutzim (Rosner, Chizik, and Shur, 1989, 118–122).

The kibbutz federations operate through an apparatus called the secretariat, which has three major functions common to all: (1) as ideological centers to the affiliated kibbutzim, a function that was meaningful mainly in formative periods when the charismatic leaders of the kibbutz federations were in power,[12] (2) as intermediaries between the kibbutzim and governmental agencies, political power bases, and major economic systems such as the banks, which played, and are still playing, a major role in the economic life of the kibbutzim, and (3) as support centers for various everyday activities in the individual kibbutz—for example, education, cultural activities, health services, and personal services. The kibbutz federations created the machinery required to fulfill these functions, acting as clearinghouses and quasi-banks to channel aid within the federation between wealthier kibbutzim and kibbutzim in need of support and of resources allocated by the government or banks. In other words, the kibbutz headquarters was the clearinghouse through which the major resources needed by the kibbutzim were allocated—for example, manpower (through the youth movements), financial resources, and political support. This gave the kibbutz federations overall control and power of intervention in the kibbutzim (Rosolio, 1994).

As political organizations, the kibbutz federations have parliamentary bodies which supervise and control the federations' headquarters. The parliamentary bodies are composed of kibbutz representatives. In the formative charismatic period, these bodies were nominated by the leadership of the federations. Today, the parliamentary bodies are composed of elected delegates from the individual kibbutzim. The kibbutz federations nominate the managers of the inter-kibbutz support organizations. The kibbutz federations' leaders, who are members of the central bodies of the federations, are also members in the major political bodies of the political parties with which they are affiliated. The centrality of the kibbutz federations and their power over the individual kibbutzim derive, on the one hand, from their function in vital resource allocation, and on the other, from the dependency of the kibbutzim on the resources allocated (a phenomenon described by Kornai [1986] as "soft budget constraints"), thereby promoting a paternalistic relationship between the federations and the kibbutzim. The economic crisis that developed in the late 1980s affected the centrality of kibbutz federations, which lost most of their power of resource allocation.

The kibbutz federations' decline in power over the individual kibbutzim can be traced to three factors: (1) the decentralization of the power structure of Israeli society; (2) the loss by the Israeli Labor and left-wing parties of their majority in the Knesset—in 1977 for twelve years and again since 1996; and (3) the effect of the kibbutz crisis. Because the kibbutz federations no longer held the balance in the struggle between change and conservation, their diminishing power has led to greater privatization in the kibbutzim. To these effects should be added the emergence of the regional organizations, which I will discuss later. The decline in the power of the national kibbutz federations is demonstrated in Table 12.2, showing the decrease of the budget of the UKM between the years 1990 and 1996.

Table 12.2 shows that in 1996, the budget of the federation was not even 30 percent of the 1990 budget, reflecting the decline of the federations as centers of activity and their influence on the individual kibbutzim—in terms of both support power and intervention power in resource allocations.

THE INTER-KIBBUTZ SUPPORT ORGANIZATIONS—
THE NATIONAL LEVEL

Together with the moshavim, the kibbutzim formed a number of cooperatives to serve as support organizations. The two major organizations are the marketing

Table 12.2
The Decrease of the UKM Budget, 1990–1996 (1990 = 00).

Year	Relative Budget
1989	85.9
1990	100.0
1991	85.9
1992	75.1
1993	74.2
1994	73.1
1995	64.7
1996	26.9

Source: Budget proposal, UKM, 1996.

cooperative Tnuva and the purchasing cooperative Hamashbir Hamerkazi (Gvati, 1981, 258–268). These two national inter-kibbutz cooperatives function under the formal umbrella of the Agricultural Workers trade union (Hamerkaz Hachaklai). Their members are the kibbutzim and the moshavim affiliated with the Hamerkaz Hachaklai, but they are controlled by the kibbutz and moshav federations. In the past ten years, as a result of the crisis in the moshav federation (for reasons similar to those for kibbutzim), the major control has shifted to the kibbutz. In 1991, Tnuva was marketing 65 percent of Israel's total fresh agricultural produce and 92 percent of the milk consumed in Israel. Tnuva's turnover that year was $1,570 million (U.S.). Hamashbir Hamerkazi supplies all kinds of goods needed on the farm—from household consumer goods to tractors and fodder for livestock. In 1991, the turnover of Hamashbir Hamerkazi was about $350 million (U.S.).

In addition to these two national cooperatives, we have to take into account the agricultural growers' and producers' councils, some ordained by law, some voluntary. These agencies act as interest groups and have legal or voluntary power over the producers. The kibbutz federations are involved in the nomination of their management.

It can be seen then that the kibbutzim created a web of inter-kibbutz organizations to lead and guide the kibbutzim (in the case of the kibbutz federations) and to support and utilize the advantages of size and organized interests (in the case of the inter-kibbutz support organizations). The effectiveness of these organizations was related to the Israeli power structure and the corporate relations within Israeli society. As long as the Israeli economic and political structure was "semi-socialist" and reflected a high degree of central planning and intervention of the government in the Israeli economy, the inter-kibbutz organizations at the national level played a major role in the everyday life of the individual kibbutzim. In the course of time, several changes took place that were related to: (1) a sociopolitical change, expressed in the political upheaval in 1977; (2) the transition from a Keynesian economy with a high degree of government intervention to a neoliberal economy (Arian, 1990, 52–83; Aharoni, 1991; Bruno, 1989); and (3) as mentioned before, the decentralization of power. The inter-kibbutz regional organizations and institutions have emerged in this framework during the last three decades.

The decentralization of the power structure in Israel is an ongoing process that has found expression in the change of the electoral system, with direct election of the prime minister and primary elections for the parties. The process stems from the development of a well-established and prosperous private sector and the plurality of Israeli society. In addition, the shift of Israel's economy from an undeveloped, preindustrial economy to an industrial, or even postindustrial, economy has brought in its wake a political shift from a semiplanned to a neoliberal economy. These general trends, as well as the economic crisis in the kibbutzim since the mid-1980s, have led to similar trends in the kibbutzim. It should be mentioned that the severe economic crisis from which the kibbutzim and their economic organizations suffered obliged them to enter a recovery contract with the government and the banks which, in consequence, stopped their support activities, such as loans and guarantees to the kibbutzim; this played a significant role in the decrease of influence of the national kibbutz federations and their organizations.

THE REGIONAL INTER-KIBBUTZ ORGANIZATIONS AND INSTITUTIONS

The kibbutzim are organized at the regional level through a web of organizations and institutions of different types. Some organizations are decreed by law (e.g., the regional municipal councils), while others developed in response to need or for the sake of efficiency (e.g., regional schools, colleges, and regional economic organizations). Most of these peripheral organizations and institutions were established by kibbutzim. Here I focus on the regional municipal councils and the regional economic inter-kibbutz organizations such as the regional purchase organizations and the regional enterprises.

The Regional Municipal Councils

The rural settlements in Israel are organized by law within fifty-five municipal councils. Table 12.3 shows the distribution of kibbutzim in the various regional councils.

Table 12.3 shows that in fifteen councils there is not a single kibbutz, while the kibbutzim have the major influence and are a significant majority in another twelve councils. In eighteen councils, the chairperson of the municipal council is a kibbutz member.

Until the mid-1980s, most regional municipal councils functioned essentially in the municipal sphere, dealing with municipal services, security matters, and investments in infrastructure through government resources. Few municipal councils were involved directly in regional economic activities. Since then, some major

Table 12.3
The Percentage of Kibbutzim in the Regional Councils in Israel

Percentage of Kibbutzim	Number of Councils
0	15
1–24	16
25–49	12
50–74	6
75–100	6
Total number of regional councils	55

Source: Bijaoui-Fogiel, 1994, 14–15.

changes have occurred: (1) the change in the election system from representative (in which the council was composed of nominees of the individual settlements) to direct election of representatives, especially of the head of the municipal council; (2) as mentioned above, the decentralization of the power structure in Israeli society and governance; and (3) the economic crisis of the kibbutzim and of the kibbutz federations and the greater demand for government resources to answer various needs of the kibbutzim. Prior to the mid-1980s, these needs were met by national organizations, including the federations and their funds. As Bijaoui Fogiel (1994) pointed out, the municipal councils became more and more active in areas in which the kibbutz federations or kibbutz regional organizations had previously exercised sole influence. Table 12.4 shows the development of the budget of the regional councils in the years 1991–1993.

In Table 12.4, we see the ongoing increase of the regional council budgets, mirroring the increase of their activities in their member settlements and their greater involvement. Activities such as education and cultural development that were formerly dealt with by the federations are now handled by the regional councils. For example, from a brochure published in 1997 by the Regional Council of Mate Asher, we can learn of the variety of services that the regional council now supplies: advanced studies for school teachers, scholarships for teachers and pupils, psychological services, a regional library, youth cultural centers, and activities for senior citizens, as well as housing and economic development. In former years, the federations through their departments were directly involved in most of these activities in the individual kibbutz. The regional councils have also established development firms to be active partners in the economic development of their regions and of the individual kibbutzim.

The Regional Economic Inter-Kibbutz Organizations

The regional purchase organizations and the regional kibbutz enterprises are linked together. The regional purchase organizations are cooperatives of the kibbutzim in the region.[13] Most of the regional purchase organizations were estab-

Table 12.4
Income and Expenditure of the Regional Councils 1991–1993

Year	Income	Expenditure
1991	1,661	1,727
1992	1,855	1,880
1993	1,896	1,979

Figures are given in millions NIS (New Israeli Shekel); prices adjusted as of December 31, 1993.

Source: Central Bureau of Statistics, 1995.

lished at the end of the 1940s and the beginning of the 1950s, a period of shortages and food rationing in the newborn state. The rationale was that regional organizations could ensure (more effectively than the large national supply agencies) the fair distribution of scarce goods to the kibbutzim (Cohen, 1970, 288–299). The needs of kibbutzim for greater efficiency in the provision of services and goods essential to agricultural production led to the establishment of regional enterprises on the basis of the regional purchase cooperatives. Because, for ideological reasons, they refrained from employing hired labor, the kibbutzim suffered from a shortage of manpower, and so they looked to the regional cooperatives (upon which the limitations for employing hired labor were not as strict) to provide services—fodder mills, packing houses, chicken slaughterhouses—at the regional level. Also, the high cost of machinery—cotton gins, heavy tractors, trucks, and so on—precluded their purchase by individual kibbutzim.

Nowadays there are eleven regional kibbutz roof organizations. Cohen and Leshem (1967) defined a typology for the regional purchase organization on the basis of centralization or decentralization—that is, whether the various activities were under one roof. They defined two types. In the *centralist* type, all the activities function under one roof, and power is concentrated in the regional municipal council, which represents the interests of the participants. In the *net* type, the different activities are not concentrated under one roof. The regional municipal councils usually function separately from the regional purchase organizations and the regional enterprises, most of which are linked together. In the competition between the kibbutz federations and the inter-kibbutz regional organizations, I found (Rosolio, 1975) the creation of a new balance of power among them involving changes in such basic assumptions as the acceptance of hired labor in the inter-kibbutz regional enterprises. During the years of hyperinflation, the national kibbutz funding organizations competed with the regional clearinghouses of the kibbutzim for the financial resources of the individual kibbutzim. As a result, a partnership of the two organizations was established to coordinate their financial activities, a significant sign of the kibbutz federations' acceptance of the regional organizations as partners. But the partnership ended in financial disaster (as a meeting on May 16, 1985, of the TAKAM secretariat showed), compoundng the overall economic crisis of the kibbutzim and their federations.

Krol and others (1989), in a document presented to the creditors of the kibbutzim and to the government, analyzed the factors in the growth of the debts of the TAKAM federation in the 1980s. The researchers found that 32 percent of the increasing debt (that is, 830 million New Israeli Shekels (NIS),[14] was incurred by the kibbutz federations and the inter-kibbutz regional organizations. The deficit and debts of the inter-kibbutz regional organizations amounted to 410 million NIS (49 percent of the overall sum) (Krol et al., 21). The main causes which left the regional inter-kibbutz enterprises in financial debt were miscalculated investment in food industries based on what proved to be a mistaken strategy of development by some of the regional inter-kibbutz enterprises, and the investments of the regional inter-kibbutz organizations and enterprises in the financial market (Krol et al., 22).

The resulting economic and financial fiasco led to a decision by the kibbutz federations to abandon industrial development of the regional enterprises and clearinghouse activities of the inter-kibbutz regional purchase organizations. In the framework of an overall recovery plan for the kibbutzim and their inter-kibbutz organizations, many of the regional enterprises were sold or, with private capital, went into partnerships. The regional inter-kibbutz organizations and enterprises reverted to service organizations for the affiliated farms, and their role in the economic life of the kibbutzim diminished—as mentioned before, some of their activities were taken over by the development companies of the regional councils.

Alongside the inter-kibbutz organizations I have described, an elaborate network of regional inter-kibbutz activity has developed, in cooperation with nonkibbutz sectors in the regions. Educational initiatives and joint ventures with private capital in industry and other businesses are providing new directions in the development of the kibbutzim.

THE SHIFT OF POWER FROM CENTER TO PERIPHERY: A THEORETICAL PERSPECTIVE

The shift from center to periphery—in other words, decentralization of the power structure of Israel as well as in the kibbutz federations—is part of an overall process reflected in western society. As Toffler (1990, 246) describes it: "As the super-symbolic economy spreads, it will create constituencies for a radical shift of power among local, regional, national and global levels; regions and localities, instead of becoming more uniform, are destined to grow more diverse."

This process is a continuation of the social change from preindustrial societies to postindustrial societies (Bell, 1973). It is also a result of the trend toward privatization which developed in the late 1980s, in the West as part of the developing neoliberalism (Deane, 1989, 168–194). Eisenstadt (1985) analyzes the changes in the power structure in Israel as a result of the transformation of Israeli society. He argues that Israeli society, in its sociological development, underwent a transformation from a pioneering Zionist ideology to an individualistic ideology. One of the results of this process was the decentralization of the power structure and the development of a civil society. The same process can be detected in the kibbutz: the transformation from social-contract relations to contract relations—that is, from a social structure in which the authority lies in the hands of the community to a social structure in which the authority lies in the hands of individuals who agree on mutual commitments through a bounded contract. In the kibbutz, as in Israeli society, the transformation from the pioneering Zionist ideology to an individualistic approach to life is linked to a liberal ideology, congruent with the ideology of the surrounding society. Or, to take another definition, Talmon-Garber (1970) defines it as a transformation from a "pioneering value-directed community" to a "consume-directed community," resulting from routinization.

We can see the process occurring in the kibbutz community itself. It finds expression in the ongoing privatization in the kibbutzim: increasing the family budgets and decreasing the communities' mutual resources so that the individual in the kibbutz now has to pay for services (food, cultural services, etc.) he or she previously received with no accounting from the kibbutz. The same trend can be found in the transformation of the power structure within the kibbutz: the decline of the power and authority of the general assembly and the diminishing range of activities in which the kibbutz organizations play a role in the everyday life of families. To conclude, it is evident from a theoretical perspective that the transformation of the kibbutz power structure from centralized to regional is part of a sociological process which is taking place in the individual kibbutz.

CONCLUSION

The inter-kibbutz organizations were an integral part of the kibbutz phenomenon. They derived from economic and sociological needs of the kibbutz way of life and from the size of the individual kibbutzim. The inter-kibbutz organization and its changes have reflected the power structure and changes in Israeli society. For a long period (from the 1920s until the end of the 1970s), the centralized economic and political culture in Israel shaped the inter-kibbutz organizations along national and centralized lines. Since the 1960s and especially during the 1970s, the change in the economic and political culture of the kibbutz environment brought to the fore the regional inter-kibbutz organizations. Both levels of inter-kibbutz organizations were centralized—one on the national level and the other on the regional level. The economic crisis of the kibbutzim and their inter-kibbutz organizations has led, among other things, to changes in the pattern of inter-kibbutz organization from exclusively kibbutz to partnerships of individual kibbutzim with nonkibbutz organizations. These partnerships are based solely on the interests of the partners in the sphere of their collaboration. In this development, the regional municipal councils and organizations are emerging as the holders of power and resources necessary for the development of the region and as efficient political vehicles for the representation of the regional interests (Schwartz et al., 1994).

It should be mentioned that voices in favor of uniting or combining kibbutzim or their economic enterprises on a regional level (Kahana, 1992) are now being raised. This is in response to demographic and economic weaknesses of many kibbutzim and goes beyond regional cooperation in joint ventures (such as chickenhouses and plantations) to the merging of communities, even if they live in separate locations. In general, the kibbutz is evolving from inter-kibbutz organizations to kibbutz partnerships on a joint level.

NOTES

1. The kibbutz and moshav federations in Israel represent a majority of the Agricultural Workers trade union (Hamerkaz Hachaklai), which is a part of the Israeli Labor Federation (Histadruth). Through this organization, the kibbutz and the moshav federations and their economic support organizations coordinate their lobbying activities to promote their mutual interests.

2. In this chapterI have not elaborated on this matter.

3. On the discussion of corporatism in Israel, see Grinberg (1991).

4. In the political culture of the Jewish community in Palestine, the individuals or individual communities had no access to the governing agencies except through the political party, the trade union, or other recognized secondary center. For direct access, one had to belong to some supra-organization. This created a corporate relationship within the Jewish society—that is, the governmental bodies had to delegate some power to the secondary centers in the same way that the Palestine government did to the Jewish national bodies. This political culture was adopted by the newborn state of Israel, and it has only gradually changed. The political upheaval of 1977 has accelerated the process of change in the direction of western civic culture.

5. Although there was an effort to create a unique kibbutz culture, it was not a peasant culture but a branch of the urbanized culture.

6. The one kibbutz which is not a member of any kibbutz federation is also supported by one of the federations.

7. TAKAM is a Hebrew acronym of the United Kibbutz Federation.

8. Kibbutz Arzi is an abridgment of the full name in Hebrew—namely, HaShomer HaZair. The name signifies that it is a nationwide organization of kibbutzim affiliated with their mother federation, which was called the Young Watchmen. In Hebrew, "nation" and "nationwide" are the same word.

9. Hakibbutz HaDati is Hebrew for "the religious kibbutz."

10. Poalei Agudat Yisrael is Hebrew for "the workers of the association of Israel."

11. I do not discuss the Poalei Agudat Yisrael federation because it is too small to play any significant role in the development of the kibbutzim or in the political life of Israel.

12. In this chapter, I shall not discuss the process of change in the pattern of leadership of the kibbutz federations (Rosolio, 1995, 45–49).

13. Parallel to the kibbutz regional purchase organizations, there are separate regional purchase organizations of the moshavim.

14. On June 30, 1988, one U.S. Dollar was equal to 1.62 NIS.

13
Summary and Conclusions

Uriel Leviatan, Jack Quarter, and Hugh Oliver

In the introductory chapter, we reviewed the past successes of the kibbutz movement in achieving its social and economic goals and suggested that the major factor contributing to these successes was its keeping to three conditions: (1) holding unchanged the basic principles and values that define kibbutz distinctiveness, while constantly adapting their concrete expressions to changing circumstances; (2) keeping a balance between the realization of values of individualism and of collectivism; and (3) having congruency among domains of life in the domains' principles of conduct.

Several chapters in this book offer insights about the extent to which kibbutzim have moved away from these conditions: Getz's chapter on the prevalence of changes, Palgi's chapter on industrial organization, Rosner's on the work domain, Gluck's on consumption, and Pavin's on governing institutions. The evidence suggests that most changes recently introduced into kibbutzim champion individualistic values. Such slogans as "let the individuals be responsible for themselves" (Getz's, Rosner's, and Gluck's chapters) accent this direction. Moreover, there is no equivalent emphasis on collectivism. Therefore, it appears that the balance between these values has undergone a major shift—a shift so pronounced that it is necessary to ask whether a kibbutz can sustain its defining qualities with such a high degree of individualism. These same chapters also demonstrate the increasing incongruence between the organization of the kibbutz economic sector in general (industry in particular) and the organization of the kibbutz as a community. Changes in the kibbutz economy that attempt to harmonize the organization of kibbutz businesses with businesses elsewhere (for example, the introduction of boards of directors, the abolition of managerial rotation, or doing away with participatory decision-making institutions at work) are incongruent with the values upon which the community is organized. Moreover, the evidence also suggests that the defining principles of kibbutzim—such as solidarity among members, collective pursuit of goals, a democratic governance, maximum self-development for every member, being of service to the larger society, and taking into account the uniqueness of each person's needs and abilities—are not supported by the changes described in this book. Most of the changes lead away from these principles.

Given that the three requirements for successful functioning of the kibbutz are not being fulfilled by the wave of changes that kibbutzim are experiencing, we pose the second question: How is the kibbutz's successful survival affected by them? This question can be answered only in gross terms—because the changes are recent and as yet no evaluative research on their effects is available. However, the preliminary evidence suggests that kibbutzim are doing worse than in the past and also in comparison to other organizations.

EFFECTS OF CHANGES IN INDUSTRY

The impact of economic changes is critical to the future of the kibbutz movement. The changes were first introduced into the kibbutz economy ostensibly to improve performance—in particular for industry, since it is now the major business of kibbutzim. In 1995, sales from kibbutz industries were about $3.1 billion (U.S.), and they accounted for about 70 percent of all the net income of kibbutzim.

The Kibbutz Association of Industries (KAI) publishes a yearly report of the economic and labor indices of kibbutz industries. The performance indicators of the last years have been dismal, particularly when compared to previous times: According to the reports of KAI, over the last four years (1993–1996), kibbutz industries show a *lower* level of labor productivity than the rest of Israel—99 percent in 1993, 88 percent in 1994, 91 percent in 1995 and 8 percent in 1996. Labor productivity of kibbutz industries was in decline from 1991 to 1995, while other Israeli industries constantly improved their performance. In contrast, sales per worker for the seven years 1982–1988 show that, for each year, the labor productivity of kibbutz industries was *higher* than that of the rest of Israeli industry, with a range of 122 percent to 151 percent and an average across the seven years of 138 percent. Even as late as 1988 and 1989 (after the crisis had hit but before the changes were introduced), kibbutz industries were still performing more efficiently than comparable industries in the rest of Israel. Rabin (1991) compared the economic performance of fifty industrial plants in kibbutzim for the years 1988 and 1989 to that of a comparable fifty firms that were traded in the Israeli stock market. He found that the kibbutz plants were doing better on all measures of efficiency.

We see similar trends with another economic indicator. Sales by kibbutz industry grew during the years 1992 to 1996 by a yearly average of about 4.1 percent, which by itself is not low. However, the real measure of economic benefits to a kibbutz from its industry is the amount of money left in the community after all outside expenses are paid (raw material, hired labor, management costs, and overhead costs). These sums actually *decreased* every year from 1992 to 1996 (by 4.5 percent, from 2,482 million NIS in 1992, to 2,438 in 1993, to 2,424 in 1994, to 2,370 million NIS in 1995 to 2,289 NIS in 1996). (all the prices of December 1996). These results look even more sorrowful when one remembers that during 1992–1995, the Israeli economy enjoyed an average yearly growth rate of 6 to 7 percent.

The data indicate that the deteriorating performance of the kibbutz industries occurred because of the decrease in their labor productivity—an indicator of the quality of management. For instance, one study (Leviatan, 1995) shows that for the first time kibbutz industrial workers (members) had a lower level of motivation and commitment than workers in farm branches. We must conclude, therefore, that kibbutz management has deteriorated; yet the changes introduced in kibbutz industries have been aimed at improving the quality of management (Palgi's chapter). It appears, therefore, that the changes have not succeeded in achieving their intended goal.

The increase in hired labor has also been important in the lower returns from the kibbutz economy. The rate of hired workers in kibbutz industries grew from 34.9 percent in 1991 to 56.4 percent in 1996, with the addition of about close to eight thousand workers. This growth in numbers has meant that the cost of payment to outside labor has doubled.

CHANGES IN OTHER DOMAINS OF KIBBUTZ LIFE

However, it is not only in the economic sphere that kibbutzim are doing worse. Commitment to kibbutz life is on the decline, and rates of leaving are on the increase (Leviatan's chapter on the second and third generations and Maron's chapter). In yearly surveys from 1992 to 1995, Palgi and Sharir (1995) asked what form of life (kibbutz, city, or village) would respondents choose if they did not have to take into account any practical considerations. Whereas only 43 percent would have chosen kibbutz life in 1992, this number declined further to 35 percent in 1995. During the 1980s, in response to a similar question, about 70 to 80 percent chose kibbutz life.

As Leviatan's chapter indicates, kibbutzim that emphasize satisfaction of members' needs without a comparable emphasis on realization of distinct values not only have a high departure rate of their youth; that departure rate also follows a tendency for negative self-selection. None of the changes introduced in the kibbutzim in recent years has aimed at strengthening either ideology or their distinct values. Social strife has occurred in many kibbutzim owing to the divisive debates about the changes (Pavin's chapter). Moreover, as Dar's chapter suggests, the educational system has surrendered its distinctiveness and its ability to prepare the younger generation for kibbutz life. Finally, kibbutz failures and changes have not gone unnoticed by the Israeli public. While support for kibbutzim and appreciation of their contribution were high until the mid-1980s, such approval has eroded appreciably in recent years. A recent public opinion survey (Smith, 1996) shows that 50 percent of the public still have a positive attitude toward kibbutzim (compared to 60 percent a decade ago), but 25 percent expressed a negative attitude (compared to about 8 percent during the 1980s). In another survey (Dahaf Institute, 1995), only 40 percent stated that kibbutz education was superior to education in the rest of Israel (previously, 70 percent thought so), and only 54 percent thought that kibbutzim contributed to the achievement of social and national goals (compared to about 70 percent in previous years).

Thus, we must conclude that the changes have not improved kibbutz functioning. If this same pattern persists, the kibbutz as a communal society may become extinct. That is not to say that the kibbutz movement is following a predetermined path. Rather, the members, in response to a crisis that at first was externally induced, have bought into solutions based upon values incongruent with those defining kibbutz life.

This particular response to crisis differs from the past. The kibbutz movement has weathered major crises by being innovative and by its members being committed to continue their form of life. However, the ideological commitment that seemed to be the major force in coming out of previous crises is much lower now. It is ironic that ideology seems to be the major force in a movement that has been so strongly influenced by the philosophy of Marxism, which tended to view ideology as relatively subservient to actual life experiences.

What is the future for the kibbutz movement? Will it continue to be "a singular nonfailure," as the philosopher Martin Buber defined it some fifty years ago, or a "singular failure," as some view it today? We think that the question should be worded differently. One should ask: What would kibbutz members want the future of their social experiment to be? It is our view that the future will depend first and foremost on the will of the members. This statement must be qualified in that the kibbutz is an open society and the members, as noted, are subject to external influences—some quite powerful. Those influences notwithstanding, the members still have a choice to make. In the past, the members' commitment to the kibbutz was such that they found solutions to crises that revitalized the movement. At present, it is not clear whether the will to revitalize the movement still exists.

One might anticipate that the current crisis will result in a much wider variability among kibbutzim in their social arrangements; some kibbutzim will turn into some other form of settlement (perhaps still retaining the kibbutz name) and others will revitalize their commitment to kibbutz principles and will attempt to restore congruence between the organization of their business enterprises and the kibbutz as a community. Although a survey by Palgi and Sharir (1995) shows that 18 percent of kibbutz members would prefer to live in moshavim (farm communities with varying degrees of cooperation in such areas as production, marketing, and purchasing), it is unlikely that this model will attract a large following because the moshav movement is beset by worse problems than the kibbutzim. Moshavim, for instance, have not grown in numbers for the last thirty years, and the producer-cooperative movement in Israel has been in constant decline and currently numbers less than thirty. Theoretically (Meister, 1984), the future of cooperatives that focus upon one domain of life (production only, or consumption only, or housing only) is much more in doubt than that of kibbutzim, which are based upon a more comprehensive model of cooperation.

LESSONS FOR INDUSTRIAL SOCIETY

Are there any lessons from the kibbutz experience for other societies? It is easy to take the view that kibbutz society is unique and therefore has no relevance for the rest of the industrial world. Yet the struggles that are occurring in the kibbutz are not dissimilar to those of other societies. For example, the conflict of values found in the kibbutz—collectivism and social solidarity against aggressive egocentrism and individualism—is found elsewhere, although the manifestations differ: for example, the political clashes about the fate of welfare programs in the United States and in Canada; the rethinking of such principles as "employment for life" in Japan; "Thatcherism" in the United Kingdom; and, of course, the revolutionary changes that are occurring in the former Communist countries. In all these examples, collectivist policies are being criticized, and individualistic solutions are being promoted. Kibbutzim struggle with similar topics, yet they offer an important methodological advantage to study the results of choosing one direction over another and of mixing them to different degrees: Kibbutz communities have now a wide range of experiences on the individualism-collectivism dimension while most other important characteristics are held constant. This makes the kibbutz experience valuable learning material.

CONCLUSION

Is the story told by the chapters of this volume telling us the end of the communal dream? Although the kibbutz movement has been weakened by the changes of the past decade, it is premature to suggest that this communal dream is at an end. The struggle between the two sets of values, communal and individualistic, is not over yet in kibbutzim. In spite of all the changes, the majority of kibbutzim still have functioning communal arrangements. Even those which have introduced the most far-reaching changes have not abolished the system of communal production, the cornerstone of the kibbutz economy (Getz's chapter). Although it is true that *Zeitgeist* trends in many societies are moving away from communal life and sharing, one has to remember that this was in effect always the case. From the time of the first kibbutz settlement and throughout their almost ninety years of history, the kibbutzim ran against the tides of time. Never have more than 7 percent of the Jewish population of Israel been members of kibbutzim (and that was only for a brief period before statehood). Moreover, for each member who stayed, there were four or five others who departed. From the perspective of outside experts, the kibbutz was always a "nonworkable" society, and yet it has successfully endured for four generations. We suggest, therefore, that there is no inherent reason why the kibbutz movement cannot continue to succeed, but the evidence suggests that this kind of life is appropriate for only a small minority.

Kibbutz history teaches the importance of ideology as a moving force. To a large extent, the future of the kibbutzim depends on their members' dreams and aspirations—dreams that are influenced by their education and socialization (particularly that of the younger generation). This is also true for communal and other forms of cooperative systems elsewhere: Success requires ideological commitment from the members.

References

Adams, S. 1965. Inequity in social exchange. In *Advances in Experimental Social Psychology*, ed. L. Berkowitz, 267–299. New York: Academic Press.

Adar, G. 1981. *Occupational Prestige: The Variables Affecting It and Its Contribution to the Social Status of Individuals* (in Hebrew). Master's thesis, Haifa University.

Adar, G. 1992. *Women of the Kibbutz in the Public Domain: A Comparison between Active and Non-Active Women* (in Hebrew). Ph.D. dissertation, Hebrew University.

Adar, G., and C. Louis. 1988. *A Survey of Women Who Are Office-Holders* (in Hebrew). Haifa: Haifa University, Institute for Social Research of the Kibbutz and the Cooperative Idea; Ramat Efal: Yad Tabenkin.

Adar, G., B. Tornianski, and M. Rosner. 1993. *Different Ways of Introducing Change* (in Hebrew). Institute for Social Research of the Kibbutz and the Cooperative Idea, Monograph no. 131. Haifa: Haifa University.

Agin, A. 1970. The kibbutznik in the army (in Hebrew). *Niv Hakvutza* 19: 50–55.

Aharoni, Y. 1991. *The Political Economy of Israel* (in Hebrew). Tel Aviv: Am Oved.

Allardt, E. 1968. Theories about social stratification. In *Social Stratification*, ed. J. Jackson, 14–24.

Alon, M. 1976. Adolescence and late adolescence in the kibbutz (in Hebrew). *Hahinuch Hameshutaf* 90: 15–29.

Alterman, L. 1973. The project method: Elementary schools. In *Collective Education in the Kibbutz*, ed. A. I. Rabin and B. Hazan, 63–98. New York: Springer.

Am-Ad, Z. 1985. Behavior Patterns of Kibbutz Elderly in Various life Domains (in Hebrew). Ph.D. dissertation, Hebrew University.

Amir, Y. 1969. The effectiveness of the kibbutz born soldier in the Israeli defense forces. *Human Relations* 22: 333–344.

Arian, A. 1990. *Politics and Government in Israel* (in Hebrew). Tel Aviv: Zmora Bitan.

Association of Kibbutz Industry—1996. 1982. *Annual Reports (in Hebrew)*. Tel Aviv: Association of Kibbutz Industries.

Atar, D. 1983. *On the Coming of Age* (in Hebrew). Tel Aviv: HaKibbutz HaMeuchad.

Avrahami, A. 1993. *Attitudes of Kibbutz Youth to the Kibbutz: 1986–1992* (in Hebrew). Ramat Efal: Yad Tabenkin.

Avrahami, A., and Y. Dar. 1993. Collectivistic and individualistic motives among kibbutz youth volunteering for community service. *Journal of Youth and Adolescence* 22: 697–714.

Avrahami, A., and S. Getz. 1994. *Kibbutz School in the Tension of Change* (in Hebrew). Ramat Efal: Yad Tabenkin.

Bar-Lev, M., and Y. Dror. 1995. Education for work in the kibbutz as means towards personal, social and learning fulfillment. *Journal of Moral Education* 24: 259–272.

Bar-Yam, M., L. Kohlberg, and A. Naame. 1980. Moral reasoning of students in different cultural, social and educational settings. *American Journal of Education* 88: 345–362.

Bar-Yosef, R. 1959. The pattern of early socialization in the collective settlements in Israel. *Human Relations* 12: 345–360.

Barkai, H. 1977. *Growth Patterns of the Kibbutz Economy.* Amsterdam: North Holland.

Bartolke, K., W. Eschweiler, D. Flechsenberg, M. Palgi, and M. Rosner. 1985. *Participation and Control.* Spardof, Germany: Verlag Rene F. Wilfer.

Becker, G. 1984. The Vandervogel movement: A challenge to the generation conflict model. In *Conflict and Consensus,* ed. W. Powell and R. Robins, 71–97. New York: Free Press.

Bell, D. 1973. *The Coming of Post-Industrial Society.* New York: Basic Books.

Belzer-Zur, R. 1996. *Linkage between Leadership and Organizational Effectiveness in the Context of the Kibbutz Crisis* (in Hebrew). Master's thesis, Haifa University.

Ben-David, Y. 1975. *Work and Education in the Kibbutz* (in Hebrew). Rehovot: Settlement Research Center.

Ben-Ner, A. 1987. On the stability of the cooperative type of organization. *Journal of Comparative Economics* 8: 247–260.

Ben-Peretz, M., and Z. Lavi. 1982. Interaction between the kibbutz community and the school. *Interchange on Educational Policy* 13: 92–102.

Ben-Rafael, E. 1988. *Status, Power and Conflict in the Kibbutz.* New Castle upon Tyne, England: Athenaeum.

Ben-Rafael, E. 1996. *A Non-Total Revolution* (in Hebrew). Ramat Efal: Yad Tabenkin.

Ben-Rafael, E., and S. Weitman. 1984. The reconstitution of the family in the kibbutz. *European Journal of Sociology* 25: 1–27.

Ben-Zeev, A. 1985. From a "camp" to a "home"—The development of the kibbutz (in Hebrew). *The Kibbutz* 11: 101–115.

Bennis, W., and B. Nanus. 1985. *Leaders: The Strategies of Taking Charge.* New York: Harper & Row.

Berman, E. 1988. The collective education in the kibbutz: The charms and the dangers in the psychoanalytic utopia. *Psychoanalytic Study of the Child* 43: 319–335.

Bernfeld, S. 1921. *Kinderheim Baumgarten: Bericht uber einen Ernsthaften Versuch mit Neuer Erziehung.* Berlin: Judischer Verlag.

Bettelheim, B. 1969. *The Children of the Dream.* London: Collier Macmillan.

Bijaoui Fogiel, S. 1988. *Regional Integration, Cooperation or Alienation* (in Hebrew). Ramat Efal: Yad Tabenkin.

Bijaoui Fogiel, S. 1994. *The Emergence of Regionalism in the Kibbutz Movement: The Kibbutz at the Turn of the Century—Report no. 13* (in Hebrew). Ramat Efal: Yad Tabenkin.

Binder, L., J. S. Coleman, J. Lapalombara, L.W. Pye, S. Verba, and M. Weiner. 1971. *Crises and Sequences in Political Development.* Princeton, N.J.: Princeton University Press.

Biran, D. 1983. *The Emotional Experience and the Verbal Expression of Emotions among Urban and Kibbutz Adolescents* (in Hebrew). Master's thesis, Tel Aviv University.

Blasi, J. R. 1978. *The Communal Future: The Kibbutz and the Utopian Dilemma*. Norwood, Penn.: Norwood Editions.

Blumberg, R. S. 1989. Toward a ferments theory of development. In *Feminism and Sociological Theory,* ed. R. A. Wallace, 161–199. London: Sage Publications.

Blumberg, R. S. 1984. A general theory of gender stratification. In *Sociological Theory,* ed. R. Collins, 23–100. Jossey Bass.

Borochov, B. 1973. *Nationalism and the Class Struggle: Selected Writings*. Westport, Conn.: Greenwood Press.

Bowlby, J. 1951. *Maternal Care and Mental Health*. Geneva: World Health Association.

Bruno, M. 1989. Israel's crisis and economic reform in historical perspective (in Hebrew). *Economic Quarterly* 40 (141): 89–113.

Buchalted, Z. and C. Klipper. 1996. Economic Characteristics of Kibbutz Industrial Plants That Have Introduced Boards of Directors During the Years 1989–1993 (in Hebrew). Seminar paper presented to the School of Business, Bar Ilan University.

Butler, R. J. 1983. Control through markets, hierarchies and communes: A transactional approach to organizational analysis. In *Power, Efficiency and Institutions,* ed. A. Francis, J. Turk, and P. Wilman. London: Heinman Educational Books.

Central Bureau of Statistics (Israel). 1954–1995 (various years). *Annual Reports* (in Hebrew). Jerusalem: Central Bureau of Statistics.

Central Bureau of Statistics (Israel). 1967. *Supplement 18(5)* (in Hebrew). Jerusalem: Central Bureau of Statistics.Central Bureau of Statistics (Israel). 1975. *Supplement 26(12)* (in Hebrew). Jerusalem: Central Bureau of Statistics.

Chafetz, S. J. 1988. The gender division of labor and the reproduction of female disadvantage. *Journal of Family Issues* 9 (1): 108–131.

Chafetz, S. J. 1989. Gender equality: Toward a theory of change. In *Feminism and Sociological Theory,* ed. (R. A.) Wallace, 135–160. London: Sage Publications.

Chafetz, S. J. 1992. *Gender Equity: An Integrated Theory of Stability and Change*. Sage Publications.

Cohen, E. 1958. Institutionalization patterns in the kibbutz's work domain (in Hebrew). *Niv Hakvutza* 7 (3): 519–530.

Cohen, E. 1963. Changes in social structure of kibbutz's work domain (in Hebrew). *Economics Quarterly* 40: 378–388.

Cohen, E. 1970. The new settlements in the Negev and regional cooperation (in Hebrew). In *The Kibbutz—Sociological Studies,* ed. Y. Talmon Garber, 264–301. Jerusalem: Magnes Press Hebrew University.

Cohen, E. 1983. The structural transformation of the kibbutz. In *The Sociology of the Kibbutz: Studies of Israeli Society,* ed. E. Krausz, 2: 75–114. New Brunswick, N.J., and London: Transaction Books.

Cohen, E. 1984. The Israeli kibbutz—the dynamics of pragmatic utopianism. In *Totalitarian Democracy and After*. Jerusalem: Israel Academy of Sciences and Humanities.

Cohen, E., and E. Leshem. 1967. *A Survey of Regional Cooperation in Three Kibbutz Regions*. Rehovot: Settlement Research Center.

Dahaf Institute. 1995. The Image of Kibbutz Society: Findings from a Public Opinion Survey September 1995 (in Hebrew). Internal Report.

Daniel, A., and A. Szeskin. 1973. *The World Cooperative Movement* (in Hebrew). Tel Aviv: Am Oved.

Dar, Y. 1968. Changes in the kibbutz school (in Hebrew). In *Education and Society in Israel,* ed. S. N. Eisenstadt, C. Adler, R. Kahane, and I. Shelach, 425–431. Jerusalem: Academon.

Dar, Y. 1993. Youth in the kibbutz: The prolonged transition to adulthood. *Israel Social Science Journal* 8: 122–146.

Darin-Drabkin, H. 1962. *The Other Society.* London: Gollancz.

Deane, P. 1989. *The State and the Economic System: An Introduction to the History of Political Economy.* Oxford: Oxford University Press.

Derekh, I. 1970. Survey of the organizational structure development of a veteran kibbutz (in Hebrew). *Hedim* 92: 154–167.

Dewey, J. 1963. *Experience and Education.* 1938. Reprint, New York: Macmillan.

DiMaggio, P. 1990. Cultural aspects of economic action and organization. In *Beyond the Market Place,* ed. R. Friedland and A. F. Robertson, 89–112. New York: Aldive de Gruyter.

DiMaggio, P., and W. W. Powell. 1983. The iron cage revisited: Institutional isomorphism and collective rationality in organizational fields. *American Sociological Review* 48: 147–160.

Don, Y. 1977. Industrialization in advanced rural communities: The Israeli kibbutz. *Sociologia Ruralis* 17: 59–72.

Don, Y. 1988. *Industrialization of Rural Collectives.* Aldershot: Gower Publishing Group.

Dror, Y. 1984. The Formation of Social Studies Curricula in the Kibbutz Movements: Ideological, Social and Educational Analysis (in Hebrew). Ph.D. thesis, Hebrew University.

Dulfer, E. 1985. The co-operatives between member participation, the formation of vertical organizations and bureaucratic tendencies. In *Co-operatives: In Clash between Member Participation, Organizational Development and Bureaucratic Tendencies,* ed. E. Dulfer, and W. Hamm, 15–39. London: Quiller Press.

Dun and Bradstreet. 1996. *Duns Guide Israel: Israel's Business Directory.* Tel Aviv: Dun and Bradstreet International.

Eccles, R. G., and H. C. White. 1988. Price and authority in inter-profit center transactions. *American Journal of Sociology* 94 (supplement): 17–51.

Eddelist, M., and B. Nevo. 1983. Creativity of kibbutz and urban children (in Hebrew). *Chavat Daat* 16: 120–135.

Eden, D., and U. Leviatan. 1974. Farm and factory in the kibbutz: A study in agroindustrial psychology. *Journal of Applied Psychology* 59 (5). [Also in *Work and Organization in Kibbutz Industry,* ed. U. Leviatan and M. Rosner. 34–42, Norwood, Penn.: Norwood Editions, 1980].

Eiferman, R. R. 1970. Cooperativeness in kibbutz children's games. *Human Relations* 23: 579–587.

Eisenberg, N., R. Hertz-Lazarowitz, and I. Fuchs. 1990. Prosocial moral judgment in Israeli kibbutz and city children: A longitudinal study. *Merrill-Palmer Quarterly* 36: 273–285.

Eisenstadt, S. N. 1985. The Israel political system and the transformation of Israeli society. In *Politics and Society in Israel—Studies in Israeli Society,* ed. E. Krausz, 3: 415–427. New Brunswick, N.J., and Oxford: Transaction Books.

Erikson, H. E. 1950. *Childhood and Society.* New York: Norton.

Erikson, H. E. 1959. Ego identity and the psychosocial moratorium. In *New Perspectives for Research for Juvenile Delinquency,* ed. H. L. Witmer and R. Kotinsky, 1–22. Washington, D.C.: U.S. Department of Health.

Etzioni, A. 1959. The functional differentiation of elites in the kibbutz. *American Journal of Sociology* 64: 476–487.

Etzioni, A. 1970. A basis for comparative analysis of complex organizations. In *A Sociological Reader on Complex Organizations,* 2nd ed. A. Etzioni, 59–76. London: Holt, Rinehart & Winston.

Etzioni, A. 1980. *The Organizational Structure of the Kibbutz.* New York: Arno Press.

Evan, W. M. 1975. Hierarchy, alienation, commitment, and organizational effectiveness. *Human Relations* 30: 77–94.

Faigin, H. 1958. Social behavior of young children in the kibbutz. *Journal of Abnormal Social Psychology* 56: 17–129.

Feldman, S. S., B. Aschenbrenner, l. Saranat, and N. Yirmiya. 1983. Perception of Child Rearing Roles: A Study of Israeli Mothers and Care-Givers in Town and Kibbutzim (in Hebrew). Unpublished paper, Haifa University.

Gamson, Z., and M. Palgi. 1982. The "over-educated" kibbutz: Shifting relations between social reproduction and individual development in the kibbutz. *Interchange on Educational Policy* 13: 55–67.

Gerson, M. 1978. *Family, Women, and Socialization in the Kibbutz.* Lexington, Mass.: Lexington Books.

Getz, S. 1994. Statistics for 1994, from the Department of Statistics—TAKAM Federation. Unpublished paper.

Gilad, Y. 1990. Development of the educational system in one kibbutz: Five years after the introduction of conventional sleeping arrangements for children. In *Kibbutz Members Study Kibbutz Children,* ed. Z. Lavi, 56–63. Westport, Conn.: Greenwood Press.

Gluck, Y., H. Goldemberg and A. Helman. 1988. *Economic Behavior of Kibbutzim under Crisis Conditions and Its Expression in Social Indicators* (in Hebrew). Institute for Social Research of the Kibbutz and the Cooperative Idea, Monograph no. 78. Haifa: Haifa University.

Golan, S. 1959. Collective education in the kibbutz. *Psychiatry* 22: 167–177.

Golan, S. 1961. *Collective Education* (in Hebrew). Merchavia: Sifriyat Poalim.

Golomb, N., and D. Katz. 1971. *The Kibbutz as an Open Social System* (in Hebrew). Tel Aviv: Sifriyat Poalim.

Gordon, A. D. 1938. *Selected Essays.* New York: League for Labor Palestine.

Gradus, Y. 1986. Centralization—decentralization: Centers and peripheries and the regional problem in Israel (in Hebrew). *Economic Quarterly* 36 (128): 496–499.

Granovetter, M. 1985. Economic action and social structure: The problem of embeddedness. *American Journal of Sociology* 91(3): 481–510.

Granovetter, M. 1991. The old and the new economic sociology: A history and an agenda. In *Beyond the Market Place,* ed. R. Friedland and A. F. Robertson, 89–112. New York: Aldive de Gruyter.

Grinberg, L. L. 1991. *Split Corporatism in Israel.* Albany: State University of New York.

Gvati, H. 1981. *A Century of Settlement* (in Hebrew). Vol. 2. Tel Aviv: Hakibbutz Hameuchad.

Halperin, H. 1963. *Agrindus.* London: Routledge and Kegan Paul.

Handel, A. 1971. Das Selbstbild des heranwachsenden Kibbutzniks. In *Kolektiverziehung im Kibbutz,* ed. L. Liegle, 230–245. Munchen: Piper, Erziehung in Wissenschaft und Praxis.

Harel, Y. 1993. *The New Kibbutz* (in Hebrew). Jerusalem: Keter.

Harif, M. 1982. Regional cooperation and integration (in Hebrew). *Divrei Haknesset* 92: 1082–1085.

Helman, A. 1982. *The Economic Factor in Members' Turn-Over* (in Hebrew). Research paper 82/10. Ruppin Institute.

Helman, A. 1994. Privatization and the Israeli kibbutz experience. *Journal of Rural Cooperation* 22: 1–2, 19–32.

Hertz-Lazarowitz, R., I. Fuschs, R. Sharabany, and N. Eisenberg. 1989. Students' interactive and non-interactive behaviors in the classroom: A comparison between two types of classrooms in the city and the kibbutz in Israel. *Contemporary Educational Psychology* 1: 22–32.

Hertzberg, F., B. Mausner, and B. B. Snyderman, 1959. *The Motivation to Work.* New York: John Wiley & Sons.

Heydebrand, W. V. 1989. New organizational forms. *Work and Occupations* 16 (3): 323–357.

Horowitz, D., and M. Lissak. 1977. *The Origin of the Israeli Polity* (in Hebrew). Tel Aviv: Am Oved.

House, J., R. C. Kessler, A. R. Herzog, et al. 1990. Age, socioeconomic status and health. *Milbank Quarterly* 68 (3): 383–411.

Kaffman, M. 1993. Kibbutz youth: Recent past and present. *Journal of Youth and Adolescence* 22: 573–604.

Kaffman, M., E. Elizur, and M. Rabinowitz. 1990. Early childhood in the kibbutz: The 1980s. In *Kibbutz Members Study Kibbutz Children*, ed. Z. Lavi, 17–33. New York: Greenwood.

Kahana, F. 1992. Kibbutz as urban alternative (in Hebrew). *Shorashim* 7: 237–266.

Kahane, R. 1975. The committed: Preliminary reflections on the impact of the kibbutz socialization pattern on adolescents. *British Journal of Sociology* 26: 343–353 .

Kahane, R. 1988. Multicode organizations: A conceptual framework for the analysis of boarding schools. *Sociology of Education* 61: 211–223.

Kanter, R. M. 1972. *Commitment and Community: Communes and Utopias in Sociological Perspective.* Cambridge, Mass.: Harvard University Press.

Katz, D., and R. L. Kahn. 1978. *The Social Psychology of Organisations.* 2nd ed. New York: John Wiley.

Keniston, K. 1970. Youth, a "new" stage of life. *The American Scholar* 39: 631–654.

Kerschensteiner, G. 1929. *The Essence of the Activity School* (in Hebrew, translated from German). Jerusalem.

Kibbutz Artzi. 1977. *Resolutions: The 41st Council Meeting of Industry* (in Hebrew). Gan Shmuel: Kibbutz Artzi.

Kibbutz Regulations (No date). *Takanot Hakibbutz* (in Hebrew), Kibbutz movements.

Kohlberg, L. 1971. Cognitive-developmental theory and the practice of collective moral education. In *Group Care: An Israeli Approach.* New York: Gordon & Breach.

Kornai, J. 1986. *Contradictions and Dilemmas.* Cambridge, Mass.

Kressel, G. 1974. *From Each One According to His Abilities: Stratification versus Equality in the Kibbutz* (in Hebrew). Tel Aviv: Tzerikover.

Krol, Y. et al., 1989. *The Economic Crisis in the TAKAM Kibbutzim* (in Hebrew). Tel Aviv: United Kibbutz Movement Economic Division.

Lakin, M., and F. Constanz, 1979. Group processes in early childhood: A dimension of human development. *International Journal of Behavioral Development* 2: 171–183.

Lanir, J. 1985. *Administration and Communication Problems of Our Epoch* (in Hebrew). Ramat Efal: Yad Tabenkin.

Larson, R. 1978. Thirty years of research on the subjective well-being of older Americans. *Journal of Gerontology* 33: 109–125.

Lavi, Z. 1973. Methods of study and instruction in high school. In *Collective Education in the Kibbutz*, ed. A. I. Rabin and B. Hazan, 131–160. New York: Springer.

Lavi, Z. 1984. The transition from communal to family sleeping arrangements (in Hebrew). *Hachinuh Hameshutaf* 114: 5–15.

Leon, D. 1969. *The Kibbutz: A New Way of Life.* Oxford: Pergamon Press.

Leviatan U. 1975a. *Factors That Determine Attachment of Kibbutz-Born to Kibbutz Life and Reasons for Their Departure* (in Hebrew). Institute for Social Research of the Kibbutz and the Cooperative Idea. Haifa: Haifa University.

Leviatan, U. 1975b. Industrialization and kibbutz values—contrast or complement? (in Hebrew). *HaKibbutz* 2: 11–26.

Leviatan, U. 1976. *Managerial Succession in Kibbutz Production Branches* (in Hebrew). Institute for Social Research of the Kibbutz and the Cooperative Idea, Monograph no. 14. Haifa: Haifa University.

Leviatan, U. 1978. Organizational effects of managerial turnover in kibbutz production branches. *Human Relations* 81 (3): 1001–1018.

Leviatan, U. 1980a. Effects of employing hired workers on the functioning of kibbutz industry (in Hebrew). In *Self Management and Hired Workers in Kibbutz Industry*, by the Association of Kibbutz Industries, 92–132. Tel Aviv: Association of Kibbutz Industries.

Leviatan, U. 1980b. Hired labor in the kibbutz: Ideology, history and social psychological effects. In *Work and Organization in Kibbutz Industry*, ed. U. Leviatan and M. Rosner, 64–75. Norwood, Penn: Norwood Editions.

Leviatan, U. 1981. Kibbutz society in the public eye (in Hebrew). *HaKibbutz* 8: 235–256.

Leviatan, U. 1982a. Human factors and economic performance. In *Work and Organization in Kibbutz Industry*, ed. U. Leviatan, and M. Rosner. Norwood, Penn.: Norwood Editions.

Leviatan, U. 1982b. Work and age: Centrality of work in the life of older members. In *Work and Organization in Kibbutz Industry*, ed. U. Leviatan, and M. Rosner. Norwood, Penn: Norwood Editions.

Leviatan, U. 1983a. *Intergender Differences in Involvement and Identification with the Kibbutz and Its Principles* (in Hebrew). Institute for Social Research of the Kibbutz and the Cooperative Idea, Monograph no. 51. Haifa: Haifa University.

Leviatan, U. 1983b. Work and aging in the kibbutz. *Aging and Work* 6 (3): 215–226.

Leviatan, U. 1985. Interpretation of sex differences in work centrality among kibbutz members. *Sex Roles* 13: 287–310.

Leviatan, U. 1988. The community as a compensating support giver to the single individual (in Hebrew). *Gerontologist* 41/42: 28–38.

Leviatan, U. 1992. *Rotation of Central Offices in Kibbutzim: A Current Picture* (in Hebrew). Institute for Social Research of the Kibbutz and the Cooperative Idea, Monograph no. 120. Haifa: Haifa University.

Leviatan, U. 1994. Leadership functioning in kibbutzim as determinants of conditions for members' commitment. *Journal of Rural Cooperation* 22: 93–111.

Leviatan, U. 1995. *The Researcher's Point of View* (in Hebrew). Institute for Social Research of the Kibbutz and the Cooperative Idea, Monograph no. 134. Haifa: Haifa University.

Leviatan, U. 1996. *Conditions for Negative Self-Selection among Kibbutz Youth* (in Hebrew). Institute for Social Research of the Kibbutz and the Cooperative Idea, Monograph no. 147. Haifa: Haifa University.

Leviatan, U., G. Adar, and Z. Am-Ad. 1981. Aging in the kibbutz—satisfaction with life and its determinants (in Hebrew). *HaKibbutz* 8: 16–42.

Leviatan, U., J. Cohen, and M. Yafa-Katz. 1983. Life expectancy of kibbutz members (in Hebrew). *Gerontology* 25/26: 45–54.

Leviatan, U., J. Cohen, and M. Yafa-Katz. 1986. Life expectancy of kibbutz members. *International Journal of Aging and Human Development* 23 (3): 195–205.

172 References

Leviatan, U., and J. Cohen-Mansfield. 1985. Sex differences in life expectancy. *Social Science and Medicine* 21 (5): 541–551.

Leviatan, U., and E. Orchan. 1982. Kibbutz ex-members and their adjustment to life outside the kibbutz. *Interchange on Educational Policy* 13: 16–28.

Leviatan, U., E. Orchan, and A. Ovnat. 1984. Success factors in absorption of youth in kibbutzim (in Hebrew). *Shorashim* 4: 199–217.

Leviatan, U., and M. Rosner. eds. 1980. *Work and Organization in Kibbutz Industry.* Norwood, Penn.: Norwood Editions.

Levy, S., and L. Guttman.1974. *Values and Attitudes of the Israeli School Youth* (in Hebrew). Research report no. 1. Jerusalem: Institute for Applied Social Research.

Liberman, Y. 1994. Kibbutz elementary schools, 1994 (in Hebrew). *Yediot* (Institute of Research on Kibbutz Education) 20: 33–58.

Liegle, L. 1980. Some remarks on deficiencies and perspectives of research on socialization in the kibbutz. In *Integral Cooperatives in the Industrial Society*, ed. K. Bartolke, T. Bergmann, and L. Liegle, 62–71. Assen, Netherlands: Van Gorcum.

Likver, J. 1947. Marking points in society development (in Hebrew). *Sefer Genigar (25 anniversary of kibbutz Genigar).*

Marcia, J. E. 1980. Identity in adolescence. In *Handbook of Adolescent Psychology*, ed. J. Adelson, 159–187. New York: Wiley.

Marcus, J., A. Thomas, and S. Chess. 1969. Behavioral individuality in kibbutz children. *Israel Annals of Psychiatry and Related Disciplines* 7: 43–54.

Margnis, D. 1976. *The Lessons of the Moth.* New York: Pushad Press, 167–168.

Maron, S. 1994a. *The Kibbutz Movement, 1993: Statistical Yearbook* (in Hebrew). Ramat Efal: Yad Tabenkin.

Maron, S. 1994b. Recent development in the kibbutz: An overview. *Journal of Rural Cooperation* 22: 5–17.

Maron, S. 1995. *Kibbutz Movement—Figures and Information* (in Hebrew). Ramat Efal: Yad Tabenkin.

Meister, A. 1973. *La participation dans les associations.* Paris: Editions Ouvrieres.

Meister, A. 1984. *Participation, Associations, Development, and Change.* New Brunswick, N.J: Transaction Books.

Melman, S. 1971. Managerial vs. cooperative decision making in Israel. *Studies in Comparative International Development* 6(3).

Messinger, Y. 1973. *Educating the Generation That Will Carry—On* (in Hebrew). Tel Aviv: Am Oved.

Michels, R. 1959. *Political Parties.* New York: Dover Publications.

Nadler, A., E. Romek, and A. Shapira-Friedman. 1979. Giving in the kibbutz: Pro-social behavior of city and kibbutz children as affected by social responsibility and social pressure. *Journal of Cross-Cultural Psychology* 10: 57–71.

Natan, M., A. Shnabel-Brandeis, and H. Peskin. 1982. Together and separate: Kibbutz-born ten years after graduation from school (in Hebrew). *HaKibbutz* 8: 105–115.

Nevo, B. 1977. Personality differences between kibbutz born and city born adults. *Journal of Psychology* 96: 303–308.

Nisan, M. 1984. Distributive justice and social norms. *Child Development* 55: 1020–1029.

Nisan, M. 1989. Children's perceptions of effort and productivity as granting a right for reward. *British Journal of Developmental Psychology* 7: 307–319.

Orchan, E. 1990. *Change in Reproduction Rates in the Kibbutz Movement, 1948–1988* (in Hebrew). Institute for Social Research of the Kibbutz and the Cooperative Idea, Monograph no. 97. Haifa: Haifa University.

Orchan, E. 1991. *Birth Giving and Reproduction Tendencies among Kibbutz Women* (in Hebrew). Institute for Social Research of the Kibbutz and the Cooperative Idea, Monograph no. 102. Haifa: Haifa University.

Ouchi, W. G. 1977. The relationship between organizational structure and organizational control. *Administrative Science Quarterly* 22: 95–113.

Ouchi, W. G. 1980. Markets, bureaucracies, and clans. *Administrative Science Quarterly* 25: 129–141.

Palgi, M. 1984. Theoretical and Empirical Aspects of Workers' Participation in Decision Making: A Comparison between Kibbutz and Non-Kibbutz Industrial Plants in Israel (in Hebrew). Ph.D. dissertation, Hebrew University.

Palgi, M. 1994a. Attitudes toward suggested changes in the kibbutz as predicted by perceived economic and ideological crisis. *Journal of Rural Cooperation* 22 (1–2): 94–113.

Palgi, M. 1994b. Women in the changing kibbutz economy. In *Economic and Industrial Democracy*. London: Sage.

Palgi, M. 1996. Kibbutz members educated in the kibbutz and youth movement: A comparison (in Hebrew). In *Education and Society—Special Issue on Kibbutz Education*, ed. I. Kashti, and Y. Dror, Tel Aviv: Massada.

Palgi, M., J. R. Blasi, M. Rosner, and M. Safir. 1983. *Sexual Equalits: The Israeli Kibbutz Tests the Theories*. Norwood, Penn: Norwood Editions.

Palgi, M., and M. Rosner. 1980. Psychological, social and organizational outcomes of self-management in kibbutz factories. In *Self Management and Hired Labor in Kibbutz Industries*, Tel Aviv: Kibbutz Industrial Association.

Palgi, M., and M. Rosner. 1983. Equalits between the sexes in the Kibbutz, regression or changed meaning? In *Sexual Equalits: The Israeli Kibbutz Tests the Theories*, Palgi et al. 255–296. Norwood, Penn.: Norwood Editions.

Palgi, M., and S. Sharir. 1995. *Public Opinion Survey of Kibbutz Members, 1995* (in Hebrew). Institute for Social Research of the Kibbutz and the Cooperative Idea. Haifa: Haifa University.

Palgi, Y. 1982. The Effect of Sleeping Arrangement upon the Components of "Family Climate" in Two Types of Sleeping Arrangement in Kibbutzim (in Hebrew). Master's thesis, Tel Aviv University.

Panebianco, A. 1982. *Political Parties: Organization and Power*. Cambridge: Cambridge University Press.

Pavin, A. 1995. *Kibbutz Changes—Theoretical Remarks* (in Hebrew). Institute for the Study of the Kibbutz and the Cooperative Idea. Haifa: Haifa University.

Peleg, D. 1980. Economic perspective on kibbutz industrialization. In *Work and Organization in Kibbutz Industry,* ed. U. Leviatan and M. Rosner, 7–16. Norwood, Penn.: Norwood Editions.

Peres, J. 1963. The general assembly in the kvutza (in Hebrew). *Ovnayim:* 76–107.

Piaget, J. 1952. *The Origins of Intelligence in Children*. New York: International Universities Press.

Pirojnikoff, L. A., I. Hadar, and A. Hadar. 1971. Dogmatism and social distance: A cross-cultural study. *Journal of Social Psychology* 85: 187–193.

Porat, Y. 1971. The ideal "I" among three generations in the kibbutz (in Hebrew). *Shdemoth* 39.

Powell, W. 1990. Neither market nor hierarchy: Network forms of organization. *Research in Organizational Behavior* 12: 295–336.

Quarter, J. 1984. The development of political reasoning on the Israeli kibbutz. *Adolescence* 19: 569–593.

Rabin, A. I. 1965. *Growing Up in the Kibbutz*. New York: Springer.

Rabin, A. 1991. *A Comparison of Economic Effectiveness: 50 Kibbutz Industries and 50 Israeli Industries* (in Hebrew). Tel Aviv: Kibbutz Artzi.

Rabin, A. I., and B. Beit-Hallahmi. 1982. *Twenty Years Later: Kibbutz Children Grown Up*. New York: Springer.

Rabin, A. I., and B. Hazan. 1973. *Collective Education in the Kibbutz: From Infancy to Maturity*. New York: Springer.

Ravid, S. 1994. Is the kibbutz undergoing a value change? *Journal of Rural Cooperation* 22: 33–40.

Raviv, A., and Y. Palgi. 1985. The perception of social-environmental characteristics in kibbutz families with family-based and communal sleeping arrangements. *Journal of Personality and Social Psychology* 49: 376–385.

Rayman, P. 1981. *The Kibbutz Community and Nation Building*. Princeton, N.J.: Princeton University Press.

Regev, A., B. Beit-Hallahmi, and R. Sharabany. 1980. Affective expression in kibbutz communal, kibbutz familial and city raised children in Israel. *Child Development* 51: 232–237.

Regev, E. 1977. Shallowness and diversification in emotional expressions as a result of the communal sleeping arrangement: A comparison among children in communal and family sleeping arrangements in kibbutzim and city children (in Hebrew). Master's thesis, Haifa University.

Ron-Polani, Y. 1960. In search for patterns of education in the kvutza (in Hebrew). In *Sefer Yosef Bussel*, ed. S. Vorm, 118–138. Tel Aviv: Tarbut Ve'Chinuch.

Ronen, S. 1978. Personal values: A basis for work motivational set and work attitude. *Organizational Behavior Performance* 21: 80–107.

Rosner, M. 1971. Hierarchy and Democracy in Kibbutz Industry: The Social Values of the Kibbutz and the Functional Requirements of Industry (in Hebrew). Ph.D. dissertation, Hebrew University.

Rosner, M. 1983a. Organizations between community and market: The case of the kibbutz. *Economic and Industrial Democracy* 14: 369–397.

Rosner, M. 1983b. Participatory political and organizational democracy and the experience of the Israeli kibbutz. In *Organizational Democracy and Political Processes—International Yearbook of Organizational Democracy*, vol. 1, ed. C. Crouch, F. Heller, and J. Chichester. New York: Wiley and Sons.

Rosner, M., J. Ben-David, A. Ovnat, N. Cohen, and U. Leviatan. 1990. *The Second Generation— The Kibbutz between Continuity and Change*. Westport, Conn.: Greenwood Press.

Rosner, M., M. Chizik, and S. Shur. 1989. *Trends in Kibbutz Socialism* (in Hebrew). Tel Aviv: Sifriyat Poalim.

Rosner, M., and N. Cohen. 1980. Direct democracy in the kibbutz (in Hebrew). *Shorashim* 2: 85–116.

Rosner, M., and S. Getz. 1994. Towards a theory of changes in the kibbutz. *Journal of Rural Cooperation* 22 (1–2): 41–62.

Rosner, M., and S. Getz. 1996. *The Kibbutz in an Era of Change* (in Hebrew). Tel Aviv: Hakibbutz Hameuchad and Haifa University Press.

Rosner, M., Y. Gluck, and H. Goldenberg. 1991. *Changes in Consumption Patterns in the Kibbutz—The Individual Level* (in Hebrew). Institute for Social Research of the Kibbutz and the Cooperative Idea. Haifa: Haifa University.

Rosner, M., Y. Gluck, and A. Ovnat. 1979. Satisfaction with consumption in kibbutzim (in Hebrew). *Economic Quarterly* 101/2: 276–291.

Rosner, M., and M. Palgi. 1980. Ideology and organization—The case of kibbutz industrialization. In *Work and Organization in Kibbutz Industry*, ed. U. Leviatan and M. Rosner. Norwood, Penn.: Norwood Editions.

Rosner, M., Z. Sheaffer, and D. Rosolio. 1993. *Hired labor in industrial plants of the Kibbutz Artzi* (in Hebrew). Institute for Research on the Kibbutz. Haifa: Haifa University.

Rosner, M., and A. S. Tannenbaum. 1987. Organizational efficiency and egalitarian democracy in an intentional communal society: The kibbutz. *British Journal of Sociology* 38: 521–545.

Rosolio, D. 1974. Patterns of Interrelations between the Government and the Kibbutz as an Economic and Ideological Entity (in Hebrew). Paper presented to the international symposium on The dynamics of interrelations between agricultural co-operatives and the government, Tel Aviv.

Rosolio, D. 1975. *The Regional Structure of the Kibbutz Movement* (in Hebrew). Tel Aviv: Am Oved.

Rosolio, D. 1993. The study of kibbutz in the process of change. Theoretical approach (in Hebrew). *The Kibbutz at the Turn of the Century* 9. Ramat Efal: Yad Tabenkin.

Rosolio, D. 1994. The kibbutz movement and the way it functions as a cause of the kibbutz crisis: A study in political economy. *Journal of Rural Cooperation* 22 (1–2): 63–78.

Rosolio, D. 1995. *Factors in the Crisis and Changes in the Kibbutz System: An Analysis of the Kibbutz System* (in Hebrew). Discussion paper no. 76. Tel Aviv: Golda Meir Institute for Social and Labor Research.

Rosolio, D. 1996. Crises, Arrangements and Changes in the Kibbutz System: Analysis of Two Periods (in Hebrew). Ph.D. dissertation, Tel Aviv University.

Ross, H. S., C. Conant, J. A. Cheyne, and E. Alevizos. 1992. Relationships and alliances in the social interaction of kibbutz toddlers. *Social Development* 1: 1–16.

Russell, R., S. Getz, and M. Rosner. 1996. Institutional Sources of Stability and Change in the Israeli Kibbutz, 1990–1995. Paper presented at the American Sociological Association annual meeting, New York.

Sagi, A., and N. Koren-Karie. 1993. Day-care centers in Israel: An overview. In *International Handbook of Day-Care Policies and Programs*, ed. M. Cochran, 269–290. New York: Greenwood Press.

Schwartz, M., L. Appelbaum, F. Keidar, and T. Banin. 1994. *Regional Councils in Time of Change: The Change of Development Planning* (in Hebrew). Rehovot: Development Study Center.

Segal, M. 1955. *Essays on Education* (in Hebrew). Tel Aviv: Hakibbutz Hameuchad.

Segal, M. 1979. Dewey's thought in the test of time (in Hebrew). *Baseminar: The Kibbutzim Teachers' College Annual* 3: 118–139.

Seginer, R. 1988. Social milieu and future orientation: The case of kibbutz versus urban adolescents. *International Journal of Behavioral Development* 11: 247–273.

Shapira, A., and M.C. Madsen. 1974. Between and within group cooperation and competition among kibbutz and non-kibbutz children. *Developmental Psychology* 10: 140–145.

Shapira, R. 1987. *Anatomy of Managerial Illness* (in Hebrew). Tel Aviv: Am Oved.

Sharabany, R., and H. Weisman. 1993. Close relationships in adolescence: The case of the kibbutz. *Journal of Youth and Adolescence* 22: 671–695.

Shatil, I. 1956. On organizational problems of the kibbutz (in Hebrew). *Hedim* 50:59–67.

Shepher, J. 1969. Familism and social structure: The case of the kibbutz. *Journal of Marriage and the Family* 31: 568–573.

Shepher, J. 1977. *An Introduction to the Sociology of the Kibbutz* (in Hebrew). Ruppin Agricultural College.

Shes, R. 1977. Division of Educational Roles between Parents and Care-Givers of Toddlers in Kibbutzim (in Hebrew). Master's thesis, Tel Aviv University.

Shimoni, U. 1983. Patterns of Kibbutz Industrialization (in Hebrew). Ph.D. dissertation, Hebrew University.

Shimoni U., H. Goldemberg, Y. Glick, and M. Rosner. 1994. *Motivation and Management Patterns in Kibbutz Industry* (in Hebrew). Institute Social Research of the Kibbutz and the Cooperative Idea, Haifa University. Ramat Efal: Yad Tabenkin.

Shner, M. 1986. The kibbutz shift from humanism to humanistic totalitarianism (in Hebrew). *Shdemoth* 9697: 25–38.

Shoham, E. 1990. The kibbutz school with matriculation exams as seen by the pupils and the educational community in the kibbutz. In *Kibbutz Members Study Kibbutz Children*, ed. Z. Lavi, 170–178. New York: Greenwood.

Shouval, R., S. Kav-Venaki, U. Bronfenbrenner, E. C. Devreux, and E. Kiely. 1975. Anomalous reactions to social pressure of Israeli and Soviet children raised in family versus collective settings. *Journal of Personality and Social Psychology* 32: 477–489.

Shur, S. 1984. *The Equality in the Kibbutz* (in Hebrew). Institute for Research of the Kibbutz and the Cooperative Idea. Haifa: Haifa University.

Smith, R. 1996. *Attitudes of the Public toward the Kibbutzim* (in Hebrew). Jerusalem: Smith Research and Consulting. Internal report, December.

Snarey, J. 1987. Promoting moral maturity among adolescents: An ethnographic study of the Israeli kibbutz. *Comparative Educational Review* 31: 241–259.

Sohlberg, S. C. 1985. Similarity and dissimilarity in value patterns of Israeli kibbutz and city adolescents. *International Journal of Psychology* 21: 189–202.

Spiro, M. E. 1965. *Children of the Kibbutz.* 1959. Reprint, New York: Schoken.

Tal, A. 1982. Differential predictors of achievement among kibbutz and urban high school students. *Interchange on Educational Policy* 13: 83–91.

Talmon-Garber, Y. 1970. *Individual and Society in the Kibbutz* (in Hebrew). Jerusalem: Magnes Publishing House.

Talmon-Garber, Y. 1972. *Family and Community in the Kibbutz.* Cambridge: Harvard University Press.

Tannenbaum, A., M. Rosner, B. Kavic, M. Vianello, and G. Weiser. 1974. *Hierarchy in Organization.* San Francisco: Jossey Bass.

Tiger, L., and J. Shepher. 1975. *Women in the Kibbutz.* New York: Harcourt, Brace, Jovanovich.

Toffler, A. 1972. Future Shock. New York: Bantam Books.

Toffler, A. 1990. *Power Shift.* New York: Bantam Books.

Topel, M. 1992. Organization, power and leadership in kibbutz community (in Hebrew). In *Kibbutz Society—Change and Continuity*, Tel Aviv: The Open University.

Topel, M. 1995. *Trends in the Process of Change in the Kibbutz* (in Hebrew). Ramat Efal: Yad Tabenkin.

Valko, L. 1985. Cooperatives and their federal legislation in the U.S.A. In *Co-operatives: In Clash between Member Participation, Organizational Development and Bureaucratic Tendencies*, ed. E. Dulfer and W. Hamm, 185–199. London: Quiller Press.

Vallier, Y. 1962. Structural differentiation, production imperatives and communal norms. *Social Forces* 40: 234–242.

Warhurst, C. 1996. High society in a workers' society: Work, community and kibbutz. *Sociology* 30 (1): 1–19.

Weber, M. 1949. *The Methodology of the Social Sciences.* New York: Free Press.

Weiseman, H., and A. Lieblich. 1992. Individuation in a collective community. *Adolescence Psychiatry* 18: 156–179.

Williamson, O. E. 1975. *Markets and Hierarchies: Analysis and Antitrust Implication.* New York: Free Press.

Williamson, O. E. 1991. Comparative economic organization: The analysis of discreet structural alternatives. *Administrative Science Quarterly* 36: 269–296.

Wyneken, G. 1913. *Schule and Jugendkultur.* Jena: Dietrich.

Yitzhaki, S. 1976. About Gustav Wyneken (in Hebrew). *Hahinuh Hameshutaf* 90: 47–55.

Yitzhaki, S. 1977. About Siegfried Bernfeld (in Hebrew). *Hahinuh Hameshutaf* 94: 52–64.

Yitzhaki, S. 1982. The contribution of psychoanalysis to the education of adolescents (in Hebrew). *Baseminar: The Kibbutzim Teachers' College Annual,* 87–92.

Yuchtman-Yaar, E. 1983. Reward distribution and work-role attractiveness in the kibbutz: Reflections on equity theory. In *The Sociology of the Kibbutz,* ed. E. Krausz, 179–193. New Brunswick, N.J.: Transaction Books.

Zamir, A. 1991. *The Sons of the Kibbutz—Realization of Their Potential and Their Integration in Kibbutz Activities* (in Hebrew). Ramat Efal: Yad Tabenkin.

Zamir, D. 1996. *Economic Success and Confrontation with Crisis—The Contribution of Organizational Culture* (in Hebrew). Institute for Social Research of the Kibbutz and the Cooperative Idea. Haifa: Haifa University.

Zellermayer, J., and J. Marcus. 1972. Kibbutz adolescence: Relevance to personality-development theory. *Journal of Youth and Adolescence* 1: 143–153.

Zilbersheid, U. 1994. Karl Marx's educational thought (in Hebrew). *Eyunim Buchinuch* 60: 373–390.

Index

Adaptability, ix, xii, 13–25. *See also*
    Change
Adar, Gila, xvii, 111–18
Adolescents, 60–61, 69–70. *See also* Education
Adulthood, 61, 69–70
Aging: demographics of, xi, 2–3; denial
    of, 134–35; effect of recent changes
    on, 142; and families, 139; and health
    care, 139; and settlement policies,
    133; single members and, 141; societal provisions for, 139, 141–42, 145,
    154; and standard of living, 125, 138–
    39; uniqueness of kibbutz situation,
    135–36; and work, 54, 140–41, 142
Agriculture: councils, 152; employment
    in, 10–11; farming produce, xiv; marketing, 151–52; purchasing, 152, 155;
    technological sophistication, 28
Asceticism, 120–21
Automobiles, 17–18
Ayelet Hashahar, 4

Banks, xiii
Bereavement, 125
Bernfeld, S., 62
Bijaoui Fogiel, S., 149
Birth rate, 7–9, 12
Buber, Martin, 162

Budgets: control of, 16–19; inclusive,
    129–30; personal, 128; privatization
    of, 18–19, 116, 128–30, 142; regional
    municipal councils', 154
Bylaws, 42

Capital, xv, 35, 46
Chafetz, S. J., 118
Change: in allocation of rewards, 22–23;
    causes of, 55–56; effect on older members, 142–43, 145; in the Nineties, 15;
    organizational structure, 21–22, 52–55,
    104–105; privatization, 14–20; relation
    to outsiders, 24–25; social and educational, 66–70; trends in, 25, 159–60; and
    value system of young members, 88–89.
    See also Adaptability
Children: age groups, 59, 69, 71 n.2, 73–
    74; caring for, 4, 31; parents' role in
    raising, 58, 67, 73–79; sleeping arrangements, 7, 71 n.6, 73–79; socialization for communal life, 31, 58, 64;
    working on kibbutz, 69. *See also* Adolescents; Education
Cohen, E., 149
Collectivism vs individualism. *See* Individualism vs collectivism
Commitment, factors determining, 81–
    96, 161–62

Committees, 101–4, 107, 134, 141

Communes: based on ownership of means of production, 25; evolution of kibbutzim from, 3–5; socialization of children for, 58

Community: and education, 59; and the elderly, 139, 141, 144; kibbutz as familial, 6–7; and relationship to economic sector, 51, 52, 108, 114, 159

Consultants, economic, xv–xvi

Consumption, 16–19, 119–30; defining the consumer basket, 123–30; issues arising from needs satisfaction, 120–22; methods of satisfying needs, 125–30

Cooperatives, 34, 151–53, 155

Coordinators, 34–35. See also Management

Cosmetics, 124

Dar, Yechezkel, xvii, 57–72

Debt, xiv–xv, 156

Decentralization, 148, 153, 156–57

Decision-making, 21–22, 36–39, 47–48, 100–109

Degania, 4

Democracy: direct, x–xi, 36–37; and restriction of managers' power, 21–22; shift away from direct, 51, 55–56, 104–7

Demographics: aging statistics, 132–33, 136–37; birth rate, 7–9, 12; divorce, 116; educational levels, 9; emergence from communes, 3–5; employment structure, 9–12; familial community, 4, 6–7; infant mortality, 137; longevity, 136; marriage, 7–9, 12, 116; membership growth, vii, xiv, 2–3, 5–9; mortality rates, 136–38, 141; per cent working outside the kibbutz, 113; population growth, 5–6

Demographic void, 133

Derekh, I., 100, 102

Dewey, John, x, 62–63

Dining hall, 17, 31, 125

Divorce, 117

Dun and Bradstreet, xiii–xiv, 50

Durable goods, 127

Economics: and birth rate, 8; budget privatization, 18–19; as change factor, 55–56; consumption level and, 122; coordination of, 100, 101, 103–104, 107; "the crisis," xiii–xvi; and the elderly, 142–43; equality vs equity, 34–35, 112; Israeli economy, viii; labor market, 19–20, 21, 29–31; ownership of means of production, 25; and relation to community, 51, 52, 108, 114, 159; transition from Keynesian to neoliberalism, 153. See also Agriculture; Industry

Education: academic disciplines, 68; attitudinal effects of, 64–66, 71 n.4; average level of, 44–45; community's role in, 59; directed toward kibbutz life, 31, 58, 64, 87, 95; equality vs individualism in, 9, 60; families' role in, 58, 67, 68; higher, xi, 9, 29, 71, 115–16, 124; Marx's influence on, 62; moral, 60, 61; new organizational culture and, 55; normative model, 57–66, 71 n.1; and occupational ambitions, 30; pedagogical approach, 60, 61–64; and psychoanalysis, 63; regionalization of, 19, 67–69, 71 n.2, 154; teachers, 60, 62, 68–69, 154; tutoring, 125. See also Adolescents; Children

Efficiency, 160–61

Eisenstadt, S. N., 156–57

Elderly. See Aging

Election systems, 22, 105–6, 154

Environment: effect on older members, 139; major changes in external and internal, xi–xii; openness to, 24–25

Equality, 112, 121, 124

Exchange rate, xiv

Exchange relationships, 83–96

Families: children's sleeping arrangement with, 67, 69, 71 n.6, 73–79; elderly members of, 139, 144; and kibbutz as familial community, 6–7; mothers' and fathers' roles in, 73–79, 116–17; in normative education model, 58; socialist view of, 62; spousal relationships, 140; transfer of functions to,

116–17; transferring budgets to, 128–30; and transition from commune to kibbutz, 4

Federations: and aging members, 134; decline in power, 151; division into, 1–2; and economic crisis, xv; gender equality departments of, 111–12; major functions of, 150–51; and members' needs, 121–22, 151; political party affiliations, 150; relations with regional organizations, 149; and structure of kibbutz, 101–2; taxing mechanism, 122. *See also* Supra-organizations

Festivities, 125

Food costs, 17, 125–26

Four o'clock tea, 125

Free goods, 125–26

Furniture, 128

General assemblies, 38, 104–5

Gerontology committees, 141

Getz, Shlomo, xvi, 13–25

Gluck, Yaakov, xvii, 119–30

Golan, S., 57–61, 71 n.1

Gradus, Y., 148

Growth rate, viii, xiv, 2–3, 5–9

Hakibbutz HaDati, 1, 149–50

Hamashbir Hamerkazi, 152

Hamerkaz Hachaklai, 152

Handicapped workers, 53–54

Hashomer Hatzair. *See* Kibbutz Artzi

Health care, 55, 125, 139

Hever Hakvutzot, 102

Hired labor. *See* Labor, hired

Holocaust, 133

Housing, 127

Ichud Hakvutzot ve'Hakibbutzim, 71 n.1, 129

Identification relationships, 83–96

Ideology: change resulting from shifts in, 55–56; decrease of emphasis on, xiii, 64, 71 n.3, 86–87, 95–96, 162; and the industrial economy, xi–xii, 42–43; need- vs equality-based distribution, 18; and work, 19. *See also* Values

Individualism vs collectivism: and commitment to kibbutz life, xiii, 86–90; economic development and, xv–xvi; education and, 9, 63–71; in Israeli society, 156–57, 159–60; in other countries, 163; in pioneer period, ix–x; and satisfaction of needs, 120; and self-realization in work, 29; shifting emphasis in, 25, 159

Industry: effect on, xi, xii, 9–11, 28; efficiency of, 160–161; evaluating suitable industries, 45–47; impetus for growth of, 43; main objectives of, 46–47, 51; normative organizational model, 46–55; and organizational structure, 47–49, 103–4 (*see also* Decision-making; Management); ownership structure, 53

Infant mortality, 137

Inflation, xiii–xiv

Interest rates, xv

Inter-kibbutz organizations. *See* Supra-organizations

Kerschensteiner, G., 62

Kibbutz Artzi: and consumption budget, 130; debt incurred by, xv; and education, 58–61, 71 n.1; membership of, 1–2; and organization type, 47, 101

Kibbutz Dati, 1, 149–50

Kibbutz Degania, 4

Kibbutzim: adapting to reality, ix, xii, 13–25; crisis of the mid-Eighties, xiii–xvi; emerging from communes, 3–5; and external society, vii, xiii; federations and inter-kibbutz organizations, 147–58; governmental system, 97–109; in the late Sixties and early Seventies, xi–xii; and needs satisfaction, 124–30; objectives of, 42–43; partnerships with nonkibbutz organizations, 157; priorities, 92; prognosis for, 162, 163; public's attitude toward, viii; retention of members, 84–96; services provided by, 19; success factors, ix–xi, 159; uniting, 157–58. *See also* specific kibbutzim

Kibbutz Meuchad, 71 n.1, 101–2

Kibbutz Regulations, 42

Kiryat Anavim, 4
Krol, Y., 156

Labor, hired: management structure and,
    34–35, 40; in normative model for in-
    dustry, 47–48; and older kibbutz
    members, 142; and productivity, 161;
    trends in use of, 32, 54, 155
Labor market, 20–21, 29–32
Leadership, local, 92. *See also* Manage-
    ment; Organizational structure
Leviatan, Uriel, vii–xvii, 81–96, 131–45,
    159–63
Libraries, 154
Life expectancy, 136–38
Longevity, 136

Mahanaim, 4
Management: boards of directors, 38–39,
    52–53, 106–7; business-oriented
    changes in, 20–22; hierarchical trend,
    xii, 38–39; monitoring, 21–22, 97;
    participatory component, x–xi, 36–
    40, 47–48, 50; plant managers, 53–54;
    relationship with workers, 50, 54–55;
    rotating, 34–36, 45, 50, 143; women
    in, 114–15, 118
Manpower, 151, 155
Marketing, 34, 151–52
Maron, Stanley, xvi, 1–12
Marriage, 7–8, 12
Marx, Karl, 62, 119–20, 129
Materialism, 88–96
Meister, A., 56
Members: aging, xi, 2–3, 54, 125, 131–45;
    attitude toward changes, 143; attitudi-
    nal traits of, 64–67, 71 n.4; handi-
    capped, 53–54; heterogeneity of,
    xi–xii, xiii; mobility of, 4; retention
    of, 84–96; second and third genera-
    tions, xvii, 7–9, 70–71, 79, 81–96;
    shared vs competitive interests of,
    109; status after mate leaves, 117. *See
    also* Adolescents; Adulthood; Chil-
    dren; Demographics; Families; Work-
    ers
Membership: growth rate of, viii, xiv, 2–
    3, 5–9; rights of, 117
Mental health care, 55, 154

Messinger, Y., 57–61, 71 n.1
Michels, R., 22
Military service, 61
Money, 129
Mortality rates, 136–38, 141
Moshavim, 1, 148, 158 n.1, 162
Motivation, 32–34, 39, 107–8, 161
Municipal councils, regional, 153–54

National Kibbutz. *See* Kibbutz Artzi
Needs, efforts to satisfy, 20, 119–30, 125

Occupations. *See* Work
Older members. *See* Aging
Oliver, Hugh, vii–xvii, 159–163
Organizational structure: development
    of, 99–105; economic vs kibbutz
    members', 103–4, 159; General Assem-
    bly, 104–5; hierarchical, 35, 40, 47; lo-
    cal leadership, 92; representative
    councils, 106; types of, 98–99; voting
    by ballot, 105–6
Outsiders: on boards of directors, 52; as
    hired workers, 32, 34–35, 40, 47–48,
    54, 142, 155, 159; partnerships of kib-
    butzim with, 157; as plant managers,
    53; relationships with, viii, 20, 23–24,
    149, 161

Palgi, Michal, xvi, 22, 23, 41–56
Panebianco, A., 148
Partnerships, 157–58
Pavin, Avraham, xvii, 13, 97–109
Payment, 22–23, 33, 55
Peer groups, children's, 59, 69, 71 n.2, 73–
    74
Pensions, 117
Pioneer period: concept of work in, 28,
    30; defining needs during, 123; gov-
    ernmental system in, 100, 102; indi-
    vidualism and collectivism in, x, 28,
    30
Plant managers, 53–54, 104
Plotnik, Ronit, xvii, 73–79
Poalei Agudat Yesrael, 149–50, 158 n.1
Political parties, 150
Polls, public opinion, 22, 23
Poultry branches, 34–35
Power structure, 147–48

Priorities, 92. *See also* Ideology; Standard of living; Values
Privatization: of budgets, 18–19, 116, 128–30, 142; of consumption services, 16–19, 128–30, 142; and the elderly, 142–43; kibbutz' definition of, 14; and neoliberalism, 156; and women, 116–17; of work, 19–20
Production, ownership of, 25, 163
Productivity, 160–61
Profit centers, 21, 108

Quarter, Jack, vii–xvii, 159–63

Rationing: inclusive budget, 129–30; and luxury items, 127–28; normative distribution, 128; personal budget, 128–29
Ravid, S., 13
Reagan, Ronald, 14
Real estate, 24–25
Regional organizations, 153–57
Relationships, exchange vs identification, 83–84, 91
Religious Kibbutz Federation, 1, 149–50
Rewards, for work, 22–23, 32–34, 36, 55
Ronen, S., 29
Rosner, Menachem, xvi, 18, 27–40, 44
Rosolio, Daniel, xvii, 13, 147–58
Rural environment, 139
Russell, R., 22

Scholarships, 154
Secretariat, 103, 105, 150–51
Secret ballot, 22
Segal, M., 57–61, 71 n.1
Self-selection, 92–95
Services, kibbutz-provided, 19, 29
Sharir, S., 22, 23
Social organizations, 83–84, 86–87
Standard of living, viii, 18, 119–30, 138–39
State services, 119
Stress, 139
Supra-organizations: agricultural councils, 152; cooperatives, 34, 151–53, 155; debt incurred by, xv, 156; economic support, 149, 151–52, 154–56;

municipal councils, 153–55; national, 149–53; national and regional, 148–149, 155–56; purchasing organizations, 155; regional, 153–57; and state's power structure, 147. *See also* Federations

TAKAM (United Kibbutz Movement): debt incurred by, xv; higher education and, 9; membership, 1–2, 6, 8
Talmon-Garber, Yonina, 120–21, 133
Tannenbaum, A., 35, 36
Tax, intrafederation, 122
Technology, xii, xv, 45
Thatcher, Margaret, 14
Tnuva, 151–52
Tourism, 10, 113, 127
Travel, 127, 128

Ultraorthodox movement, 1
Unemployment, xiv
United Kibbutz Federation. *See* TAKAM
Urbanization, 1

Vacations, 128
Values: and communal consumption, 18; consistency in adhering to, x–xi, 86–88, 159–60; and member's commitment, 90–92; and social arrangements, xiii; as success factor, ix. *See also* Ideology
Voting, 22, 105–6, 154

Women: education, 115–16; kibbutz's view of gender equality, 6, 111–12; life expectancy, 137, 139–40; as office holders, 114–15; and work, 113–14, 117, 140
Work: aged members and, 138, 140–41, 142; allocation of, 20; changing concept of, 28–29, 55; efficiency vs egalitarianism in, 36–40; individual vs community needs, 29–32, 39; motivation to, 32–34, 39, 107–8, 161; occupational changes, 140, 143; outsiders hired to perform, 32, 34–35, 40; payment for, 22–23, 34; privatization in, 19–20; women's, 112–14

Workers: alienation of, 54–55, 108–9;
    children as, 69; handicapped, 53–54
Workers' assemblies, 37, 51, 52
Work groups: changes in, 34–36; com-
    pared to workers' assembly, 37; role in

plant management, 48; and social co-
    hesion, 32–33
Wyneken, G., 62

Youth, 134–35, 154

About the Contributors

GILA ADAR is a member of kibbutz Gaaton. She is the current manager of the Institute for Social Research of the Kibbutz and the Cooperative Idea at the University of Haifa. She is the coauthor of *A Survey of Women Who Are Office Holders* (in Hebrew). Her current research interests are in women at work and in politics, women on the kibbutz, and regional development.

YECHEZKEL DAR is a member of kibbutz Degania Aleph. He is a professor in sociology and education at the department of education in the Hebrew University of Jerusalem. His research interests are in educational and social inequality, educational integration and segregation, transition to adulthood, and kibbutz education. He is the editor of *Kibbutz Education—A Bifocal Socialization* (Hebrew).

SHLOMO GETZ is a member of kibbutz Gadot and a research associate in the Institute for Social Research of the Kibbutz and the Cooperative Idea at the University of Haifa. He is the coauthor of the recent book *The Kibbutz in an Era of Change* (in Hebrew). His current research is in the domains of changes in the kibbutzim and education and vocational choice.

YAAKOV GLUCK is a member of kibbutz Kfar HaChoresh and a research associate in the Institute for Social Research of the Kibbutz and the Cooperative Idea at the University of Haifa. He is a lecturer in the department of sociology at the University of Haifa and the Emek Izrael and Oranim colleges. His major research interests are in the domains of consumer behavior on kibbutzim and turnover of members in kibbutzim.

URIEL LEVIATAN is a member of kibbutz Ein HaMifratz and an organizational psychologist. He is the head of the Institute for Social Research of the Kibbutz and the Cooperative Idea at the University of Haifa and a professor at the department of sociology at the University of Haifa. His current research interests are organizational behavior, turnover, and commitment, leadership, and social gerontology. He is coauthor of *The Second Generation in the Kibbutz—Between Continuity and Change.*

STANLEY MARON is a member of kibbutz Maayan Zvi. He is a research associate with Yad Tabenkin (the research institute of the United Kibbutz Movement), and associated with the Institute for Social Research of the Kibbutz and the Cooperative Idea at the University of Haifa. He specializes in social anthropology and social economy. He recently published *Kibbutz in the Market Society.*

HUGH OLIVER was the founding editor of the teacher journal *Orbit,* a former managing editor of the scholarly journal *Interchange,* and editor-in-chief of OISE press. His stone carvings have been exhibited in numerous galleries; and for his recorded lyrics, the Beatles contributed to the backing music for two of them. He is currently working on *After the Tempest* a three-act play. He is a coauthor of *The Canadian Limerick Book.*

MICHAL PALGI is a member of kibbutz Nir David. She is a former head and current research associate in the Institute for Social Research of the Kibbutz and the Cooperative Idea at the University of Haifa. Palgi is a lecturer in the department of sociology at the University of Haifa and the Emek Izrael and Oranim colleges. Her current areas of research are organizations, immigration, gender roles, and kibbutz. She coauthored *Participation and Control.*

AVRAHAM PAVIN is a member of kibbutz Genigar. He is a research associate in the Institute for Social Research of the Kibbutz and the Cooperative Idea at the University of Haifa. His current research interests are social change, democracy, and stratification. He is the author of *Stratification and Change in a Society of Equals* (in Hebrew).

RONIT PLOTNIK is a member of kibbutz Mishmar HaSharon. She is the director of the Kibbutz Center for Child Development (T.L.M.). A developmental psychologist, she teaches at the Kibbutz Teachers College in Tel Aviv. Her current research areas are parenthood (kibbutz parenthood in particular), ecological psychology and its application in educational systems, and the application of developmental psychology in the field of education.

JACK QUARTER is a professor at the Ontario Institute for Studies in Education of the University of Toronto (the graduate school of education at the University of Toronto), where he specializes in the study of workplace democracy, cooperatives, and community development. He recently coauthored *Building a Community Controlled.*

MENACHEM ROSNER is a member of kibbutz Reshafim and professor emeritus of sociology and anthropology at the University of Haifa and former president of the Israeli Sociological Association. He is a former head, and currently active head, of the Institute for Social Research of the Kibbutz and the Cooperative Idea at the University of Haifa. His current research interests focus on changes in kibbutzim. He is coauthor of the recent *The Kibbutz in Times of Change* (in Hebrew).

DANIEL ROSOLIO is a member of kibbutz Kabri and a research associate in the Institute for Social Research of the Kibbutz and the Cooperative Idea at the University of Haifa. He is a former Knesset (Israeli parliament) member, and general secretary of the Kibbutz Meuchad Movement. Rosolio is a lecturer in the department of sociology at the University of Haifa and the Western Galil Regional College. His current research interests are in political economy, regional development, and the management of kibbutz industry.

ISBN 0-275-95838-8

90000>

EAN

9 780275 958381

HARDCOVER BAR CODE